THE PSYCHOLOGY
OF
HUMAN CONFLICT

The Clash of Motives Within the Individual

❧❧❧❧

BY

EDWIN R. GUTHRIE

Beacon Press   Boston

To

H. M. G.

Notes

Guthrie's chief other books are (with Stevenson Smith) *General Psychology in Terms of Behavior* (1921); *Psychology of Learning* (1935, rev., 1952); (with G. P. Horton) *Cats in a Puzzle Box* (1946); (with A. L. Edwards) *Psychology: A First Course in Human Behavior* (1949); (with F. F. Powers) *Educational Psychology* (1950).

His theory of learning is explained and criticized in a chapter by C. G. Mueller, Jr. and W. N. Schoenfeld in W. K. Estes and Others, *Modern Learning Theory* (1954), and in E. R. Hilgard's *Theories of Learning* (2d edition, 1956). The modern development of some of his ideas is reflected in W. K. Estes, The statistical approach to learning theory, in S. Koch (ed.) *Psychology: A Study of a Science*, Vol. 2, 1959, 380-491.

CONTENTS

Contents

PREFACE

This book attempts a simplified description of the ways in which men adjust themselves to circumstances. Much use is made of the writings of Pierre Janet and in particular of his notions of mental energy and the effects of its depression. Janet, however, has refused to speculate concerning the physical basis of such energy. In the present account it is suggested that the physiological mechanisms for the reinforcement of action as they have been described by W. B. Cannon and by E. J. Kempf are adequate explanations for the behavior that Janet describes. To this combination of Janet's descriptive psychology and current physiological notions of the sources of action has been added an objective theory of learning.

My debt to Janet, Cannon and Kempf is equaled by my debt to the fellow members of my own department in the University of Washington. A twenty-three-year association with Stevenson Smith has been responsible for many of the positions taken in this book. The typescript has been read by Dr. Homer Wheelon and by Roger Loucks and advantage taken of many suggestions. It has also been read by my wife with profit to its form.

EDWIN R. GUTHRIE

Seattle, November 4th, 1937

FOREWORD TO THE BEACON PRESS EDITION

Those who knew the distinguished psychologist Edwin Guthrie (1886-1959) found him friendly, wise, humorous and self-effacing, yet standing firmly on the ground of a theory of learning that pervaded all of his thinking. Only a somewhat anecdotal theory could have been ever-present, in living room and classroom, without pedantry, and there was no pedantry in Edwin Guthrie. The present book makes Guthrie relive for those who knew him, and it will introduce him to those who did not have this privilege, for he could not write without infusing his writing with his own personal idiom. The simple informal style will come as something of a surprise to those who expect ponderous writing in serious psychological books.

In his preface to this book, Guthrie suggests that he has combined three approaches to the understanding of human behavior: Janet's descriptive psychology, Cannon and Kempf's physiological mechanisms and his own objective theory of learning. A word about how he uses each of these.

Pierre Janet (1859-1947) was a distinguished French psychologist, successor to Charcot at the Salpêtrière and a contemporary of Sigmund Freud. Janet called attention to many of the phenomena dealt with by Freud, but he remained at a somewhat descriptive level. Some of his cases were used extensively in William James's *Principles of Psychology* (1890), and his work was well known to American psychologists throughout his long life. Yet, as Guthrie indicates, Janet was greatly overshadowed by Freud, perhaps because of the very "depth" metaphors in Freud that Guthrie deplores. Guthrie sides himself with those who stay on the surface, who deal with what man actually does, who are not concerned with his private consciousness or his (more private!) unconscious. This is a difference in preferred mode of scientific description; it does not necessarily mean "superficiality" in any other sense. Guthrie had long been impressed by Janet, so much so that he and his wife had translated Janet's *Principles of Psychotherapy* into English in 1924. The reader will find many references to Janet in this book, but he will learn curiously little about Janet: most of the references use Janet as a source of case illustrations, and the theoretical views attributed to Janet make him sound much more like a contemporary behaviorist than he sounds in the original.

The main notion from the physiologist Cannon is that of *homeostasis*, that is, a basic level or steady state at which the body operates best; when there are departures from this state there are efforts to restore it. Kempf enters the picture because he was interested both in autonomic and glandular functions (in common with Cannon) and in psychopathology. There is not actually much physiology in this book, for Guthrie could never interest himself very much in more "central" processes. His interest lay in *emotional excitement* as one of the conditions of behavior modification; in this he felt that some of the views of Cannon and Kempf gave substance to Janet's vaguer ideas about mental energy.

The nub of the interpretations in this book, as in Guthrie's other writings, is the theory of learning that is associated with his name. It developed over the years, first in association with Stevenson Smith as early as 1921. The theory is influential in some contemporary developments in psychology, as in statistical theories of learning, such as those associated with the name of Estes.

The learning theory is disarming in its simplicity. New associations occur in a single trial; whatever the organism happens to do gets attached to whatever stimuli are present. This is associative learning with but a single law, but a single law that in Guthrie's hands comes to encompass all of personality development. Skills, defined by what they do, are collections of habits. Guthrie's position is a confident one; his examples illustrate a *thesis*; they do not test a *hypothesis*. This confident and finished nature of the theory is annoying to many psychologists who are struggling with the little that we know, and who are trying very hard to find out more. Guthrie did not mean to slow them up, but he does not need them or their findings: see what a man has done and you will know what he will do. The firm of Dun and Bradstreet is a better predictor of behavior than are students of personality traits.

This associative learning theory is set in the context of a confident behaviorism, a behaviorism that defines mind as learning, and thinking as speech. Many contemporary objective psychologists will find fault with the glibness of these equations, but it is instructive to see how far an advocate can go with a theory of this kind. Guthrie goes very far very gracefully, and this must be acknowledged by those who disagree fundamentally with his position.

The pervasiveness of learning in his conception of mind and personality accounts for the long running start — ten chapters on learning and motivation — before we reach personality. Then we get into the content that we expect in a book concerned with conflicts: the types of adjustment problems which cause people to seek help. We must not ask Guthrie to do what he will not do: he will not give statistics on mental illness, nor will he indicate whether or not some conditions will resist psychotherapy. A considerable optimism about change is reflected in the fact of learning: if we can learn, we can also relearn. That is the essence of psychotherapy.

The Psychology of Human Conflict is a serious book, originally intended for students in courses. Though it is not an effort of a psychologist to write for a wider public, it is readily understood and appreciated by non-psychologists. It is written anecdotally, as Guthrie always wrote and lectured, whether as a contributor to a learned symposium or as the president of the American Psychological Association addressing its annual meeting. Because of this anecdotal nature of his writing, there is a timelessness about what Guthrie says. His occasional references become outdated, but they are few in any case. His stories about people are as valid as they ever were. The reader can learn from these, and in the process become acquainted with a wise and delightful psychologist.

ERNEST R. HILGARD

Stanford University

THE NATURE OF LIVING ORGANISMS

M AN is by nature smug, and it is not modesty that makes him willing to share an adjective with other objects in his world. For man must acknowledge that he is like stones and planks and vegetables, because occasional collisions establish that he also has mass, and he must at least be measured for his coffin in the same foot-lengths that he uses for the boards of which it is made.

Man is forced to share more qualities than mass and length. There is a limited class of objects which he must acknowledge to be as alive as he is himself. This admission that there are living beings that are not men is also not pure benevolence on man's part. It is an admission which the other living creatures force upon him by their own behavior. Just what behavior it is that distinguishes man and other living beings from non-living objects is hard to put into words. We are so used to the difference that we recognize it and take it for granted, but a good description of it is another matter. One psychologist of a generation ago asserted that we call some things living because they are capable of surprising us. We are, Baldwin said, ready and prepared for what inert objects will do, but not for what living things will do.

This is not a very good statement of the difference between living and non-living things. Whether anything will or will not surprise us depends more on our own state of knowledge and readiness than it does on the object itself. It is possible to be surprised by a stone or by a machine; and it is possible to be quite prepared for the daily growth of the living vegetables in our garden, or for the conversation and acts of our friends There must be some other mark that will distinguish what is alive from what is not. Perhaps that mark can best be sought in those cases in which an object changes its class and resigns from the group of living creatures to join the inanimate world. Just what is it that the dead organism has stopped doing?

For one thing, the object has not stopped changing; in fact, death may start a period of rapid and far-reaching change. Nor has the body at death stopped responding to changes in the outer world. It can still be warmed or cooled or moved. Even a stone is sensitive to changes in temperature or to the impact of other objects. What the living thing does that the inert object does not is something else. A living man responds to temperature changes about him or to impact, but his response is often just what a non-living thing would not do. If the sun shines on a stone, the stone grows warm. If the sun shines on a man, he may respond in various ways, but it is fairly certain that his temperature will not go up.

There is a small county seat in Canada where county business has for many years been at a minimum. There are few deeds to record because little property changes hands. The county clerk, the judge and the bailiff, the peace officer and others employed at the court house used to lead during the summer months a highly predictable life. They spent most of the official day in the shade of a large oak tree on the grounds of the court house. When the shadow of the oak moved so as to expose one of the crowd to the direct rays of the sun, it was the business of that one to propose that all move to the nearby inn for a drink. When this was finished, all returned to the shade of the oak and there they remained until the sun again overtook them, which was the signal to adjourn to the inn. The sun's threat to raise their temperatures was regularly foiled. It is true that the sun made them respond; it altered their positions, changed their conversation, and started an elaborate series of events that included muscular contraction, the burning of glycogen to produce lactic acid and carbon dioxide, and had other results that would take volumes to describe. But the one thing that the sun did not do was to raise their body temperatures. They responded to its radiant heat not by being warmed, but by elaborate measures to keep their blood temperatures between 98 and 99 degrees.

Our idle gentlemen have, in their answer to a threatening sun, illustrated what we mean by the word "life." They have behaved in such a way as to preserve their body temperatures against a threatened change. It was essential that they should thus behave because if they had been warmed by so much as ten degrees it is highly probable that they would have left the company of the living. Our whole internal economy is adjusted to a temperature between 98 and 99 degrees Fahrenheit. A few degrees above this or a few degrees below this, and there will be a general breakdown of physiological processes.

Blood temperature is not the only state that must be preserved in order that life continue. Cannon introduced the term "homeostasis" to name a long list of such constant states which living organisms defend against change. On the preservation of such constant states the living thing depends for continuing its own identity. We can define life in terms of these constant states. A living organism is a structure capable of maintaining its identity for an indefinite time against a limited range of threatening changes in the world about it. This maintained identity is achieved by maintaining certain physical and chemical states within a narrow range. Most living organisms can do more than this. They can give rise to other living structures of the same kind, and so maintain their species as well as their individual identities; but this is not essential to life. We still call an individual alive if it can resist change in its constant states, even though it is incapable of reproduction.

When we speak of a living thing as maintaining its identity in a changing world we do not mean to imply that it does not change. The very devices by which it remains the same are, of course, differences. And in the course of its life it may so alter its gross appearance that it can be recognized only by someone who has watched its development or the development of similar organisms. An oak is very different from the acorn which was its beginning. No man at forty suggests very strongly the infant he was at the age of six months. But there is a day-to-day resemblance that serves to establish his identity, and it is this identity that is served by the detailed changes that Cannon calls homeostasis.

Even if the gentlemen under the oak tree had not moved they might still have remained themselves. Their bodies have more tricks in reserve than the one device of moving to the bar and then to the shade when the sun threatens. Continued exposure to the sun would have activated the county clerk's sweat glands, and evaporation from his skin would have kept him normal. This activity of sweat glands would eventually offer a new threat. The loss of salts from the blood stream would eventually produce heat stroke which could be avoided only by new supplies of salt. Reports from Boulder Dam state that heat prostration has been practically eliminated by requiring that the workers exposed to the sun have an extra ration of salt to compensate for what is lost in perspiration.

Living creatures differ from non-living creatures in that they react to change in circumstances by so changing themselves as to preserve certain of their essential characteristics constant. For the most part this requires activity and constant change. There are certain seeds and germs which can maintain the essentials for starting a new organism almost without activity, and for long stretches of time. We call this suspended animation. But in most living creatures the maintenance of identity requires active changes. The blood sugar used in our muscles when they contract must be replaced by food, and this demands more muscular activity and still more food. Water is used in eliminating waste through the kidneys or the sweat glands, and this requires that new supplies of water be discovered and taken in. The oxygen which reacts with glycogen in the muscles to produce contraction is left in an unusable combination and must be eliminated if the muscles are to continue to contract. It leaves the blood stream in the lungs and is forced out into the surrounding air in breathing.

The integrity that living things achieve by all these processes is, of course, temporary. In the end they all succumb and disintegrate; all lose their form and identity to rejoin the dance of atoms about them. We cease, as Montaigne expressed it, to live *en masse* and begin to live *en détail*. But to live *en détail* is to cease to live at all. All individuals are mortal. Eventually they fail to maintain their constant states. But the kind goes on. Not always, however, for there are many remains of extinct species. The kind goes on often enough for us to include this maintenance of the species as one of the characteristics of life. The living creature that cannot reproduce or take a direct part in reproduction either contributes to the life of the group, like the worker ant, or is regarded as a casualty. We think of living creatures with few exceptions as being destined for reproduction of their kind, whether by division into two, by budding, or by the intricate process of sexual union.

The continued identity of a species is, like the identity of the individual, a relative matter. The horse has developed from a small creature scarcely knee high to its present size. Species change, but that change is so slow and systematic that we find it possible to call the members of a species by the same name, just as we use a name, John Doe, to identify a series of states from infancy to old age. If change in species or in individuals were abrupt, language could not keep up with it and we should be limited to naming only certain features of the organisms we encountered. There would be no familiar kinds, or familiar individuals. No dog is exactly like either parent, but any dog is sufficiently unlike any cat and sufficiently like other dogs to make the word "dog" a useful element of our vocabulary.

We have described life as a certain way of behaving; it is not a juice or an essence, or a principle, or a substance. When we see a calf walking across a pasture browsing on the green grass, this browsing is part of the behavior that *is* the life of the calf. Browsing is one of the ways in which the calf remains a calf. Veal does not browse. The difference between veal and a calf is that the veal no longer breathes, drinks, digests, browses; it is not that some "principle of life" is now missing that was once present. It is that the structures by which life's activities were carried on are broken up.

The grass, which is quite as alive as the calf, is meeting circumstances which it is prepared to resist. Grass will survive great variations of temperature, light, moisture and soil composition. It is also prepared to restore its leaf area when this has been removed by the calf, and its vital activities will continue. The portion that is cropped by the animal loses its identity as grass and rapidly becomes calf. It is subdued by the digestive apparatus of the eater and within a day or two is gamboling about the field and perhaps taking part in the cropping of the plant to which it once belonged. What Singer has called the pulse of life has engaged the substance of the grass in a new form. The behavior program which we call the calf has overtaken and enmeshed the program which was grass. For the purposes of science the conception of life as an agent or power or hidden substance which is in some mysterious way responsible for the behavior we see is quite useless. Science is the reduction of what we see and hear and feel to rules which will enable us to know what to expect to see and hear and feel in similar cases in the future. It has no place for hidden principles. For science, life is a mode of action.

In this book we are to be concerned with a very special and interesting form of life, our fellow men, and some of their less ordinary and routine ways, some of the more bizarre forms which the pulse of life takes in them. We shall find these also understandable in terms of homeostasis, the exhibition of constant states. Man, like all living things, meets change by himself changing, but at the same time remaining in certain essentials unchanged. The variety of ways in which men keep warm or cool, or replenish their supplies of sugar and other necessary chemicals is infinite. Men beg, borrow or steal; they work for wages or they may refuse to work; but the normal outcome of any human activity is to restore some disturbed balance, physical or chemical, in the human organism. Most of man's behavior is adaptive. By that we mean only that it serves to maintain his constant states. We shall find that even the delusion of an insane person may be his method of keeping himself intact. A patient in a local clinic who was diagnosed as suffering from that form of insanity called schizophrenia once remarked: "Schizophrenia is not a disease but a cure." He meant that the strange behavior he exhibited, his detachment from the affairs of the world and his indifference to his family and friends were his own way of meeting his troubles. We shall find that much behavior that appears totally unreasonable and bizarre is understandable when it is viewed as adjustive reaction to circumstance. It may be the normal and expected retort to unusual suroundings, the method by which the organism preserves its essential constant states in face of unusual threats. The organism is working perfectly, but working to compensate for an extraordinary situation.

Most of the constant states against the disturbance of which man and other living creatures are defended by their structure are, like the temperature of the blood, not absolute. If the body is invaded by destructive germs, its reaction may include not only an increase in the number of white blood cells which attack the germs one by one, but also a rise in the body temperature, a change in the norm itself, which change may slaughter the invaders by the wholesale. If the reaction is successful and the invading germs are eliminated, the blood temperature will return to its optimum point, the point at which the processes of growth and metabolism are most favored.

Among the homeostatic or constant states described by Cannon in his recent book, *The Wisdom of the Body*, many reflect the primitive environment of living forms, the ocean, and are concerned with the condition of the blood which offers the cells of the human body an environment approximating the sea water to which the early forms of life were adjusted. We do not think of ourselves as marine animals, but we are. By means of an outer sac of skin we manage to get about on dry land with our "innards" still enjoying the saline water bath in which our remote ancestors swam or floated. The pressure of this blood, the quantity of the blood, its supply of sugar, of water, of salt, of protein, fat, calcium, oxygen, carbon dioxide, its acid-alkaline balance, all are constant states which are protected by a multitude of reactions.

Physiology is the science concerned with these constant states and with most of the means by which they are maintained. Our present interest lies in the way in which such states are maintained through behavior or the integrated reactions of the organism brought about through its nervous system. The nature of this integration will be sketched in the third chapter. Our friends, the gentlemen under the oak tree, were defending themselves against the sun through behavior as well as through the processes described by the physiologist. Sweating is primarily a physiological event. It is the business of the physiologist to describe its mechanism, the sweat glands, their nerve connections, the conditions under which these operate, and the effect of sweating on the body temperature and the body economy in general. Saying "Let's have a drink" goes beyond the material of a textbook of physiology. It shows, we say, evidence of mind, or, at least, of the beginnings of mind. Our friends have become subjects for the psychologist.

The plant and animal physiologists investigate the structures of living things and learn the circumstances under which self-preservation will occur and the means by which it is accomplished. When, for instance, we are injured and lose a considerable amount of blood many adaptive changes promptly occur. Cannon (pp. 41 ff.) describes some of these. There is a local clotting of blood at the wound and a local constriction of blood vessels which together protect against further loss. The medulla of the adrenal glands is stimulated through sympathetic nerves to discharge adrenine into the blood stream. The blood vessels and the spleen, which is a large reservoir of blood, contract to maintain pressure. If this pressure should fall beyond a critical point many organs will cease to perform their functions because of lack of the necessary oxygen. A loss of blood is also compensated for by replenishment of water and salts from the lymph supply. And the animal will have a consuming thirst which originates in the dryness of its throat. The most urgent request of wounded men on the field of battle is for water. In this last item we find ourselves again confronted with a new form of reaction which we call mental. The next chapter will undertake to describe what it is that we mean by the words "mind" and "mental."

—II—

THE NATURE OF MIND

THE ability to compensate for change, to meet threatening changes in the world about by a reaction that preserves identity through the preservation of the essential constant states, is what we mean by life. Men share this with plants and animals. There is, however, a more elaborate form of this compensation that defines an exclusive class of living creatures. Some living creatures have mind as well as life.

We all agree that mind is not present in plants. Celery and parsnips live out their lives and make their adjustments to weather and soil; they give rise to new individuals of their kind. They react to the conditions surrounding them. The growth of roots is in the direction of greatest moisture. The stalks grow toward the light. But these reactions do not lead us to endow celery and parsnips with wit. Mind, wit, intelligence, so far as we know, are limited to certain kinds of animals. One of their essentials seems to be the possession of a central nervous system. Jellyfish and sea anemones move about more briskly than do plants, but there is nothing in the quality of these movements which would entitle them to be classified as mental. The response of the leaves of a sensitive plant to a touch or the sudden contraction of a sea anemone when it is prodded about the mouth opening is not evidence of mind. Something more is required.

This something more is that responses shall show evidence of profiting by experience. If we should find on the beach a sea

10

anemone that, after being prodded a number of times, changed its answer to this stimulus and contracted as the shadow of its tormentor fell across it instead of waiting always for the actual prodding, we should say that this anemone gave signs of mind. Inanimate objects respond to the forces about them, to blows, to heat, but their responses are not adaptive. Living creatures respond to a limited range of forces with adaptive changes, changes like the protective contraction of the sea anemone. Those living creatures that have minds do more than this; they improve their adaptation with experience. This is something that never happens in the anemone. No matter how often we prod it, it does not improve its device for meeting this disturbance. It may grow fatigued and fail to respond. This is not learning, because as soon as rest has restored it we will find its response what it was before. The anemone and its descendants will continue to have only one answer to being prodded. The anemone has no capacity for changing its answer to our attack, and therein consists its mindlessness. It is, like the radish, a living being but a witless being.

The mental character of a response does not lie in the adaptive nature of the response because all living beings are capable of adaptive response. Responses are mental when they are subject to modification. This modification lies in the capacity for attaching responses to new stimuli. Organisms which can learn to give their adaptive reactions to new cues have at least the rudiments of mind. So far as we know, such a capacity is limited to animals that have nervous systems which include a central ganglion where there are available connections for the rerouting of impulses. The sea anemone which we have denied a mind, has nerves. That is, it has specialized cells whose chief use is the rapid conduction of a disturbance from one part of the animal to another. When sensitive areas about the mouth opening are touched or otherwise stimulated, a disturbance which is called the nervous impulse travels along a fibril to muscle fibers along the stalk. When the impulse arrives at the contractile muscle fiber this shortens and the whole animal takes on a more compact shape. This is a defensive response and is obviously useful to the animal in protecting its vulnerable tentacles and mouth area. Most of the cells of a living animal are capable of conducting disturbances like the nervous impulse. The advantage of specialized nervous tissue is that in such tissue conduction is a specialized function and is brought to such a point of perfection that nerve fibers in man can transmit signals at speeds up to four hundred feet per second.

In animals that learn by experience the specialized conducting system has a very important feature. Nerve fibers take their start in sensitive organs placed at strategic points over the body, at points where threatening changes are likely to be first manifest. This is true also in creatures that are incapable of learning. But in animals that learn, these sensory or receiving fibers lead to a central ganglion, where they have—and this is the characteristic essential for learning—connections with many possible routes through the nerve center and out to muscles and glands. In this central ganglion or brain rerouting is possible. The tracks are there to begin with; some physiological device whereby the setting of nerve "switches" can be achieved is also there. Learning consists in such resetting of switch connections in the central brain. Herrick estimates the number of nerve cells in the human cortex, or the part of the central system which is in man most concerned with learning, at 9,200 million, and the number of possible different routes (*Thinking Machine*, p. 116) through this maze is, he believes, so large that the figures would convey no meaning. The possibility of learning lies in the possibility of change in these through connections.

From the myriads of connections in the central nervous system there lead other myriads of nerve fibers out to the structures of the body in which adaptive effects can be produced, to muscles which contract and take the animal to food or away from harm, and to glands which secrete; in the electric eel nerves lead to cell groups which can produce severe electric shock, or, in the cuttlefish, to groups of cells with many ramifications through which minute pigment spots are spread when the nervous impulse arrives. The cuttlefish can by this device respond to light stimulating its eyes by a radical change of color.

In these effector organs, which contract, secrete, or otherwise respond, the animal makes its adjustment. This adjustment may or may not be adequate to the threatening situation and may or may not result in the survival of the animal. In our own case these adjustments have been thus far adequate, and adequate for all our ancestors, at least to the point of allowing each of them to reach maturity and beget offspring. No living creature ever had an ancestor that succumbed in infancy. But we must remember that many do succumb, and many do leave no offspring. For this reason we cannot accept survival or self-preservation as a law of nature. As a law it works only when it works. Many whole species have disappeared from the earth and others are undoubtedly on their way to extinction. Another increase in the radiation of the sun, which is a mildly variable star, and the increased evaporation and precipitation on the earth's surface would bring another glacial epoch with tremendous ice caps at the poles. In such an event, many species would again find themselves unprepared for the changes in temperature, humidity and food supply that would result and would disappear like the mammoth.

But to return to our nerves. The ability to learn by experience is limited to those fortunate animals that have central nervous systems. And this learning by experience in its elementary forms, and, I am convinced, also in its most elaborate and sophisticated forms, consists in changes in the central nervous system that result in new routings of nervous impulses between sense organs and effectors and so in new ways of responding to the world about. It would be more exact to say that learning consists in responding in old ways to new stimuli.

Some of the more tender-minded psychologists have recently taken to saying that learning consists in responding to new situations in an adjustive or adaptive way. It is true that this is what usually happens. What we learn is often to our benefit, but it is not necessarily to our benefit. Learning often gets us into trouble as well as getting us out of trouble. I am convinced that we can be much more definite. We can say that learning consists not simply in responding to new situations adequately or appropriately, but in responding to new situations with a specific response which has in the past been associated with some feature of the new situation. Lloyd Morgan's newly hatched chick pecked at a cinnabar caterpillar. With the caterpillar in its bill there was a new stimulation, a taste which entomologists pronounce bitter. To this new stimulation the chick responded by a movement analogous to what in a man we should call spitting. Our language has not yet furnished a word to describe what a bird does when it hastily rids itself of something in its bill. If the chick were incapable of learning, it would continue indefinitely to peck at and then reject cinnabar caterpillars. This is an adaptive response, and chicks could conceivably manage to get along with such behavior indefinitely. But the chick has a central nervous system in which learning can take place. It sees the caterpillar while it is "spitting." On the next sight of a caterpillar the chick shakes its bill vigorously in a movement of rejection. It does this instead of pecking, which was its first response to the sight of a caterpillar.

Learning by experience depends on a past response. As a result of that past response the organism may now respond to cues or signals which attended that response. If we were confronted with a new situation that included no familiar features, nothing resembling learning could be in evidence. Careless talk about "insight" or the supposed ability of the higher animals to adjust themselves to completely new situations is very misleading. Just how a man or an animal could behave wisely or adequately except in responding to some familiar character of the new situation as on some previous occasion, is very hard to understand. All wisdom, all improvement of adaptation that shows intelligence, all use of human wits, depends on past experience and familiarity. From the day-old chick to the competent scientist, the successful anticipation of events depends on responses which have been given to past events and the evocation of these responses by stimuli which accompanied them.

To endow a sea anemone with mind, several additions would be necessary. One of these would be a new receptor, a new sensitive area. Another would be a connection through nerve fibers with a central ganglion in which impulses from the new sensitive area could be routed to the muscle effectors. If the added sensitive area were a pigmented spot conveniently placed to receive the shadow of an approaching enemy and this were sensitive to light, and, further, if the central ganglion were so constructed that activity in the pathway leading to the muscle led to the establishing of connections between the nerves from the pigment spot and the nerves to the muscle, the conditions for learning would be satisfied. The anemone would not at first contract when the shadow fell upon it, but if the shadow accompanied the touch and the contraction which follows the touch, the next occasion would find the animal prepared. The shadow would be a cue for the defensive contraction and the touch on the open intake would be avoided.

The anemone of our illustration would be, of course, capable of learning only one thing, whereas most men have astonishing possibilities of learning. Instead of one response to begin with and one possible new cue for that response, human beings have a large number of responding organs and an almost infinite number of possible new cues for these, with a practically infinite variety of combinations of both cues and responses. An intelligent adult can, among other things, discriminate between perhaps a hundred thousand words and an unlimited number of their combinations.

If life is described as adaptation to change, mind may be thought of as a special form of that adaptation. Living things which are mindless react over and over again in the same way when they are disturbed in the same way. Their behavior is in general adaptive and achieves the result of protection, but they do not improve. Mind consists in the ability to improve this adaptive behavior with experience, to make better and better adaptation to recurring change. This idea of mind Humphrey has described at length in his recent book, *The Nature of Learning and the Living System*. I am in hearty agreement with the definition of mind as progressive adaptation with recurring experience. But this definition of mind does not coincide with the suggestion made above, that mind is equivalent to the capacity for associative learning. The relation between these two divergent statements of the nature of mind is this, that mind is best *defined* in terms of adaptation, and that we *discover* that the means by which progressive adaptation is accomplished is associative learning. For this discovery there is a very impressive body of evidence. And it will be found that the few psychologists who do not hold to the notion that learning proceeds through association of response with new cues do not hold to any alternative theory of the way in which progressive adaptation is achieved, but are contented with trusting to the fact that progressive adaptation can, however it is brought about, be trusted to occur in most cases.

This is quite true. In certain species of animals, progressive adaptation does occur in most cases. But to be contented with this observation is to be like a physician who does nothing but trust in the *vis naturae curatrix* for his cures. Most people recover from all but one of their illnesses. This is a comforting observation. But it is the business of medicine and physiology to do more than to observe that most people recover from most of their disorders by themselves. These sciences must set to work to find out *how* these natural recoveries proceed. When this has been discovered it is possible here and there to lend a hand to the process. To be content with the observation that human behavior is adaptive is to be like the Moorish caliph who, to a French proposal to collect vital statistics in his area, objected that the death rate of Mohammedans was already known. Allah had provided that there would be one death for each inhabitant.

If Cannon in his absorbing book, *The Wisdom of the Body*, had been contented to observe that organisms tend to resist destruction, or to describe the various detailed constant states which are maintained in any given species, this would be no guide to the physician. The physician would be reduced to passive observation and uniformly hopeful prediction. But Cannon goes on to the description of the detailed mechanisms by which these constant states are maintained. With such information, active interference and assistance are possible.

Since this book undertakes much the same problems in the mental field which Cannon has dealt with in the physiological field, we shall be concerned not only with the fact that adjustments occur and that mental states closely resembling Cannon's constant states are to be found, but also with the means by which these adjustments are brought about. We must understand *how* adjustments are arrived at. This will require an examination of the nature of learning and habit formation.

Several pages ago it was hinted that learning is much the same process in newly hatched chicks and in scientists. This is both true and false. It is true in the sense that learning is, in all organisms capable of learning, a process of association of responses with new stimuli. It is false in that men have an enormous superiority over worms in their capacity for learning. What a man can learn depends on many things. It depends first of all on his repertoire of responses, on his equipment of effectors and their variety. No organism can do anything except through the action of its muscles and glands and other effectors. And no effector can do anything but respond in its characteristic fashion. Muscle fibers contract or relax. Glands either secrete their characteristic secretion or they do not. Man and other living creatures are limited to the responses for which they have effector organs. New behavior can consist only of new combinations of the action of effectors.

What a man can learn depends also on the variety and extent of sense organs. It depends particularly on the structure of the brain and central nervous system in which new associative pathways can be established. In all these respects man has a superiority over all other forms of life. One undoubted source of man's superiority is not yet well understood. This is the arrangement of connections in the human brain that makes possible differential responses to the patterning of stimuli.

In the retina of the eye, for instance, there is an immense number of the sensitive rods and cones which respond to light. These are connected with an area in the brain in something approaching a point-for-point correspondence. But they may act, not as separate elements but according to the pattern of stimulation affecting them. The stimulation of points A, B and C may have one effect, and the stimulation of points A, B and D have a radically different effect. Somewhere in the brain the impulses from receptor elements can be combined to act as functional units. Rashevsky has described purely speculative arrangements of pathways and connections which might achieve such results, but whether the actual brain structures resemble his scheme we simply do not know.

Species differ in their capacity for learning, and so differ in the degree to which they possess "minds." There are also great differences between the members of a species. Some dogs are more intelligent than others. Among men these differences reach a maximum because of man's higher position in the range of intelligences. There are human beings who have not the learning capacity of an ape. The bases for differences in learning capacity between species and between members of the same species are various. The capacity for learning has already been said to depend on the repertoire of action made possible by an animal's structure. Between a human hand and the paw of a dog, for instance, there is an enormous gap. The hand has more muscles and there are undoubtedly more possible combinations of action in these muscles. The number of separate and distinct movement patterns in a human hand is probably some thousands of times greater than the corresponding number in a dog. On the sensory side man has not such a great advantage. The vision of hawks and pigeons is, according to some studies published by Gundlach, probably more acute than man's. The dog may equal or surpass man in the number of smells that give rise to different stimulation of the dog's nose. Man's greatest advantage probably lies in his ability to establish more complex patterns of stimuli as functional units. His next greatest advantage probably consists in the complexity of his hand musculature and the complexity of his vocal apparatus. Between a feeble-minded man and a man of average intelligence no necessary gross differences in brain have been observed. But what the feeble-minded man probably lacks is not nerve connections from sense organs or to muscles, but the central mechanism for integrating the action of specific combinations of stimuli.

THE INTEGRATION OF BEHAVIOR

WHEN a honeybee is collecting honey from a flower its abdomen can be removed and the forward end of the bee will go on drawing honey, only to have it discharged into the open air. This is a failure on one part of an animal to take into account what the condition of another part is. The illustration is not a perfect one because, even if the forward end had wind of what had happened to the rear, it is possible that there would still be nothing better to do in the circumstances. But at least the unfortunate bee will serve to illustrate a failure of communications which interferes with the coordination of action. The interaction of the parts of an organism so as to conserve the identity of the whole we may call integration. Such adaptive interaction may take place on the physiological level. The maintenance of physiological constant states described in the first chapter is a form of physiological integration. When blood from active muscles reaches the breathing center in the medulla, nerve impulses increase the breathing rate and the deficiency is made up. Heart action increases at the same time and circulation is more rapid. Here are many organs cooperating to the end that the normal oxygen content of the blood be restored. In this book our interest will lie in those forms of integration which are achieved through the nervous system, and particularly through the progressive adaptation which we call learning.

The structure responsible for learning is the system of intercommunicating nerve fibers which enables man to respond to conditions in one part of his body with changes in a distant part. In a living sponge such a system is lacking. For its nourishment a typical sponge depends on a current of water which is kept circulating by beating cilia placed around the outlets in the walls of the sponge. If the intake is closed, these cilia continue to beat, though their beating now accomplishes nothing. If there were nerve connections between intake and cilia which could incite or depress the activity of the cilia according as the intake is open or closed, a waste of energy could be avoided. The sponge is imperfectly integrated by reason of its lack of a nervous system.

In syphilitic invasion of the ganglia where sensory nerves enter the spinal cord, nerve impulses from the muscles and joints of the legs fail to reach the central system. On these nerve impulses depends the coordination of the movements of walking. Without such nerve impulses the action of the muscles used in walking cannot be fitted to the actual position of the legs. The walk of the victim becomes uncoordinated and confused. Unless he is trained to keep his eyes on the position of his legs and to regulate his movements by what he sees, he will be unable to walk.

This is a failure of coordination on a comparatively simple level. The same notion of integration may apply to more complex behavior. A man whose taste for alcohol interferes seriously with his business ambitions may also be looked on as a failure of integration. One interest may so interfere with the other that he becomes neither a good business man nor a good serious drinker. We are judging his conduct by social standards, but we are still concerned with the adaptive interaction of the drinker's movements.

We take for granted the elaborate and precise integration of most of our own behavior. We notice it only when it fails.

Much of this complex integration we have acquired. Many of the lower animals come into the world with their behavior much more "of a piece" than is the behavior of a new-born infant. In the rabbit or the cat a very early age finds them able to right themselves when dropped from a height of a foot or so. This is not learned; without any previous experience the ability appears at a certain stage of the animal's growth.

Many of these instinctive integrations are complicated and involve many muscles. This is true of the righting reaction in rabbit and cat. It is also true of the dog's scratch reflexes. A little irritation with the point of a nail on a dog's back will bring up his leg on that side in rhythmic movement, while the other leg is stretched out in such a way as to support the dog if he is standing. It is easy to fail to notice the extent and elaboration of this reflex response, or its nice coordination. There must be thousands of dogs that are irritated by flea bites on both sides, but no one has ever seen a dog bring up both hind legs at once. If one leg is scratching, the other is extended. The scratch reflex elicited by the bite of a flea may for a time result in the coordinated activity of muscles in all regions of the dog's body, the neck and jaws, the front legs, trunk, rear legs and tail. If one leg is scratching, the other rear leg is somehow prevented from scratching, or from moving in such a way as to destroy the dog's balance.

The German physiologist Magnus has described in great detail many elaborate postural reflexes. Standing erect in animal or man is a complicated performance. It means that numerous muscles are working together. Walking is similarly complicated. And the presence of any coordinated posture places strict limitations on the actions that can be performed. A man cannot jump unless he is in the posture for jumping; he cannot walk without a preliminary shift of posture; he cannot throw a ball without getting set for the action. Our freedom of action is regularly limited by our postural sets.

Many of our important integrations are learned. It requires much practice to swim, to dive, to ride a bicycle. Early efforts betray the fact that the muscles of the body may work at cross purposes. Behavior can include confusion and interference, conflicting postural adjustments. To the sources of such confusion and to the results of such confusion we must give some attention.

Human acts normally begin with the stimulation of a sensitive area and the initiation of a nervous impulse which follows a group of nerve pathways to muscles. The stimulus acts as a goad which releases energy along the communication path and finally in the muscle. If we are interested in knowing what a man is about to do, it is the stimulus that we must observe. Stimuli are only the occasions for action, not the full causes of action. Action derives in part from the energy contributed by the meals we eat; but knowing what calories a man has consumed will not serve to predict his next movements. The weather signs which indicate action are stimuli. Our chances of controlling the behavior of others or of ourselves depend on knowing the stimuli which serve to release that behavior and on our ability to control such stimuli. If we know that a friend responds to an argument with heated defense, we can avoid or produce that defense by withholding or offering the argument. So far as can be observed, nearly all action is occasioned by stimuli. The muscles which serve to move our members contract only as the result of nerve impulses, which are normally set up in sense organs. It is true that some of the most important stimuli to which we react are stimuli furnished by our own movements, but these are none the less stimuli. They are hard to observe. The man seated opposite us in the railway coach, the traffic officer approaching us after whistling us to a stop, the baby lying in his crib, the customer listening to our persuasion, the patient listening to a physician's directions are all controlled by the stimuli that they are receiving, but only a limited portion of the stimulation to which they are responding can we note. If they surprise us by their next act, they are none the less responding to events to which their sense organs are sensitive. But each person has a multitude of sense organs in his viscera, in his muscles and joints, as well as eyes, ears, nose and skin receptors whose stimuli are more or less stimuli for us also.

For most stimulus patterns there are no names and there never will be names. Words are used only for a few outstanding types of situation. This interferes seriously with our ability to predict behavior. But we must do the best we can with the weather signs at our disposal. It is this difficulty in prediction that leads psychologists to speak of stimulus-response *tendencies* or action tendencies. By the word "tendency" we indicate that we are not too certain what will happen. Other stimuli are always acting along with the ones we name or the ones we observe. The sensitive areas of the body are being continuously assailed. There are always conflicting tendencies to be considered. We can never be sure of any response. If we assert that men *tend* to scratch mosquito bites, we say this knowing that no one scratches while chasing his hat down a windy street.

In spite of our inability to take account of any total situation or to be accurate in the description of any stimulus, we find our fellow men predictable. We greet others on the street, fairly certain of having our greeting returned. Students trust that the instructor will have followed his routine and appear to deliver his lecture. The behavior of the insane may be even more predictable than the behavior of the normal man.

With these cautions, we may go on to consider the nature of the interplay of human actions. If a stimulus combination which has in the past been an occasion for a certain action no-again occurs, we expect the action to recur. But there are a number of things which may interfere with that action. Other stimulus patterns may also be present and other action tendencies aroused. In general, one action system may affect another in one of two ways. It may *facilitate* the other. If you grip your hands just as your patellar tendon is struck, your resulting knee jerk will be much exaggerated. Blows directed at fighting dogs may be intended to break up the fight, but may have the effect of making the struggle all the more fierce. A sudden noise which catches us in the course of a movement will ordinarily exaggerate that movement. A loud and unexpected whistle just behind a man who is starting to raise his coffee cup to his lips may make him splash its contents about with a too vigorous lift. Action that is under way tends to enlist reinforcement from whatever stimuli accompany it. It is the lasting effects of this enlistment that are the basic phenomenon of learning.

Psychologists have in the past given the name "dynamogenesis" to this phenomenon, but it has not received the attention that it deserves. We know only that something of the sort takes place. A few studies have measured increase in work done when loud music is played. The added speed and energy of city dwellers may depend on the noise of city streets. Those high school and college students who have in the last few years taken to studying with the radio sounding in the room undoubtedly often benefit by this. Noise and disturbance in our environment which do not interrupt our activity are very likely to add to the energy we give to what we are doing. We might paraphrase the old expression that possession is nine points of the law. An action system under way has the advantage. Unless new stimuli force in a competing action system these new stimuli will simply contribute to the energy of the going act. We fail often to realize this. We argue bitterly with our friends, not knowing that our efforts only add to the strength of their convictions.

We scold or punish a child, not taking into account the fact that our scolding or our punishment only contributes to the child's determination. In both cases, argument and scolding, the essential goal should be to change the action, not to intensify it. We should look for a distraction that would bring about this change, find something on which we can agree with the friend in order to do away with his hostile set, or offer the child a lollypop that would take his attention from his annoying purpose.

Students who work to the accompaniment of the radio almost unanimously report that this is possible only with musical programs. When the music is replaced by a lecture or by an advertising talk, study becomes difficult or impossible. This is because music can be followed by keeping time with muscles which do not interfere with study, by foot-tapping or swaying the body, or by nodding. But our responses to the sound of words occupy our own muscles used in speech, and these very muscles are necessary in reading the textbook. We cannot pronounce to ourselves two different words at the same time because the slight tongue and throat movements which we use in inner speech conflict and interfere. Any person who is not convinced through self-observation of the reality of these movements which accompany inner speech or thinking will find convincing evidence in the work of L. W. Max reported over the last four years. Muscular action is accompanied by slight action currents which can be amplified and recorded. Max attached electrodes to the lips and to the fingers of deaf-mutes and of normal persons. When either "thought" a sentence, action currents were discovered in the appropriate place. The lips of deaf-mutes were inactive, but their fingers busy. The fingers of normal persons were quiet, but their lips registered muscular activity. In neither case were the slight muscle contractions accompanying thinking always visible nor were the subjects always aware that such activity had been going on.

When added stimuli do not increase and facilitate a going act but diminish or suppress that act, this effect is called *inhibition*. The notion of inhibition takes an important place in psychoanalytic explanations. Unfortunately it has never been objectively defined by the psychoanalysts. The term *inhibition* is best reserved for the situation in which one of two competing action systems suppresses the other through the central nervous system. G. R. Wendt has marshaled the evidence for the view that "an activity is inhibited when some other behavior system takes its place." This is my own opinion. In the dog's scratch reflex Sherrington demonstrated that the contraction of the muscles that flex the leg has a positive restraining effect on the opposed muscles which would extend the leg. If the flexors are in contraction, the extensors are not only prevented from contracting but they lose what little tonus they had. In the nerve center the extensors are deprived of impulses. Sherrington believes that inhibition is achieved by actual inhibitory or relaxing impulses over the motor nerve. Others believe that muscles are inhibited by being deprived of exciting impulses at some point in the central system. It is not necessary to decide between these two theories, since the practical effect is the same. One action can, through the stimuli it gives to sense organs in muscle and tendon, prevent a competing action. This is what we mean by *inhibition*.

Not all interference between rival action systems is the result of inhibition. The rival systems may fail to settle the rivalry in the central system, and both systems appear in muscles. The effect is a tug of war, a state of conflict in which two incompatible systems are both active. *Conflict* is a failure of inhibition. And conflict may have distressing results. Action may become confused and inefficient. Prolonged conflict causes exhaustion and exhaustion may in turn exaggerate and prolong the conflict. Stage fright is such a condition. Set for a public appearance at the piano, the unfortunate player is disturbed by the sight or sound of the audience. Tendencies to seek cover, or to look at the audience may compete and interfere with attention to the piano. The result may be a pitiable state of confusion and an emotional storm.

There is considerable evidence that conflict is the most important source of exciting emotion. Excitement is a bodily condition in which the general musculature is tense. In such a state any action which occurs will be exaggerated. Such states of tension activate endocrine glands, the adrenal medulla and possibly the thyroid. The effects of the adrenal secretion in the blood stream are to speed up heart action and to raise blood pressure, to release blood sugar from the liver, and to counteract the effects of fatigue in muscle. The result of all this is that the state of excitement is increased and maintained.

Conflict is not the only means of arousing excitement and general tension. Any intense stimulation will do it. Sherrington believes that the possibility of throwing the whole body musculature into activity from a single receptor by intense stimulation is evidence that from every receptor there are direct paths to every effector. This does not follow. The effect may be a reverberation of neural impulses from the muscles directly activated. Every muscle contains many sense organs which are stimulated by the contraction of that muscle. When any single muscle contracts vigorously, volleys of sensory impulses are discharged into the central nervous system and the tonus of other muscles will be increased.

A number of years ago Watson wrote that fear in human beings had only two original and instinctive stimuli, loud sounds and falling. Dunlap promptly called attention to the fact that the response of babies to these stimuli is not properly described as fear. It is better described as "startle," the rather stereotyped response which Landis has made familiar by taking extremely rapid motion pictures (over 1500 per second) of people who have been startled by the noise of a pistol shot. When the baby does more than "start" at a noise he is probably responding more to his own self-stimulation from the start than to the sound. Watson's statement was misleading in another respect. The effect of startle can be produced by a sudden douche of cold water, a flash of a bright light, a bump, or by many more of those unfortunate mishaps to which babies are exposed.

In the physiological laboratory it has been established that stretching a muscle or offering sudden resistance to the contraction of a muscle is responsible for volleys of sensory impulses from that muscle which traverse the central nervous system and emerge as motor impulses to the first muscle and to other muscles. This is the physiological basis for the exciting nature of conflict. In conflict, muscles are working against each other. The result of conflict is a general increase in tension.

Intense stimuli and conflict give rise to excitement. Resistance to any movement or obstacles to action likewise cause excitement. Excitement may also result from what may be called *accumulation*. Sherman and Sherman report that drawing the edge of a card along the sole of a baby's foot will at first result only in a local response in the foot, a plantar reflex. But if the stimulus is repeated at short intervals each repetition leaves the baby with a slight increase in general muscular tonus. The effect of a series of stimuli is to produce a state of excitement and crying that cannot be distinguished from the effect of a single intense stimulus. This accumulated effect of stimuli is nicely demonstrated in one of the studies of Max already mentioned. If a sleeper receives a series of stimuli (tapping on the bed) the responses to the last of the series are greater than to the first. If the tapping occurred during one of those restless periods which Johnson had described in his studies of sleep, there was a much exaggerated response.

States of conflict and states of excitement play an all-important part in directing learning. They determine to a great extent what it is that we will learn to do, what habits we will form, what interests we will acquire. How this is done will be described in the chapters to follow.

ASSOCIATIVE LEARNING

THERE are two problems of learning. One of them is *what we learn*; the other is *how we learn*. The first problem concerns the results of learning and will be deferred for a few chapters. The second, the description of the circumstances under which learning occurs and the description of the learning process itself, will be considered in this and the two chapters following.

These two problems are somewhat like the two general tasks of the physiologist. It is important that he note and describe accurately the constant states of the organism that he is studying. It is also important that he do more than list these constant states; he must find *how* these states are maintained in the organism. This is essential before his information can be of any use to a physician. Similarly it is not enough for the psychologist to discover what sorts of things men are prone to learn; he must also find how that learning is done. Before we can attack any problems of training or problems of mental readjustment we must know how the obnoxious behavior came about and how we can be rid of it. It is not enough for a dog trainer to know that dogs tend to learn to retrieve or to point. He must, if he is to assist at the business or is to interfere with it and direct it, know how dogs come to do these things. If he is to prevent a dog's becoming gun-shy, he must know the circumstances under which a dog learns this annoying habit. We know already that many persons develop annoying fears or phobias. We cannot prevent or cure phobias unless we know how such habits are acquired.

The scientific description of how learning proceeds brings out immediately a very remarkable fact. This is that in the history of psychology to the present time only one theory of the way in which learning occurs has been so much as proposed. This is the theory of association. Among scientific theories the theory of associative learning has the unique distinction of having opponents but no rivals. Psychologists who are not associationists do not offer rival theories of how learning occurs; they are content to point out *that* learning does take place and then to describe the expected results of learning or the normal results of learning. It is important to know what we can expect the average man to learn, to know the list of goals that human beings tend to attain. It is even more important to know how these goals are attained. Information that men in general tend to discover food somehow is of no assistance in dealing with a man who refuses to eat. Information that organisms tend to self-preservation (which is true enough) does not relieve the public school teacher from the necessity of training her pupils to be cautious in the city traffic. There is a strong tendency for those psychologists who are contented with observing goal attainment in men to neglect cases of failure and maladjustment. A number of psychologists have made a curious use of the association theory. They use it to explain failure but accept success as a variety of natural law.

John Locke was the first psychologist to follow this last course openly. In his *Essay Concerning Human Understanding* published in London in 1690 Locke added as an obvious afterthought a chapter on the association of ideas. The reason for the addition of this chapter was that when he had finished his brilliant account of what the mind could do he realized that not all minds worked thus by the light of reason. There were men who had opinions contrary to his own. If all minds worked alike, how was this to be explained? This was the occasion for the added chapter. It explained that there was a certain low form of mental activity which crept into the reasoning of certain ill-equipped men and led them into error. This was the association of ideas.

This disposition of Locke's to consider how men think only when it was necessary to explain the errors of other men is a disposition we all share. When the outcome of an activity is the achievement of a goal or purpose, there is no need to explain it. We did it, and take the credit. But when we fail, we find objective reasons for that failure, reasons which others will understand. If we succeed in getting the engine of the boat started, this success needs no explanation other than that we intended to do just that; we are a person of insight. If we fail to start the engine, we go into mechanical details and put the blame on the physical mechanism of the engine, or we talk in terms of forgetting or the association of ideas. Even the most modern studies of maze learning are likely to explain wrong turns as "position habits" and right turns as just natural tendencies to reach the goal. But right thinking and right choices in a maze must happen somehow; and it is quite probable that they happen according to the same rules of learning that are involved in wrong choices and in mistakes.

Although the association theory has no rivals, it has more than its share of difficulties and ambiguities. For many centuries it was thought of in terms of the association of ideas, and ideas are very difficult to observe and record, whether they are our own or are the ideas of others. There were consequently almost no controlled experiments on associative learning until the last of the nineteenth century when Ebbinghaus made his elaborate study of the memorizing and the forgetting of nonsense syllables. Since Ebbinghaus was his own subject and was observing his own performance, his experiments did not bring into the open the question of just what it is that is associated, ideas or speech, and whether the ideas or the speech were supposed to be associated with the printed symbols which Ebbinghaus had before him, or with the ideas of the words which were presumably aroused by the sight of the list.

It was not until the beginning of the present century that the problem of association was attacked by objective methods and divorced from metaphysical issues of how ideas are related to stimuli or to actions. In 1902 Twitmyer at the University of Pennsylvania published a report of a laboratory experiment in which he had succeeded in associating the knee jerk with the sound of a bell, after sounding the bell as he tapped the patellar tendon. Twitmyer succeeded, after many pairings of the two stimuli, in getting the knee jerk as a response to the sound of the bell alone.

Twitmyer's work has been rather lost sight of because soon after its appearance the late Russian psychologist, Pavlov, began the publication of work done by himself and by his students which by its tremendous volume and its interesting new methods captured the attention of psychologists. Pavlov's more important experiments are described in every modern textbook of general psychology, and the details will not be repeated here. To the "new" phenomenon, which was new only in the sense that it was attacked by a new laboratory method, Pavlov first gave the name "psychic secretion," recognizing that associative learning of this sort is the kind of thing we mean by the word "mind." For this name he soon substituted another. A correct translation of the new name would have been "conditional reflex" on the ground that the secretion of saliva depended or was conditional on the training given. The first English translation of the new name, however, was the phrase "conditioned reflex" and the prestige of Pavlov's new method has fixed this as the scientific term for this form of associative learning. This is un-fortunate, for the name does not indicate the nature of the phenomenon without elaborate explanation.

The extent and originality of Pavlov's work established him as a leader in the investigation of the conditioned reflex. His conceptions of its nature and his descriptive formulas have been accepted until recently by most of the psychologists and physiologists working on problems of conditioning. This has had a number of extremely unfortunate results. It has committed many other investigators to very questionable theories and awkward and misleading formulations of experimental methods. One of the chief objections to Pavlov's work is that throughout his experiments he assumes that the items that are associated are two stimuli, an "unconditioned" stimulus, usually the taste of food, which is instinctive or native in the animal and provokes the flow of saliva without any training, and the new or conditioned stimulus, which becomes the new cue for the response.

In Pavlov's typical experiment a dog is placed in a loose harness in which he stands before a food receptacle. The room is protected from stray noise and disturbance. The experimenter is in another room and can view the dog through a window but cannot be seen by the dog. A bell or other stimulus is used. Some two seconds, more or less, after the bell, food appears in the receptacle, and the dog, which has been kept hungry, eats. Saliva flows and is collected and its flow recorded. The duct of one of the salivary glands has been led through the dog's cheek to a tube to facilitate the recording of the flow. After ten to fifty "pairings" of bell and food, the bell alone will cause saliva to flow.

One objection to Pavlov's description is that the so-called "unconditioned" stimulus has a rather obscure relation to the flow of saliva. The dog must be hungry; he must be accustomed to the apparatus. It is possible that the taste of the food is not the direct cause of the flow of saliva. It may be the movements of chewing which bring this about. It is very hard to be sure just what stimulus is primarily responsible for any response. It is also highly probable that what Pavlov should have observed was the connection of the cue and the response, not the connection of the new and old stimuli.

Pavlov found that the bell could be sounded as long as thirty minutes before offering the food. If this was repeated often enough, the dog would eventually secrete saliva some thirty minutes after the sounding of the bell, even though no food was offered. In cases of such "remote" association it is highly probable that the real associative cue for the secretion is not the bell; the direct effects of the bell on the nervous system are probably over within a fraction of a second, and the actual associative cue is some indirect effect of the sound on the dog's posture and movements. The bell starts the dog to listening, and a regular series of listening movements has one component which accompanies the secretion of the gland. This component movement becomes the signal for secretion. If the dog is disturbed in the meantime so that this component movement does not occur, no associative response will occur.

Another objection to Pavlov's descriptions of his results is his use of the term, "reflex." The total effect of the bell-food situation on the dog is an elaborate complex of movement as well as of glandular secretion. The dog changes his position, eats the food, licks his chops, or, at first, cocks his ears in the direction of the bell. Confining observation and record to the one isolated factor of secretion has hindered the understanding of the event. Behavior in general offers no well-defined and stereotyped "reflexes" which have clear-cut "unconditioned" stimuli.

In the theory presented in this book we shall speak of conditioned response or associative response rather than of conditioned reflex; and we shall understand that the two items associated are not two stimuli, but a stimulus pattern which we shall often call the cue or signal, and whatever complex of movements is going on at the time of the association. The associated cue tends to call out not a stereotyped reflex, but whatever the animal was doing at the time. Motion pictures of experiments like Pavlov's show that the single record of salivary flow gives a very restricted and inadequate notion of what the dog has really learned to do.

Many psychologists in past generations have pointed out that different forms of associative learning could be readily described in terms of one basic principle, association by contiguity in time. If thinking of Jones whom we met at the railroad station calls to mind Watson, whom we met also at the railroad station on another occasion, this could be described as association by virtue of sameness of place. But it can better be described as two associations: thinking of Jones reminds us of the station, because Jones and the station were experienced at the same time; thinking of the station reminds us of Watson because on another occasion the station and Watson were experienced at the same time. Associations have been described as due to similarity: thinking of a new car reminds us of someone's new yacht. Or they can be described as due to contrast: thinking of black reminds us of white, or "small" reminds us of "large." All of these can plausibly be explained as based on coincidence or contiguity in time. A restatement of the principle of association by contiguity which makes clear what is associated is as follows: *Stimulus patterns which are active at the time of a response tend, on being repeated, to elicit that response.*

In the explanations which follow, this will be assumed as a general principle analogous to the use of the principle of gravitation in physics. The present account will attempt to use this principle as a tool of investigation, to carry it to the problems

which lie in the field of mental disorder and maladjustment. It
has the disadvantages of any general principle. One of these disadvantages is that generality is achieved by a certain amount of
indefiniteness. But the principle also has great advantages. It
tells what to look for as the weather signs of any action in which
we are interested. If a dog sees us as we stone it or kick it, its
response to stoning or kicking may be in part or in whole restored on the next occasion that we are seen. If a slight puff of
air is blown on the cornea of the eye as a light is flashed, the
light may become the signal for the blinking originally caused
by the puff. If, in Pavlov's laboratory, a pin prick just precedes
the appearance of food a number of times, the dog will learn to
approach the food dish and to secrete saliva when he feels the
pin. The pin prick has become an appetizer or *hors d'œuvre*
which starts appetite and eating.

Of course, this might not happen. All depends on what response is made, not on what stimuli are offered. If the pin prick
is lively enough to cause the dog to jerk and struggle in his
harness and to disregard the food, instead of the pin's becoming
an appetizer, the food will become a signal for struggle. Pavlov's
conception that it is the two stimuli that are associated would
conceal this possibility, while the principle of association as
stated above would make clear what to expect. It is always a
response, no matter how produced, which is associated with
some new stimulus cue which has accompanied it. It is never an
isolated bit of muscular contraction or glandular secretion, but
the response that is associated and tends to follow the associative cue *is the response that occurred in all its complexity.*
When the response is recorded in the laboratory, the record
picks out some detail of the total response. This detail is never
more than a fraction of the associative response.

It has just been stated that the response that *tends* to follow
the associated cue is the response that occurred with that cue.

The word "tends" in this statement betrays some doubt of the event, and this doubt is justified. The organism is continually beset by stimuli in many regions. There may be, in fact, there always are present cues for other conditioned responses. These are not necessarily compatible with the conditioned response for which we were looking. The result is always compromise. No associative or conditioned response (these words are used interchangeably) is ever a perfect repetition of a previous response. There is only a rough approximation of repetition. If we have made a hostile move toward a friend's dog on our first visit, and the dog has barked at us, we cannot expect the dog to repeat on our second visit the identical movements that he went through when he saw us before. Some details of those former movements will be impossible because we have caught the dog in a different stance. A dog cannot jump from a sitting position. He cannot bark with a bone in his mouth. His master may be in sight on the second occasion, and this will make his reaction to us a compromise. But we can be fairly sure that some essentials of his former hostility will be in evidence.

A child is frightened by a barking dog while playing on the lawn. The child screams and runs. On the next occasion that the child sees the dog the child is walking with its mother. We do not expect it to run away from the dog. It will probably turn and cling to the mother, or get behind her. Her presence alters the situation and habitual attitudes toward her interfere with the exact repetition of the former behavior. But we may well expect the child to show some signs of fear. Some part of the former response to the dog will be present.

When care is taken to set up again the total situation so far as possible, the response is much more likely to be a close approximation to what happened before. And when responses have become dependent mainly on stimuli within the person himself, stimuli from muscles and joints which are furnished by movements, we may have astonishing repetitiousness in behavior. Our signatures tend to resemble each other. We acquire many habits which are just as characteristic of us as are our signatures.

All this seems very discouraging for the prediction of human behavior. It is really not so. In many situations some features of the situation are outstanding, and likewise some features of the response. A woman has acquired a cat phobia. This means no more than that she is afraid of cats. On some occasion she has been frightened when a cat was conspicuously present. She already had many responses associated with cats and her perception of the cat accompanies her fear. On a later occasion the mewing of a cat, not heard at all on the occasion of her fright, may be enough to reinstate terror and flight from the neighborhood.

Such a person may never show her fear twice in exactly the same way. Whether she is with companions or alone, in a strange house or at home, whether the cat is close by or only heard at a distance, will all determine differences in the way she shows her distress. But who will doubt after being associated with such a person that there is a core of response which is enough the same on these various occasions to justify one name for the successive exhibitions of terror. Both stimuli and responses, the signs of cats and the terror, are roughly identifiable, enough so for practical purposes, at least. Even a man is never twice the same, but we find it convenient to refer to him by the same name in successive days or successive years. The word "two" never conveys exactly the same meaning to any two persons, or to any one person on different occasions. But this does not justify us in dropping it from our vocabulary.

After these tedious and discouraging remarks about associative learning, it is high time to turn to the question: What are the basic facts of association? How does it operate in bringing about mental adjustment? We may begin with a few illustrations from common experience. A practical animal trainer in teaching a horse to stop at the word "whoa" utters the word and pulls back on the reins. The horse stops in response to the pull. After a number of rehearsals of word and pull together the horse will stop at the word. A careful trainer follows the instructions to be found in an army manual: Never give a command that you do not expect to be obeyed. The reason for this is, of course, that a command that is followed by disobedience becomes an associative cue for the disobedient action. To train a dog to come when his name is called, the dog must first be induced to come. This can be done in various ways, and it is in his knowledge of these ways that the man who knows dogs shows his superiority. But whether he shows the dog food, or pulls the dog toward him with a check line, or starts away and trusts the dog to follow, it is the repetition of the name as the dog starts to approach that establishes the name as a cue for approach.

To undo this training all that need be done is for the trainer to do as many owners do, call the dog's name while he is preoccupied with something else, or just as the dog starts off to chase a car, or in any circumstances in which the dog could not be expected to obey promptly. The name then becomes a cue for this particular form of disobedience and loses all its drawing power. Children regularly called while they are running away learn to run away when called. We associate the name of a person with his face by uttering it while looking at his face. We fail to remember names by failing to do this; embarrassment keeps our eyes downcast or causes us to mumble indistinctly instead of speaking the name clearly.

A student told me several years ago that his Czech grandfather had a large flock of chickens, some white and some black. He enjoyed mystifying visitors by demonstrating that one call

would bring all the white chickens running to his feet, leaving
the blacks indifferent, while another call would bring the blacks
running and leave the whites attending to their previous affairs.
This was, of course, easy to bring about by keeping the whites
and blacks in separate pens and using different calls while scat-
tering their grain.

Association is between cue and response. This means that we
learn only what we were caused to do on the previous occasion.
Three persons have recently described to me their visit to
Mexico. There is practically no overlapping in the descriptions,
which might well concern three different countries. One is
resolved never to return. Mexico means for her only death, disease, and unsanitary food. A second was enthusiastic. The Indian food was appetizing and interesting. The people seemed
happy and friendly, whereas the first visitor reported them dour
and hostile. From the third visitor I have heard almost nothing
but descriptions of church architecture. I neglected to ask him
whether or not he had seen any Mexicans during his trip. From
these descriptions we can reconstruct their behavior while in
Mexico. The first was not in good health when the trip was
undertaken; a gastro-intestinal disorder dominated her behavior.
The food was nauseating only because she was nauseated. The
second was in good health and ate with good appetite. The food
was therefore well recommended. The third tourist had gone to
Mexico looking for churches and with a large architectural
vocabulary already in his stock of habits. The phrases were
already in his repertoire. All that he needed to do was to attach
them to the names of churches, and his trip consisted largely in
doing just that.

Razran has recently published a selected bibliography of over
a thousand studies on conditioning which have been printed
since Pavlov called attention to his "psychic secretion." These
studies have brought out much information about the phe-

nomenon of associative learning, but many mysteries remain. Very little is known of the brain mechanisms for learning. Some types of stimulus patterns serve more readily as associative cues than do others, but we do not yet know why. We cannot be concerned here with the finer points raised by this mass of experimental work. We must be contented with the statement that all learning involves the establishment of new cues for response by virtue of the association of these cues with response, and that these new cues retain their associative connections until they are associated with new responses. I am familiar with no experimental results which need be interpreted as contradicting the generality of the principle of association by contiguity: Stimulus patterns tend to elicit on their recurrence whatever response they accompany.

Associative learning must be described as a mechanism. By this is only meant that in itself its action is not planned. It is not an agency with foresight and intelligence. Associative learning is the *basis* of foresight and intelligence, not the result of these. It is possible to construct a machine which will perform the essential task of associative learning, and many such machines have been built. An electric buzzer can be so connected with a push button that a touch on the button will not activate the buzzer until on some occasion the button is touched while the buzzer is sounding. After this, a touch on the button will be effective. It is, of course, impossible to duplicate the learning of real organisms. The complexity of their structures is beyond our artifices.

One of our students, Thomas Ross, has pointed out that if a device were constructed that would resonate to the sound of the voice in a sufficient variety of patterns corresponding to the qualities of the sound, it would be possible to build a typewriter which would, if words were pronounced as they were typed, eventually "learn" to take dictation. This would probably take several lifetimes to build, but it is not beyond possibility.

If the basic phenomenon of association is mechanistic, how is it that it can result in foresight and intelligence? How can any mechanism be adaptive? Many mechanisms are, of course, adaptive. The governor of an old-fashioned steam engine regulates the steam supply to maintain the speed for which the governor is set. The thermostat of a modern heating plant keeps the temperature of the house within a narrow range. When the temperature rises above the point for which the instrument is set, the heat is shut off. When the house cools, the heating mechanism is put into action. The constant states of the physiologist are undoubtedly maintained by a variety of such regulators.

But a capacity for associative learning, a capacity for connecting actions with new signals simply because these new signals have happened to accompany the action, is not, on the face of it, adaptive. Why should it lead to the defense of the organism against danger or to provision of food and mates? Part of the answer to this is that associative learning is not always fortunate in its results. Animals and men can acquire conditioned responses that lead directly to trouble and to death. Many forms of unhappiness and maladjustment in human beings are direct results of habits, and the capacity to learn may establish bad interests like morphine and heroin which are destructive in their effects. The delusions of the insane are acquired by associative learning, and a high intelligence often means only more elaborate and successful defense of the delusion. The person with a phobia learns to maintain the phobia, to avoid situations which would lead to his retraining and his return to normal. The annoying behavior of the hysteric, the despair and anxiety of the neurasthenic are in large part the products of learning. Intelligence, which is sometimes used in the sense of a capacity for learning, may even defeat the biological ends which we assume gave rise to it in the first place. It was developed by virtue of its contribution to survival, but it can threaten survival. A man may learn to avoid food or to question the value of his own life and end life by his own efforts. He may learn to avoid the trouble and care of children, and thus intelligence, which developed in the course of evolution because it meant generally more adequate protection of self and children and so furthered survival, might conceivably lead to what E. A. Ross has called race suicide.

If all this gives the impression that associative learning is not an advantage to a species but a danger, that impression is mistaken. The disadvantages of an ability to learn have been mentioned only because it is usually assumed that such an ability is an unmixed benefit. Intelligence is like the other devices produced in the course of evolution, generally serviceable or it would not exist. Legs are useful but they can carry a man into trouble as well as out of it. The great advantage of the ability to associate lies in the fact that it enables its possessor to react to the signs of good and evil events instead of reacting only when actual harm and actual benefit have been realized. The defensive reaction can be given before the misfortune. The organism can be prepared for food before food is swallowed. Man's eyes, ears and nose are sometimes called his distance receptors because the objects which furnish stimuli to these organs are not in contact with the body. In a new-born child practically no responses are associated with stimuli to these distance receptors except looking, listening and sniffing. Stimuli to these sense organs accompany all activity and all response, whether approach or avoidance, and become cues for such responses. The new infant is not blind, but it has accumulated none of the associations with things seen that make vision useful to the adult. His only sign of having vision is that he will follow a moving object with his eyes, but he does not perceive what such objects are. That means only that seeing leads to no action because it has no associations. He soon learns to blink when something approaches his eyes, because approaching objects have at other times touched his lashes or his eyes and this is a native stimulus for blinking. The approaching object becomes a substitute cue for blinking. By association the infant acquires a repertoire of learned response.

The possibilities of learning are limited only by the indefinitely various combinations of muscular contraction and, on the side of the senses, by the capacity of the infants' brain to respond differentially to patterns of stimulation and to establish patterns as functional units for the release of action. It is probably in this last feature that bright persons differ in structure from dull ones. No characteristic differences in the number and the nerve supply of muscles have been noticed, or in the structure of sense organs.

Associative learning is thus not identical with adaptation, but it is a means by which adaptation may, under favorable circumstances, be achieved. Under unfavorable circumstances associative learning may lead a man far astray from health and virtue and from cooperation with his fellows.

——V——

ASSOCIATIVE INHIBITION

O NE action can inhibit or prevent another by virtue of stronger stimuli, more complete integration or through priority. Such inhibition is achieved in the central nervous system, either by depriving the rival action of its motor nerve impulses or, as Sherrington believes, by arousing an inhibitory state of some kind at the motor centers which would relax the rival muscles. When any act is under way, the contraction of the muscles used in that act stimulates their muscle sense organs, and it is probably the effect of this stimulation which "captures" the motor centers in the central system and excludes the rival act.

Such inhibition can be very complete in spinal reflexes. If the scratch reflex is stimulated in a dog whose brain has been disconnected from the rest of the central nervous system, other spinal reflexes are thoroughly eliminated so long as the scratching continues. But in ordinary human behavior such complete elimination of rival action is very rare. The rivalry may not be settled in the brain and may be carried on to an actual contest in the muscles. One set of muscles may be actually pulling against another. This state we have called *conflict* and *such conflict is a failure of inhibition*, or a failure of inhibition to be complete. A man contemplating a jump from a high place may be in such a state of conflict. The jump is all set to go. The muscles that will be used are tensed in readiness. But the muscles used in holding back are also tense. The result may

be a long pause, and eventually the fatigue of the tensed opposing muscles results in muscular tremors.

Some time ago I was idly watching a laboratory kitten stalking a beetle on the floor of the laboratory. It occurred to me
to interfere and I brought my hand sharply down on the desk
top with a loud slap. The kitten jumped almost instantly, but
landed at some distance from the beetle. Obviously the cautious stalking included two opposed action systems, one which
was carrying the kitten forward toward the beetle, the other a
preparation for a quick get-away. Neither system had fully inhibited the other. Both were present in the form of muscular
tension.

The prevention of one act by another can thus be either
through inhibition or through the interference of actual muscular contraction. In either case it is evident that such prevention
is subject to associative learning. We can learn not to do something at a particular signal by learning to do something else
which will interfere with the first act, either through inhibition
or through active muscular interference. Negative reactions to
a stimulus are merely positive actions from a different point of
view.

That the dissociation of a cue from a response is actually
the association of the cue with a rival response has until recently escaped notice in the laboratory. This is for a reason
very easily understood. A certain response is being investigated,
for instance, a tendency to jerk away the hand when a buzzer
sounds. The conditioned response has been established by
sounding the buzzer just before an electric shock is applied to
the fingers. As the buzzer is sounded again and again without
reinforcement from the shock, the tendency to jerk away the
hand may gradually disappear. It would in this case be difficult
to find the response that is substituted for jerking away the
hand. But that careful observation will often disclose the substi-

tute is made very probable by the fact that several recent experiments have made clear the new response which takes the place of the one subject to associative inhibition. Wendt discovered that nystagmus, the peculiar eye movement which can be set up by rotating a person in a chair and which serves to hold the eyes directed on one point of the surroundings for a moment, then shifts them rapidly to another fixation point, tended to disappear with practice. But this disappearance of nystagmus was accompanied by the appearance of a competing movement. With repeated slight rotation the subjects formed a habit of moving the eye forward instead of backward. Only by searching for it would this substituted response be found, and most investigators, interested only in the presence or absence of a particular response, have failed to note all that happened.

If the laboratory experiment consists in establishing an association between the two members of a pair of syllables, so that the sight of the first syllable will recall the second because the second had regularly appeared after the first, a loss or a forgetting of this association is probably the effect of some new association acquired by the first word. But this is extremely difficult to prove, because the record shows only whether or not the second word was given in response to the first. If it fails to be given, it is hard to identify the response which presumably took its place.

In a great many instances the substitute response is clear and obvious. When we have heard a ribald version of a familiar song it is often impossible from then on to recall the true version. The wrong phrase has taken the place of the original. A young man whose hero was a famous American orator had the misfortune to see his hero in an extremely undignified position, and complained to me that from that time he has no longer been able to think of him in his impressive platform appearance without having this episode suddenly intrude itself and deflect his train of thought. A quarrel with a friend may substitute for our former friendly attitude a new constraint. It is my own conviction that forgetting is based on associative inhibition. A number of facts strongly indicate that this is the case. We may define forgetting as the tendency of a response to cease following its former cues. The sight of a certain person's face no longer calls up his name. The examination question has ceased to be a cue for the answer. The memorized piano selection now "goes wrong" at some point and cannot be played through. The mention of the name of a dead friend ceases to call up grief.

Until very recent years it has been assumed by psychologists that forgetting is a simple effect of time. The lapse of time was supposed to include metabolic changes in the nervous system which gradually erased the effects of associative learning. Against this belief stand many instances in which the expected forgetting does not occur. It has been remarked by many experimenters that laboratory animals have kept certain conditioned responses over a period of months or years without any practice. In our own laboratory, cats which have learned to escape from a puzzle box, each cat in its own individual way, will promptly go through its act even when its only experience of escape had been several months before and its practice had been limited to a few trials on a single afternoon.

It has long been known that different kinds of learning disappear at different rates. A list of nonsense syllables may be learned by repeating it sufficiently often to give it once through without consulting the list, for example, *nem, geg, fov, dib, hov, pum, gor, toc, buk, rog, maf, kos.* If such a list is rehearsed to the point of one repetition without error or prompting, it will, for most persons, require several repetitions to bring it to this point again after an hour has passed. It may have taken thirteen rehearsals to learn and possibly eight to relearn. This is a saving of five repetitions and this represents what was not forgotten. But if the same persons hear the sentence, "The New York Giants won their game two to nothing," they can repeat this without rehearsal, and may be able to recall the sentence years later. The sentence, of course, was composed of parts which had been learned before hearing the sentence on this particular occasion; the nonsense syllables demanded many new associations.

The "fading" of memorized nonsense syllable series is often a fairly regular and orderly process. It is possible to represent it by a curve if too accurate a fit is not demanded. But the curve of forgetting of the meaningful sentence would be very different in shape. If forgetting is essentially relearning of interfering activities, why should the nonsense syllables disappear in so regular a fashion? The answer probably is that after the syllables have been once learned, most persons use similar linguistic patterns in speech and thought, but with different associations and different following syllables. This "sidetracks" the associative sequence and the series cannot now be correctly repeated because of these new connections. Forgetting is, for nonsense syllables, very rapid at first and progressively slower. After one day, very little has been saved, but very little of that very little is being forgotten. The probable reason for this is that just after the series is learned there are many associative cues which assist the memory, and these are alienated by new associations. Many cues are alienated during the period just after learning because there are many cues to alienate. Fewer are being alienated after twenty-four hours because there are fewer to alienate. I once used as an analogy the budget system of two Philadelphia artists about which I was told some twenty-five years ago. The two painters occasionally, but only occasionally, sold a picture. When they did, they took the check to a bank and drew their money in dimes. These were taken to their garret studio and flung about everywhere. During the first few days afterwards dimes were easy to find and they could dine well. After a month, dimes were still to be found, but, being fewer in number, they took more time and effort to locate. The cost of dinners was automatically reduced to fit the available funds. Similarly the effects of learning fade rapidly at first, but the cues remaining after a period of months are likely to be cues which are not readily run across in daily life and so do not occur in other connections.

Jenkins and Dallenbach have established that even for nonsense material far less is forgotten during a period of sleep than during a period of waking, and others have confirmed this observation. Everyone is familiar with the experience of waking with the events of the evening before clearly in mind, only to have them become somewhat uncertain and vague before the day is over. This is strikingly true of children, who recall bedtime stories (provided they were still awake when the stories were told) in the morning in great detail; but a story told in the morning will be far less perfectly remembered. The experiences which we have during the visit of a single day to a strange city remain fixed in memory. If we stay on for an extended visit, other associations with the same surroundings erase some of the first associations, and we are more vague about our first day's program.

In functional nervous disorders the inability to forget is often one of the outstanding difficulties. A phobia is a special type of fear in which the victim has learned to avoid the fearsome stimulus. As a result he cannot unlearn his fear, because unlearning or associative inhibition *requires that the stimulus be present* and that some other response be attached to it. If a person who was afraid of cats were forced to live among cats, the fear would be lost. But a "phobic" person is just the person who will not submit to such retraining.

Similar inability to forget may occur in grief. A mother whose interest had turned from her husband to her young son was overcome with grief at his sudden death in an influenza epidemic. The situation was complicated by the fact that she had come to resent the presence of the husband. This may or may not have been influenced by the fact that he had grown fat and bald and lost the interest in variety and adventure evident during courtship. She also had what will in another chapter be described as an hysteric personality and had been used to getting her way by indirect means and to acting under motives of which she was not clearly aware. Her grief took on the nature of a civic event. By this is meant that she made use of it to annoy her husband and to impress the world with her loss. The boy's possessions were left undisturbed in their places in the house, except for an occasional dusting. At dinner a place was regularly set for him as it had been during his life. Her conversation was devoted to the lost son. This state of affairs continued for many years. In a normal household or among normal persons grief is a very different affair, and leads to new habits and a new adjustment. This particular person was unable to forget.

This inability to forget consisted only in arranging her life so as not to forget. A move to another home or to another city, the acquiring of new interests, even keeping on with the ordinary household routine in the same home, would lead to forgetting. A room with sad memories loses these memories if we work in it or if we continue to live in it with thoughts on other things. But in the case of the mother, grief had become a self-conserving state analogous to the constant states described by the physiologist. This tendency of all habits will be considered in a later chapter. The mother learned to take care to preserve her emotion or, to be more exact, the habits of its public expression, and to keep it alive. All that was required was that she allow no new associations to displace the old.

All learning involves associative inhibition. Acquiring a tendency to respond in any manner whatsoever to a situation must involve losing other conflicting tendencies already established. Breaking one habit always means establishing another. In many cases it is a matter of indifference what the new habit shall be, just so that it is not a new annoyance. We thus lose sight of the substitution and remark only that the old habit is gone.

It has been stated that forgetting and the loss of associative learning are always caused by the substitution of new learning. A number of psychologists would not agree to this statement, and for their opinion they can offer excellent reasons. Humphrey in his *The Nature of Learning* argues that there is an independent principle involved in the tendency of a cue to lose its associative connection with a response. He believes that the repetition of an associative cue leads to what he calls "habituation." By this term he means a gradual loss of the effectiveness of the cue.

Pavlov in his *Conditioned Reflexes* describes a characteristic of the conditioned salivary reflex which was illustrated in many experiments. Once the conditioning was established and the signal had become effective in causing saliva to flow, the repetition of the bell or other cue at short intervals "extinguished" the conditioning, and the number of drops secreted at each ringing of the bell gradually diminished to zero. It could actually pass through the zero point and the bell would exert an inhibitory effect on other stimuli. This effect he called "experimental extinction" and he found it temporary in nature. After a short rest period or after a disturbance of any kind the conditioned reflex was again present in almost its original strength.

To my notion, Winslow has explained this "temporary" or "experimental" extinction without recourse to a new principle of learning. He points out that the dog has been accustomed to eat after the bell rings and that to have the bell ring time and again without the presentation of food leads to a state of irritation and excitement which it is well known will inhibit the flow of saliva. The rest period is sufficient for a recovery from the excitement and the uninhibited reflex can again appear. This does not explain the similar effect on blinking which can be illustrated by striking a person across the forehead with a light roll of paper. As the light blows continue, the subject gradually ceases to blink each time that he is struck. An unexpected slap on the back will restore the tendency to blink to its full strength. This case of extinction, I believe, depends on the gradual practice by the subject of holding his eyes motionless and this replaces the blinking. The slap on the back upsets the cues for this substituted response and leaves him in his original state.

Menzies has recently published an account of the conditioning of some vasomotor responses. When one hand is placed in cold water, the surface blood vessels of both hands contract and the skin of the dry hand becomes cooler. This is, of course, brought about by nerve connections between the skin sense organs of the one hand and the surface blood vessels of the other. It may be described as a reflex. We have very little information about such vasomotor behavior and its amenability to associative learning. Menzies attached a thermocouple to the skin of the dry hand and recorded its changes in temperature. He succeeded in associating both this response and its complementary one, the dilation of blood vessels when one hand is put in warm water, with a number of cues, a bell, a buzzer, a word pronounced by the experimenter and whispered by the subject, a movement of the arm and a movement of the hand.

All of these became cues for the response after more or less practice with the water bath. When Menzies repeated the cues without reinforcement by the water, which is the method Pavlov used to get temporary extinction, only the arm movement and the hand movement showed extinction of their responses. The other cues lost none of their effectiveness; in fact, they gained effectiveness.

All of the instances of temporary extinction so far reported are, in my opinion, instances of associative inhibition; and their temporary character means only that their cues, the cues for the inhibiting substitute responses, are dependent on temporary stance or posture or other temporary features of the situation. When temporary extinction fails to appear, as it does in many cases, this is only because no inhibitory response has been set up. Menzies could have extinguished his vasomotor responses quickly enough by associating their cues with water of the opposite temperature.

But there is some new evidence for Humphrey's "habituation" which cannot be interpreted as associative inhibition. Prosser and Hunter have found something quite similar to "habituation" in the gradual extinction of "startle" in a white rat. They recorded activity in the leg muscles of a rat electrically and found that when a sharp clicking noise was repeated every fifteen seconds there was a gradual elimination of the response. That this was not simple fatigue of the muscles was shown by the fact that the opening of the door of the box in which the rat was confined, or the flashing of a bright light before the rat, restored the start and this required many repetitions to extinguish again. Similar extinction could be brought about in a spinal rat. Prosser and Hunter believe that this extinction and its disinhibition by new sensory disturbances are based on events in the central nervous system between the sensory nerve cell and the outgoing motor nerve cell.

To what extent such extinction leaves permanent effects has not yet been investigated. So far as is now known, it is a state which disappears after rest or on any disturbance of the animal. I am not convinced that it is necessary to accept "habituation" as a characteristic of learning of general application. There are so many cases on record of responses which fail to extinguish with repeated stimulation that such a generalization would be questionable. The laboratory instances of clear extinction all involve frequent stimulation at intervals of a few seconds.

Whether or not this temporary extinction as described by Prosser and Hunter can enter into relatively durable learning effects is not now known. It is quite possible that in spite of the fact that the animal recovers from it after a short rest or after a shock of any kind, cues which operated during the period of extinction would be alienated from the response and would contribute their effect to other activities going on at the time. So far as the evidence now shows, such extinction does not operate to reduce the response to stimuli which occur only at occasional intervals. It could not, for instance, be invoked to explain the behavior of Thorndike's cats.

Many years ago Thorndike, as an amusing variation of his puzzle-box experiments, placed a cat in the box and waited until the cat sat down and started to scratch. He then opened the door by a distant release. When this had been repeated a number of times, the release always being postponed until the cat had scratched, the cat would, on being placed in the box, promptly begin to scratch. But as the routine was continued a change came over the cat's behavior, a change that indicates a strong resemblance between cat behavior and human behavior. The scratching became more and more perfunctory until the cat would finally make only a feeble pass with its hind leg and then look at the door. The new office boy, the new student assistant, or the new teacher behaves much like this. The new broom sweeps clean. Humphrey and Wheeler would dignify this reduction of effort with the status of a general principle of learning. The time and energy, they would say, that any animal expends in reaching a goal reduces to a minimum.

One objection to this is that the time and energy used by animals and men in attaining their ends does not reduce to any ascertainable minimum. Studies of bricklaying show that new instruction will make it possible for the most experienced brick-layers to halve the time required for laying a thousand bricks. We all conserve useless movements in our best performances. For those interested in nervous breakdown and functional nervous disorders, or in the failures of human beings to make successful adjustments to their situation, such a principle appears to have a slightly mocking quality.

What common sense names "habituation" is without any doubt based on associative inhibition. The old sailor no longer feels qualms when there is a slight blow. It is well known that a landsman who ships as a member of the crew on a vessel and has duties to perform is less affected by rough weather than the landsman who ships as a passenger and has nothing to keep him from devoting himself to enthusiastic nausea. The medical student may lapse into unconsciousness at his first sight of a major operation, but nearly all get promptly over this. They get over it through the competition of their duties. Attempts to fix in memory what they see eventually displace the behavior that leads to syncope. They learn to follow the surgeon's knife instead of the stimuli for distress. An experienced pilot in the naval air service once did me the dubious favor of showing me "what it was really like." I gratified him by losing all interest in the scenery, particularly when it appeared overhead. After it was over he unbent to the extent of confiding to me that when he himself went up as a passenger, a stunting pilot could put him in the same condition that I had lived through. Piloting his own ship he was occupied with his job and properly anticipated the movements of the plane because he was himself putting it into those movements. With another pilot he would be caught unawares by the plane's motion and would have the same tensions as a groundling.

The driver of a car is seldom affected by car-sickness on a winding road. He is ready for the eccentric motions of the car; but the passenger, especially if not used to riding with that particular driver, finds himself in great tension, bracing himself for turns that do not come, unready for others that do. I have, in the early days of driving, had my passenger push his feet through the floor board. He evidently would not have used just the same driving tactics that I was using at that particular intersection.

We recover from grief because we are compelled eventually to go about our duties in the presence of stimuli for grief. Unfortunately we can recover from affection by the same method. Not simple "habituation" determines this, because our recovery depends on the acquisition of new and inhibiting responses. Objects about whose beauty we were once enthusiastic lose their thrill because we have been led to other behavior in their presence. The new car whose first flyspeck is carefully removed with a handkerchief is allowed, after some months, to go unwashed and untended. This is not simply because experience with it brings automatic habituation but because we have by that time seen the car often when we were preoccupied with other affairs. If there is no such preoccupation, and we are persons of leisure, we may demand that the car be regularly spotless.

The gist of the whole matter is that we learn to respond to a cue as we were caused to respond to that cue. If a reminder of an embarrassing incident causes us shame and depression and we are later led to confess it to a friend who laughs at us, we may come to laugh instead of blush when the incident is recalled. Many practicing physicians dealing with mental cases owe the bulk of their good results to an air of cheerfulness and confidence to which the patient responds. The patient in this state can discuss his troubles, being always steered aside when he shows signs of upset. The patient is much surprised later to find himself thinking calmly of his difficulty. He has mentioned his trouble without distress, and so his trouble can now be mentioned without distress. Associative inhibition has replaced distress by the state encouraged by the physician. The patient, to use the current jargon, has been reconditioned.

There are three ways by which a stimulus can be prevented from eliciting a given response. The first of these consists in introducing the stimulus at such weak strengths that it will not cause the response and then gradually increasing the intensity of the stimulus, always taking care that it is below the "threshold" of the response. A gradual introduction to the motion of a ship which, unfortunately, cannot be controlled by human means, but depends on the gradualness of change in the weather, can bring about tolerance of a considerable storm. Most children react to the taste of green olives by spitting them out. But if they begin with small nibbles, not enough to cause rejection, whole olives will eventually be taken with pleasure.

This is distinct from sense organ adaptation, which is a temporary affair. The visitor to a chemistry laboratory is assailed by many smells. Within a few minutes after entering, these are much less obtrusive. The receptors for smell in the nose have adapted and no longer give rise to sensory impulses. But there is another more permanent effect which has nothing to do with sense organ adaptation. From this temporary adaptation there is recovery in a few minutes in the open air. But the chemist who enters the laboratory every morning may no longer notice the odor even as he enters. In the presence of that odor he has been occupied with his work, and this preoccupation establishes new responses to the stimulus of the odor. It is not that he does not smell it, but that he ceases to comment upon it and goes to work. He no longer wrinkles his nose in distaste or rushes to open a window; the odor is now simply another reminder of his work and may become part of the conditions essential for absorption in his problems.

Members of families learn to make use of this type of associative inhibition in dealing with their housemates. The proposal to send the daughter to an expensive school is "broken gently" to the father. Casual mention of the school's advantages without directly submitting the issue, criticism of the present school, at first so mild that it will not stir defense, prepare the father so that when the question is at last put squarely before him he does not make a scene over the expense. He is by this time used to the idea and there will be no violent reaction.

This is the method of gradual increase of the stimulus, it being kept within the point of tolerance, and it results in gradually increasing tolerance. The second method for preventing an undesired response to a stimulus is more direct. This consists in presenting the cues for the unwanted action in a strength that would ordinarily cause the response, but at the same time preventing the response by other controls of the situation, seeing to it that the response is inhibited. The simplest practical application of this is illustrated by the method used by the old-fashioned blacksmith in shoeing a horse that shows a disposition to kick. The blacksmith's helper uses what is called a "twitch." This is a loop of rope at the end of a stick. The loop is placed around the upper lip of the horse and the stick is twisted until the loop is tight. In its preoccupation with this annoyance at its forward end the horse disregards what is going on at the stern. Response to the twitch inhibits kicking in response to the shoeing of the rear foot. The horse eventually may learn to submit to being shod without showing resentment.

When the husband in a family reads aloud items from the newspaper to his wife while she is occupied about the affairs of the household, listening and replying are inhibited by her more pressing activities. If this is kept up, she will eventually reach a state in which she is adapted to his habit by the ability to disregard his voice. She no longer hears what he says. A student attending a lecture who is preoccupied with some current serious problem concerning his funds or his evening diversion is kept from responding to the lecture and may in time form the ability to sit through any hour without hearing what is going on. We must learn to listen to music, and if music is heard while we are preoccupied with other affairs, we learn to disregard it. The practice of keeping the radio going continuously makes the members of the household practically music-proof.

We have already described the method of many psychoanalysts and physicians who see to it that some pleasant or at least cheerful attitude is maintained while troubles are discussed, with the result that the mention of troubles no longer causes distress.

Besides the method of keeping within the subject's tolerance and gradually increasing the stimulus and the method of inhibition, there is a third way to develop associative or conditioned inhibition. This is to present stimuli for an act at a time when some of the instruments necessary for carrying out the act are not present. We cannot drink without water, or drive without a car, or go hunting without a gun. The lack of the means of execution prevents the act as well as would direct inhibition or inadequate cues. If the means of execution are absent, something else will be done, and this becomes the associated habit.

All three of these methods are, of course, only one method. All of them consist in presenting the cues of an undesirable action and seeing to it that the action is not performed. Since there is always other behavior going on when we are awake, the cues we present become stimuli for this other behavior and are alienated from the obnoxious response.

It is probably only the lack of activity that reduces learning during sleep to a minimum. Association is between stimuli and action, and when action is not present, associations are not established. Experiments on learning during sleep were undertaken on the mistaken assumption that the associations would be established between stimuli. When records of a foreign language are played in the room with a sleeper who is really asleep, they become associated only with the behavior of sleep. If sleep is light and the sleeper is restless, he may respond to the records with some slight speech activity and slight learning is not impossible. In general, the new language would come to act only as a lullaby.

HABITS

WE ARE still occupied with the question: How do men learn? That question has been partially answered by the description of association. Learning proceeds by new associations of stimulus and response. If we are asked to predict how a man will behave in certain circumstances, the answer will be that we expect him to behave as he did on the last occasion when these particular circumstances were present. The child who has been frightened in the dark will show fear in the dark. The child who has been caused to run to his mother when the neighbor's dog entered the yard will do this on the next occasion. The man who has taken morphine or alcohol when in a state of extreme tension will tend strongly to repeat this method of relaxing. The man who rose promptly when his alarm clock sounded will probably rise at its signal the next morning. The man who turned over for another forty winks when he heard its bell will repeat this the next day.

At first sight this rule of associative learning has all the appearance of a solution of the problem of learning. Actually, prediction in terms of the principle of association will not carry us very far. The reason for its inadequacy is that on most occasions there are complications in the situation. Stimulus patterns which have been associated with different acts are both present. The situation does not tell us unambiguously which of a number of conflicting actions will take place. All of them have cues present and it is clear that not all of them can prevail. A small

boy has several times smoked with his companions. Will he repeat this with his younger brother present? The prediction of
behavior would be extremely simple if we could always refer
back to a previous situation just like the present situation, and
know that there had been no intervening repetitions of any of
the parts of the situation. This information we almost never
have.

Human behavior is more predictable than this would indicate.
It is predictable in terms of habit as well as in terms of association. Habits themselves are the products of associative learning,
but they are a very special form of association and enable us to
go much further in understanding our fellow men than would
the principle of contiguity alone. A habit means a tendency to
respond in a particular way *to a wide variety of circumstances.*
We do not need to inquire much about the present situation if
we know that a man is an habitual smoker, or that he is a stut-
terer, or that he is an hysteric who has a habit of losing consciousness when he is in a tight place. The essence of a habit is
that it can be depended on in spite of contrary cues. The habitual smoker will smoke even if others are inconvenienced.
He will smoke even if the tobacco supply is a mile distant.
Habits seem to surmount obstacles and cues for conflicting responses. The small boy may eventually smoke in the presence of
a stern father who has forbidden the practice. We describe
people as being the slaves of habit. By that description we mean
that the habit will prevail over associative signals for other acts.
The morphine addict gets his drug in spite of the opposition of
his friends, his family and the police.

If there is any outstanding characteristic of human behavior
it is its repetitiousness. It is more repetitious than the world
about us. We ourselves change less than our environments. The
habits we form in prosperity tend to go on in depression. The
habits we form in childhood tend to last into adult age. One of

life's greatest surprises is to find that our childhood notions of our elders were mistaken and to reach middle age only to discover that the "grown-up" was a myth. Many habits we preserve for most of our lives though they have become meaningless. We bite our nails, twiddle our thumbs, draw the same sketches over and over on the paper of the letter we had intended to write, vote the same ticket though it has become the same in name only, feel hostile toward a neighbor though all occasion for hostility passed long ago.

Habit involves much more than a tendency to repeat the same behavior in similar situations. It becomes a tendency to repeat the same behavior in highly dissimilar situations. We begin drinking under very special circumstances and end up by drinking anywhere and any time. Drinking has become so fixed that we may expect it where social considerations and manners would forbid it or other interests are subordinated to it.

Several years ago college women, at least in my own institution, were wearing their hair down over one eye. One young occupant of the front row of a lecture class I particularly noticed because she frequently responded to the contact of her hair with her face by running out a long underlip and blowing a blast of air that carried back the offending hair. The following year college coiffures had changed and eyes were no longer covered. But the young blower, now seated on the front row in another lecture class, continued to run out her lip and blow at intervals, though the action now had no longer any meaning or use. A misplaced habit like this, if it is sufficiently annoying or embarrassing, is called a *tic*. Such tics were originally adaptive acts, but they have later become a useless byplay of conduct. All persons have such useless habits, but most people are fortunate enough to keep them more or less inconspicuous. The more exaggerated and disturbing forms, the winks and grimaces that get unfavorable attention from others, are often marks of some deep-seated failure of adjustment.

For the present we are interested in tics only as illustrations of habit. A *habit* is an action series that has become comparatively stereotyped and can now be released by a comparatively slight cue. The best description of the process by which habits are established is in terms of a word which Hollingworth has revived after it had for many years ceased to be used by psychologists. This word is *redintegration*, and by it Hollingworth means the tendency of an action to be reinstated as a whole when a part of its former stimulus situation recurs. This describes what happens in the formation of a habit. An action takes place; the action is the complex resultant of all the stimuli acting at the time. The action in its turn stimulates at every stage sense organs in the body itself. Each contraction or change in contraction in a muscle and each bending of a joint, each strain on a tendon contributes to the pattern of stimuli offered by the reaction itself. There is a continuous procession of movement-produced stimuli intimately associated with the action.

The action therefore not only establishes associations between what is seen, heard, smelled, or touched and the movements that accompany these stimuli, but also establishes associations between movement and movement, that is, between movement as a stimulus to proprioceptors and movement as a response to that stimulation. By virtue of these associations, the action becomes self-sustaining. If it is only once started, it will keep itself up. Cues inside the body take the place of cues outside. At the piano after a pupil has learned to read the notes, playing a selection following the notes may establish associations between one movement and the next so that the tune can be played without looking at the music.

In repeated actions many associations are set up which do not relate to the environment, but serve to knit the action into an integrated whole, to effect redintegration. Any stimulus which starts the action will be followed by the action without reference to outside cues, or with only occasional reference. The reinstatement of the first part acts as the cue for the next.

The act is now somewhat independent of the pattern of stimuli offered by the outer world. It can "run itself off" once it is started. The dog lying asleep on the hearth illustrates this reinstatement in almost complete independence of environmental stimuli. He is lying down, but goes through the movements of running after a rabbit. His legs work in proper order, if not to the proper extent. Muffled "woofs" issue from his mouth. We say that he is dreaming because he is so obviously out of touch with his surroundings. And this is undoubtedly the stuff that dreams are made of. They are stray action systems running through their paces, each movement offering the cues for the next, until something breaks up the sequence. At some point the dog's position makes impossible even a small degree of the movement that was next in the original series, or his master's voice causes him to open his eyes and look about, and the dream is gone. Dreams are made up of bits of past action.

In the establishment of a habit we have a progressively closer knitting of the parts of an action until the action can be reinstated almost as a whole by a slight cue from the environment. Once, on a dull afternoon in the classroom, the lights went out for a moment. One of the students jumped to his feet and stumbled over others on the way to the aisle. When the period was over he came up to explain. He worked at a city power house on a night shift. One of his duties was to pull a certain switch as soon as possible if the lights went out. The nature of my lecture and, I hope, the lack of sleep because of his night job, put him in a doze. When the lights went out he was already sufficiently out of touch with the classroom to allow his experience at the power house to be in some part redintegrated.

His awkwardness and stumbling were undoubtedly because the movements linked together at the power house did not fit his classroom position.

Mind has been defined as progressive adjustment to recurring situations. This progressive adjustment results in habits which take care of recurring disturbances. The final habit represents the adaptation that solves the recurring problem. It is only on the basis of past experience that we can meet any problem. If we confront a situation that is new, we react to familiar parts of it as we have in the past reacted to those parts. If the problem is not solved and the hurt or the hunger continues, these first reactions will be eventually checked by fatigue, or by their own completion which changes the situation, and we will change our attack; but we are forever limited to action in terms of our habits. It is absurd to speak of solving a new situation by immediate insight or by intuition.

According to the explorer Stefansson, the unfortunate Franklin Expedition to the Arctic starved to death in the midst of plenty. In that region Eskimos live on the country. But the British explorers, when their British food was gone, had no equipment of habits which could have led them to fish or hunt. A friend who is a geologist tells me that one of the difficulties he encountered in managing an exploration across Central America was that donkeys from one region became unfit for work in the next district because in the next district the habitual forage was not to be had. His animals starved while the local donkeys were thriving. Habit adjustment includes much more than action and movement. Vasomotor conditioning has been mentioned before. The new recruits in a Canadian kiltie regiment were issued their kilts on a winter afternoon. Many of them, after their experience with the new uniform, turned up the next morning on the line at reveille wearing kilts, but also wearing under the kilts their long woolen underwear. It took many days of enforced exposure of their knees to establish new local vasomotor habits in that region.

Our diets become habits, not only habits in the choice of food, but habits in the digestion of food, so that we may suffer real distress when we visit a foreign country. Our thinking is as fixed by habit as is our action. We are by habit in sympathy with liberals or with conservatives. By habit we are contented or discontented, loyal or disloyal, thrifty or careless, selfish or generous, and, to a greater extent than most people will believe, sick or well. One well-informed physician asserts that by habit many people are fat or thin. We know that habit plays a heavy rôle in determining how much we shall eat. But this authority states that when weight has been reduced for a long period by means of a diet, an increase in the diet will very often not result in an increase in weight. A new endocrine adjustment of weight has been established.

All disturbances of mental health are habit maladjustments. Physical defect may be a contributing cause in the great majority of nervous breakdowns, but the establishment of bad habits is as essential a part of the disorder. A visit to an orthopedic hospital will demonstrate what can be accomplished by habit adjustment in the face of physical weakness and injuries. Children accommodate themselves to chronic pain, to weakness, to prolonged months in casts. They do not have the handicap of long-established habit systems which make their state intolerable. Men adjust themselves to the loss of vision, the loss of hands or legs, to paralysis and life in a wheeled chair without nervous breakdown. Other men "go to pieces" when their income is cut to five thousand, or the authority to which they have become used is gone, or their standing in the community is lowered without any loss of essential comfort.

A distinction must be made between habit and *skill*. Skill is defined as an ability to achieve some end result, hitting the target, driving the car, training a race horse, managing a child, teaching, skiing, performing a surgical operation, filling teeth. Such skills are made up of thousands of habits. Skill at chess depends on years of playing in which different responses have become attached to thousands of different patterns of the pieces on the board. The skilled chess player makes without hesitation the move that experience has last attached to that situation. How the unsuccessful moves tend to be eliminated with practice and only the successful retained will be discussed when we turn to consider *what* we learn instead of *how* we learn.

Most of the undesirable behavior of the nervous breakdown, the anesthesias, paralyses, compulsions, tics, seizures, that make life a burden to the psychoneurotic and to his friends are habits. They illustrate the fact that habit, as contrasted with skill, is blind. Habits mean primarily mechanical responses to set cues which are little affected by the rest of the situation. Skills are not blind because they include discriminating habits which adapt behavior to a variety of situations. Knowing when to talk and when to keep silent is a skill. Chronic talkativeness and chronic silence are habitual attitudes. Knowing when to run up to the net and when to stay back is tennis skill, two sets of habits which adjust to two sets of situations. Smoking is a habit, but the person who smokes and yet never annoys others by it has learned a skill.

A paralysis of the legs may be a habit. A woman who had been through a illness that made walking impossible spent her days in a wheeled chair. When she recovered she still could not walk. She had formed habits of relying on the chair, habits of giving way when she tried to walk, and these survived her physical recovery. One day she saw across the room her two-year-old baby about to put the iodine bottle to its mouth. She was up and across the room in an instant, seized the child and put the bottle out of reach. Then she noticed that she had walked. This served to lead to renewed efforts to walk which were successful. Neurotics develop skills as well as habits. They learn to manage their families to their own satisfaction by illnesses, by fainting, by headaches, by scenes. A person who has learned when to faint and when not to faint, who can "take it or leave it," has acquired a skill. The person with a phobia develops a skill in avoiding the object of his fear. By this is meant that he establishes in the course of time a large number of habits that all serve this end.

A habit may be established on one occasion. This is true of paralyses, tics (where these are learned and not based on lesions in the central nervous system), or of such trivial habits as button twirling or a food distaste. But a skill always takes practice because it requires that many discriminating habits be established and fitted to the circumstances. The boxer must not only learn to swing or jab; he must learn when to do this and when to do something else. He must attach to the movements he sees his opponent make the proper responses. To establish such discriminating habits and the associative inhibition of bad habits takes long practice.

There are in general two methods of breaking habits. One of these leaves the habit in a very real sense whole and unimpaired, but at the same time gets rid of it. This apparent paradox is explained when we understand that it is possible to discover the initial cues for a habit and to associate other behavior with those cues, leaving the habit with its internal organization undamaged. It is there and ready to appear, but its usual cues have been alienated. We are rid of the habit only in the sense that we will not be any longer embarrassed by it. It is not gone, but merely retired. The habit has been sidetracked.

A man leaves off smoking or drinking by such a method. His difficulty in doing this comes from the fact that these are not single habits but large groups of habits and include some minor skills, such as not spilling from the jug, or keeping the pipe burning. But smoking and drinking habits acquire in the course of years a thousand reminders, a thousand cues, and it is very difficult to redirect all of these cues. The smoker, with the best intentions in the world, is caught by reminders that were not reconditioned. When a man who has smoked for many years succeeds in breaking off and does not smoke again, this means that he has reconditioned the initial acts of smoking itself, and that he follows these with some substitute movement, even if it is only a grim expression.

Habits may also be broken by a process that does not merely "sidetrack" the action but breaks up its internal associations so that the habit is actually gone, not just retired, and would have to be relearned in order to reappear. A pianist may try to increase the tempo of his piece and may introduce a confusion that remains even when the former slow rate is attempted.

Dunlap's method of negative practice probably involves both sidetracking and some breaking up. Dunlap attacks an undesirable habit by having its possessor practice it. But the conditions of practice must be very definitely controlled. If the bad habit is a facial grimace that, left to itself, is repeated every few minutes or seconds, the grimacer is directed to carry through the movement shortly before its usual occurrence. It is to be done with attention and a thorough understanding that the grimace is undesirable. Repeated practice under these conditions builds up a strong interest in not grimacing and the time comes when this rival behavior can be carried through. Now the victim of the tic has associated his substitute action with the beginnings of the tic, and, because of his negative practice, these beginnings are attached to words or their equivalents. They are now under voluntary control.

By grimacing on request of the psychologist rather than to the

obscure and unnoticed cues which had been causing the tic, the
victim becomes aware of these beginnings. The clear understanding of the undesirable nature of the response on which
Dunlap insists serves to prepare a substitute act and to cause
this substitute to be practiced in advance. After practice on
command of the psychologist, the act can be controlled because
the substitution can now be made.

A psychologist has recently described to me the successful
issue of a case of negative practice which illustrates these points.
A country boy of ten went swimming with some older boys
who indulged in much talk of sex. On the way home by a se-
cluded woods road where he assumed he had no hearers, the
boy shouted an obscene word. But the daughter of a neighbor
was just entering the road from a path. She had overheard, and
she promptly announced that she was going to tell the boy's
father. The boy realized that if she carried out her threat he
would be severely beaten, his father being an irascible man.
During the day the boy developed what some writers have
called a "psychic tic." After a spasm of his respiratory muscles
he would shout the word. This happened in spite of his efforts
to control himself. These efforts merely added to the severity of
the spasm and the energy with which the word was shouted.
This behavior was intolerable at school and led to his dismissal.
Eventually the neighbors refused to allow him to step foot on
their premises and the boy was confined to his own back yard.
Much later his family brought him to the clinic.

The parents were first persuaded to modify their attitude of
horrified resentment. The psychologist then took the boy into
a separate room and induced him to shout the forbidden word
some hundred times. Toward the end this required strong urging. The whole performance was repeated with the parents
present. The tic seemed to have disappeared and the boy was
sent to a parental school for a week's observation. There it was

reported that the tic was not gone but was materially changed. The respiratory spasm was still present, but the obscene word was now replaced by spitting. Brought again to the clinic with this new tic, he was made to repeat the treatment. Before long the boy was very loath to go on. From that time on there were no further occurrences of the tic. Of course, no progress had been made toward correcting the original conditions which gave rise to the tic, the fear of the father and the relationship to the older boys were not materially changed by what had happened at the clinic, but the compulsive act had disappeared. Negative practice had succeeded in first substituting spitting for the word, and finally in substituting something else for the spitting and the respiratory spasm.

Dunlap warns that the method in unskilled hands may be ineffective or harmful, but it is a method that can often be used. Practice of a habit in order to get rid of it seems on the face of it absurd; but it turns out to be just a special application of the general rule for all habit-breaking: find the associative cues responsible for the start of the habit, the conditioning stimuli, and to these cues or conditioners practice some less undesirable response. The old association will give way to the new.

In such tics as that just described one of the outstanding features of habit is well illustrated. A person subject to a tic can restrain the movement, but only for a limited time. During this attempt at control he becomes visibly tense and agitated. He can give his attention to nothing else. He is, of course, meeting the tendency to grimace by some rival action; he holds his face set against the tic. Gradually tension increases and eventually the tic occurs. This is followed by relief. The conflict of the two action systems is over and relaxation can follow. The redintegrative nature of habits based on their interconditioning of the parts of the habit gives them an advantage over rival action systems. If the habitual movement is started, the habit tends strongly to go through to completion. Blocking the movement by a competing action produces excitement which will continue so long as the blocking continues or until there is complete inhibition of the beginnings of the habitual action. Habits thus are self-conserving, and their blocking tends to produce minor variations which overcome the blocking. Many habits which are successful substitutes for undesirable ones preserve the main features of the suppressed action. The smoker often finds that chewing a straw or sweet is the easiest method of avoiding a smoke.

When disturbed, an organism reacts in such a way as to minimize the disturbance and maintain its identity. But the reaction itself was a change in the organism. It is now a new creature with its new habit. This also tends to be defended and to be resistant to change. Habits are thus like the homeostatic states described by Cannon. Interference with them tends to reinforce them. Habits become parts of our personality and new habits will be developed in their defense.

THE EMOTIONAL REINFORCEMENT
OF ACTION

DANCING is a widespread human occupation and serves a wide variety of interests. One of its most interesting forms is the war dance which serves to stir enthusiasm to the point necessary for confronting a hostile tribe in battle. At least one African tribe prepares for a lion hunt by a dance which undoubtedly is necessary for the method of hunting used in that locality. The men of the tribe armed only with short spears charge the lion and depend on their numbers for victory. The death of a huntsman or two is a fairly common result. It is interesting to speculate concerning the nature of a lion dance which would serve to make a group of American stockbrokers rush out and confront a lion with spears.

Every person may notice during the day changes in his energy level which affect his behavior. The student pouring over his textbook of psychology late at night may find his eyes heavy. Reading is a strain and requires much effort. Attention flags. He cannot make himself follow the sense of the print. He finally gives up. Before going to bed he casually picks up the mystery story which he had begun the day before. He becomes absorbed in it. Reading goes easily. His eyes no longer feel heavy. All the feeling of strain and effort is gone. At the tense moments of the story his finger is ready to turn the page with a sharp rustle of paper when his eye has reached the bottom line.

What is the difference in the bodily condition of a huntsman before and after the lion dance, or the student before and after picking up the exciting tale? A great many somatic conditions are changed. The pulse is quickened and stronger. Blood pressure has risen. There is added blood sugar in the blood stream and oxygen supply is increased. The adrenal glands are discharging adrenine into the blood and this counteracts fatigue effects in muscle and prepares the blood for more ready clotting. This last effect, of course, has more usefulness for the lion hunter than it has for the novel reader, but it is present in both cases. One of the most striking changes in the onset of excitement is in the nature of movement. This is energized. The voice of an angry man is changed and becomes louder. His least actions are either very energetic and exaggerated, or they show the effects of tension in their restraint. He does not simply close the door, he bangs it. He paces the room or makes useless gestures. There is energy to spare. His body is prepared for action by a large number of physiological mechanisms.

The most direct and immediate of these preparations for action is in the increase in tonus of body muscles. Some of the origins of this increase are clear. Any intense stimulus has this effect. Its first effect may be confined to a small muscle group, but the contraction of the muscles of this group is also a stimulus to the muscle sense organs and this stimulation adds to the total stream of afferent impulses carried to the central system. If the intense stimulus is sudden in its onset, there is evidence for a tendency of the resulting volleys of sensory impulses to "spill over" and energize many muscles. Landis has recently taken many motion pictures of human subjects thus stimulated by an unexpected revolver shot. His pictures, taken at a rate of over 1500 a second, show details of the "startle" response which quite escape the observer who merely watches the subject. The pattern of response is highly stereotyped and predictable. Whether the same pattern would be obtained by a sudden slap on the back or a douche of cold water, we do not know. It is evident, however, that in all such intense stimuli part of the response of the subject is to his own movement. His first action stimulates him further and he is left in a state of increased muscular tension. The dozing husband at the symphony concert may be roused by a sharp prod from his wife's elbow, and the effects of this will be evident for many minutes. He is for a time alert and conscious. His general tonus is higher. But as one group of muscles after another relaxes, the stream of stimulation from this group diminishes. The result is that these and other muscles lose still more of their tonus, for they were dependent on the stimulation from the contraction which is now diminished. Relaxation is progressive, and the concert lover gradually resumes his normal peaceful condition. A sudden *fortissimo* passage with the orchestra's brasses may have the same effect as a poke in the ribs. The final number of the program should be loud and lively if the audience is to be aroused to animation as it leaves the hall.

The physiological preparations for action are continuously adjusted to action. If a record of heart action is made over a period, constant fluctuations are evident. These coincide with demands on the subject. If someone enters the room and attracts his attention, if he makes a slight motion of hand and arm, if he recalls that his car was parked near a fire hydrant, the heart shows more vigorous activity. Just how, in detail, this regulation is accomplished is not completely known. The nerves responsible for increased and diminished pulse are known, but not the full description from beginning to end.

It is not only intense stimulation that can increase the tension of muscles and incite to activity the physiological supports of that tension. Laboratory studies have established that any muscle which meets sudden resistance to its contraction, or any muscle which is suddenly stretched, is the origin of sensory impulses from its own receptors. One effect of stimulation by resistance or stretching in a muscle is to increase the tonus of that muscle itself. This occurs through "circular" reflexes from muscle back to the same muscle. E. B. Holt first pointed out that even if such were not the rule in a young organism, it would be one of the first and most certain effects of associative learning. The contraction of a muscle is always accompanied by the stimulation of its own receptors, so that associative pathways are established by the very first activity in muscle.

Resistance to the contraction of a muscle or the stretching of a muscle is furnished by obstacles to action. If the door opens easily, the movement which we make to open it may be slight. If it unexpectedly sticks, our movement is almost automatically energized. When we pick up a weight our first effort may be determined by association with the appearance of the weight. We learn to judge how heavy an object is by looking at it. But if the first contraction of the muscles used is not sufficient to lift the weight, the resistance to the action of muscles serves to increase their contraction. Obstacles then become occasions for excitement as well as intense stimuli.

States of excitement may also be built up by accumulation. One stimulus may have little effect, but leave many muscles in a state of slightly increased tension. The added stimuli may be no stronger than the first, but one of them finally has an effect out of all proportion to its intensity. Rage may thus be built up by a series of annoying incidents. No one incident by itself would have been effective, but the effects of the series accumulate and finally a storm of excitement may be produced. What we call a temper tantrum in small children is often built up in such a fashion. Once the child's muscles are in this state of general tension and the physiological accompaniments of it in heart action and adrenal action and other mechanisms are present, the tantrum state is self-maintaining. Tension is self-main-

taining because muscular contraction is self-stimulating. Adrian
has succeeded in isolating a single muscle sensory cell and its
afferent fiber. This sense organ showed little evidence of the
adaptation which appears on stimulating a touch receptor. Continuing the stimulation of the muscle receptor continued its
response, whereas continued touch on a touch receptor soon
puts it in a state of adaptation in which it no longer responds.
This throws light on the tendency of many action systems to be
self-sustaining.

A man who has just been slapped will be found to have a
much exaggerated general muscular tonus. This may be indicated by increased reflexes like the knee jerk. His actions, whatever they are, will be more vigorous than they were before. Just
after the ferry whistle has blown, there is a sudden stir of movement among the passengers on the upper deck, and this stir
will require some time to disappear. For the first instant the
passengers were responding to the whistle. Now, they are responding to their own response to the whistle. The effects thus
only gradually die away.

If a baby is teased into a gradual increase of muscle tonus,
there comes a point at which crying occurs. This is probably
governed by impulses originating in the mid-brain and depends
on the degree of tension in muscles. It serves in its turn to
maintain and intensify excitement. Crying keeps the baby crying and time is required to bring relaxation. The general tonus
of muscles and the chemical changes in the blood stream do
not disappear with the original stimulus which was responsible
for them.

A child's temper tantrum is a state in which all the body's
agencies for reinforcing action are in evidence, and the energetic action resulting is the maintaining stimulus for continuing
the state. As the child grows older, his behavior may be modified by learning. This is not necessarily the case; many adults

are subject to such tantrums until they reach an age at which the body's capacity for reinforcing action is diminished. A recent bride, married just after graduation from the university, surprised her husband by lying on the floor and kicking and screaming whenever there was a difference of opinion between them. This was a form of tantrum which she had preserved from early childhood. It refused to be unlearned because it had been for years successful in getting what the child wanted from her family and in reducing it to submission. Had it not been successful, she would have remained in the same situation and the tantrum would have worn itself out. Associative inhibition would then have suppressed the tantrum. The fact that the end of each tantrum had seen the situation change, had been accompanied by family surrender instead of family opposition, left family opposition the cue for the tantrum.

In most adults, the behavior accompanying one of these emotional storms shows great modification through learning. The expression may be affected by its reception in the group to which the individual belongs. Conventional behavior in the logging camp of a generation ago was for an enraged logger to throw his hat on the ground and to riddle it with holes by jumping on it with his calks. One social caste may tend to show rage by vituperation, another by frigid restraint. The manner in which the surrounding folkways guide the action of the individual will be considered later in this book.

Many nervous breakdowns in adult life are essentially tantrums. The origin of the excitement may be very occasionally intense stimulation from the environment. There is an occasional man who cannot survive the noise of a machine shop, and an occasional soldier who may give way under continued noise of modern artillery. But the cause of the onset of a breakdown is more likely to be not merely intense stimulation from the environment, but the presence of obstacles to deep-seated desires and interests. The breakdown is still more likely to be the result of conflict in the individual himself. The opposition of action systems within the individual first activates the mechanisms for reinforcement of action, and then, when the conflict is unresolved, exhaustion follows.

It is fashionable at present for psychological texts to refer often to the lack of emotional maturity and the consequences of that lack. By this is meant that many adults have never learned to conform to the approved ways of expressing emotional excitement. There are many such approved ways, and states of excitement form the core of many social institutions. Dancing has been mentioned. In primitive society this unites the group in energetic pursuit of a common cause. The college "pep rally," the political meeting, the revivalist's tent performance are all means of working up a common excitement in order to further a common enterprise. There are even social institutions for working off the effects of excitement which serve to bring the group back to normal routine. Primitive groups have triumphal dances which serve to expend the energy still available after the victory. Janet has pointed out that the behavior of triumph occurs when victory has not been too hard won and there is surplus energy remaining after the need for it is gone. This is dissipated by the ceremonies of triumph, the celebration of victory. Without such ceremonial, it would be impossible to settle down to work. Individuals manifest the behavior of triumph as well as groups. When the news of success arrives and finds the individual still worked up to a level of energy far above normal, the surplus may be expended in one manner or another.

There are a number of ways in which the individual may bring about relaxation after excitement has been worked up to a high point. Tensions may be relaxed by direct "progressive relaxation," as Jacobson has described it. Jacobson's method of progressive relaxation requires long training and much supervision. Other methods tend to be learned by individuals without instruction. Crying, laughing, sighing, yawning and stretching all serve to relax the skeletal musculature. The Freudian doctrine that yawning and sighing are essentially sexual in origin is oblivious of the fact that they may become associated with tensions from any source, not only sexual tensions. It is not only lovers who sigh. Inexperienced orators, babies waiting for a delayed bottle, job-seekers sitting in the anteroom of the employment office all sigh and by sighing effect a temporary relaxation of their tense state.

Waiting is a very interesting condition. A person who is waiting is in a state far different from the state of a person who is just resting. Waiting means being in a state of muscular readiness for an action and at the same time deferring that action. The "waiter" is restless and tense. If he can sigh or yawn that tension will be reduced.

We speak of laughing things off or of having a good cry. Both actions are capable of erasing a pattern of tension. We recognize this in our distrust of public servants who laugh too easily. The dictator should not be able to laugh, nor should the doctor or the plumber. We prefer that they continue to worry until they find the solution of our troubles. It is very significant that the neurotic person is almost never jolly and has no true sense of humor. He is often desperately sincere and earnest. His habits do not include hearty laughter. They may include its superficial imitation, the sort of laughter that we all indulge in when the joke is "on us." Or neurotics may be able to laugh occasionally at severe misfortunes to their friends or at the statement that some acquaintance or relative is a fool or a knave, but their own troubles they cannot laugh off.

Laughter, is important because it can be used to displace states of irritation or anxiety. With such states it is somehow incompatible. By means of laughter associative inhibitions can be set up that help to restore mental balance and mental health. Laughter is more available for the cure of tension and anxiety than it is for the cure of grief because in grief and depression there are no tensions to relax and laughter depends on initial tension. In embarrassment the tensions are already present and laughter is easy. Social tabus enter into most social laughter. The reason for this is that the tabu creates the tensions that are necessary before laughter can occur. The baby's first joke is to be tickled. This requires a state of tension which results from a conflict of defense and friendly attitude. Crying and tears serve to resign us to misfortune as well as laughter, and by the same means. The captive weeps long and often, and in weeping is reconciled to fate.

About the states of excitement in which action is energized we have a considerable amount of physiological information. This is not true of states of depression which are also characteristic of human behavior. Men are capable of entering into a condition in which action is hard to elicit and if elicited is diminished in vigor. In so far as such states of depression are merely failure of one or more of the mechanisms for excitement—a failure of the heart to respond, or a failure of endocrine secretion, or a failure of blood sugar supply, or of respiration—depression is understandable. But we are forced to recognize that the human being has distinct mechanisms for the depression of action and that these mechanisms may be set in action by associative cues. Bad news, the death of a loved one, the complete failure of a cherished enterprise may put the individual almost immediately into a condition in which the energy of action is diminished. The criminal sentenced to death is frequently in this condition for a prolonged time. As his hour comes near, movement becomes difficult. He may have to be supported on his way to the scaffold. In order to get from him a reply to a question it may be necessary to shake him by the shoulder. This produces enough increase in tonus to make him for a short time attentive and responsive. His facial expression is characteristic. The expression of grief and shame appears to be the simple result of a loss of tonus in those facial muscles which are, when we are in the company of other persons, kept in a state of contraction. The depressed individual gives the same impression to an observer that an exhausted or weakened person gives. But depression can occur when muscles are not in the least fatigued. The physiology of depression remains rather a mystery.

Depression is an adaptive response. That is to say, it can in many circumstances be of great utility to the organism. It keeps down the useless expenditure of energy and avoids exhaustion when an individual is confronted with a complete and hopeless blocking in his conduct. It is the reaction by which we give up hopeless undertakings. The normal occasion for depression is a situation in which all lines of action are closed to us. If it were not for depression, the prisoner in his cell would wear himself out in vain efforts to escape. On the death of a loved one, depression prevents a vain struggle with the inevitable.

Excitement and depression are the two general physiological states which are of most importance in understanding and dealing with human conduct. They are the two general emotional conditions which are of prime importance in the mental hospital. We use many other words to describe emotion. Disgust, passion, shame, rage, fear, are all useful in describing behavior but these do not describe general physiological states so much as the sources of those states, and the type of behavior that we expect to accompany them. The emotional condition present in each of these is excitement or depression. Hunger and passion are, for instance, both states of excitement. Their specific origins are different. The persistent stimulation which accounts for the excitement of hunger has its seat in the stomach and the hunger spasms of that organ. The persistent stimulation which accounts for erotic passion originates in the genitalia. But the two states of excitement, in so far as these reinforce action and involve heart, breathing, endocrine secretion, and other physiological mechanisms, are not distinguishable. Rage may be described as a tendency to attack accompanied by excitement, and fear as a tendency to flight or avoidance accompanied by excitement. The general physiological reinforcement of action is alike in both.

There are, of course, fears which are more related to depression, in that action is paralyzed; but the real distinction between rage and fear lies in the nature of the action systems involved, not in the blood pressure changes, the glandular secretions, and other internal effects.

In the temper tantrum we are dealing primarily with a state of intense excitement in which the physiological mechanisms for reinforcing action are at work, but learning has not directed the action into approved channels. The energy available is being wasted, or used to the extreme annoyance of others. The temper tantrum is neither fear nor rage, unless it includes attack or flight. The addition of attack or flight does not change the nature of the general physiological condition which is the essence of the tantrum.

Until the last generation psychologists spoke of rage, love and fear as if they were distinct patterns of response released as functional units by instinctive stimuli. Attempts were made to describe the natural expression of fear and rage. These attempts were unsuccessful. It is true that in the cat there appear to be areas in the mid-brain which on being directly stimulated will produce attitudes and action directly connected with postures of attack or postures of withdrawal, together with excitement. Stereotyped emotional expressions have not been demonstrated for man except for laughter and weeping and nausea. Man's forms of attack are learned, not instinctive; so are his forms of avoidance and flight. It is more proper to speak of rages than of rage, and to speak of fears than of fear. Learning shapes the action, and there is not much in common between our fear of the dentist's chair and our fear of infection or our fear of thunder, save in the state of excitement which may be common to all. Love takes many forms of action depending on training. The most bizarre perversions may be included in its expression.

The common names for emotion are useful, even though they do not name physiological states but include references to the cause of the physiological state and to the behavior to be expected. Love, rage, fear, jealousy, humiliation, awe, pride, are better described as sentiments than as emotions because they include many details of learned attitude. The actual emotional condition of a lover at any particular moment is not indicated by the word with which we name him. He will be excited if obstacles stand in his way. Associative learning has made him responsive to a particular person. If his interest is balked by the presence of a rival he may sulk and grow depressed, or he may storm and threaten. The mere fact that he is in love tells nothing of his present emotion.

MOTIVES

MEN learn to be plumbers, drug addicts, psychologists, golfers, pinochle players, diet cranks, theosophists, fly fishermen, head-hunters, yachtsmen, camera enthusiasts. The variety of things that men learn to do appears a hopeless confusion. But there have always been efforts to classify the behavior that men are prone to learn. Such classifications have been in terms of urges or motives, passions, desires, interests. One of the early classifications was offered by the Greek teacher Epicurus. He declared that men have three kinds of wants. There are natural and unavoidable wants which even the wise man cannot avoid because they are essential to life itself. These natural wants of Epicurus remind us of the constant states of the physiologist which are a condition of continued living. Others of our wants are conventional and artificial, imaginary, according to Epicurus. These are obviously the wants which are based on habit only and which could be dispensed with. Their disappearance would not threaten our welfare. Other wants, which make up, Epicurus held, the great majority of human desires, lie between these two classes. They are natural but not indispensable. By these he obviously means those habitual desires which serve essential needs which could be served in other ways. We cannot get along without food, but we can get along without our favorite kinds of food, or our favorite ways of being served. The wise man, Epicurus taught, puts away from him

those artificial desires which have no basis in nature and controls his natural wants in such a way as to live a life of quiet
enjoyment, avoiding being the slave of his desires.

More than nineteen centuries later Hobbes made a different
attack on the explanation of what men are prone to do. Both
Hobbes and Epicurus were, of course, drawing on common-
sense notions that had been available since men began to discuss human nature. The theory of Hobbes was that we learn to
do what brings us pleasure and we learn to avoid those actions
that bring us pain. He roughly identified pleasure and pain with
conservation and disturbance of those conditions essential to
life which Epicurus described as natural wants and which modern physiology describes as constant states. Hobbes assumed
that all human desires grow out of pleasurable and painful experience and association with such experience. He made no al-
lowance as Epicurus did for purely artificial and conventional
wants which have either lost or never possessed any connection
with real biological need.

Descartes, writing as Hobbes did in the seventeenth century,
tried to be more specific. Human desires and interests all grow
out of six basic passions. These are wonder or curiosity, love,
hate, desire, pleasure and pain. These are men's drives, the
forces which direct action and learning. In our own generation
McDougall has offered an extension of this list. He represents
man as governed by certain impulsions which he calls instincts.
These include flight, repulsion, curiosity, pugnacity, self-abase-
ment or subjection, self-assertion or self-display, parental care,
reproduction, the tendency to seek human company, acquisition, and construction. All human interests can, he thinks, be
classified under one of these headings or under a combination of
these.

There are many other such lists. The most interesting recent
one is suggested by Knight Dunlap, who calls these impulsions

desires and who includes in his list desires for excretion, protection, activity, rest, love, children, for being noticed, for conformity to the ways of those about us. This is more complete than the list of an unknown Greek sophist of the fifth century B.C. who writes of "food-loving, drink-loving, love-loving" man. Such lists have their uses. They help to describe behavior. But they have severe limitations. There are many desires and interests which cannot be classified under any of these headings. Amateur gardeners, for instance, have secret gratifications of their own which are misrepresented when we try to classify them as desires for construction or for activity. Even the desire for love turns out to be not just a desire for love, but an enormously complicated sentiment that has just one person, not love, as its object. If we wish to understand the driving forces which direct human behavior and direct the modification of human behavior through learning, these instinct lists are not enough. They are even misleading. Not all persons desire food or children. Men may learn to avoid the company of their fellows. If our only information is that men have a gregarious instinct, we shall be misled. Curiosity and pugnacity are not simply universal desires, but are classes of behavior which may or may not be exhibited in a particular man under particular conditions. If we wish to be able to predict human behavior we must find the circumstances under which men will exhibit curiosity and the circumstances under which they will not exhibit it. We must know the conditions under which men will fight and the conditions under which they will refuse to fight. This knowledge obviously includes an understanding of learning.

There is a much better line of attack on the question of human motives. This lies in understanding the sources of human activity and the conditions which direct that activity through associative learning. If we take this course, it is evident that the most profitable weather signs of action are stimuli to sense organs. These are the immediate occasions for movement in men and in animals. Human motives can best be described in terms of such stimulus goads to action. If human behavior were not complicated by learning, the problem of motives would be extremely simple. All that would be necessary would be to observe the effects of various stimuli on the individual. This can be done for the sea anemone, and the problem of its motivation is so simple that it hardly deserves being called a problem. A poke at the oral opening, and the animal contracts into a compact mass. No elaborate instincts need be assumed. We do not need to invent a "libido" which is somehow aroused by the poke into an active wish for security. We do not have to account for the movement of the animal in terms of pleasure and pain. The animal simply responds in this fashion to the poke.

But a man is in much the same case. It is not necessary to invent a desire for food, if we can show that the activity we are interested in originates in hunger spasms in the stomach. When a man hammers his thumb we do not explain his dancing movements and vocalization in terms of an aroused "ego" or aroused "libido," nor do we say that his activities are an expression of the self-preservative instinct. It is simply that men who hammer their thumbs usually become very active for a time and the source of the activity is not desire or instinct, but the impact of the hammer on a sensitive area.

The problem of motives arises when it is necessary to explain how behavior becomes directed at certain ends, and this is a problem of learning, not merely a question of placing the end attained under one of the items in our list. How motives can be attacked from this point of view may be illustrated by some experiments which G. P. Horton and I have recently been conducting in our laboratory.

For psychologists whose first interest is human behavior, animal experiments require some justification. We are well satisfied that they have this justification in that they give us an added understanding of certain elementary learning processes in human beings. These processes are much more obvious in the behavior of our cats because that behavior could be controlled in ways to which human subjects would object. We could be sure of the regular attendance of the cats on the experiment and of the fact that they were fed and ate a fairly standard ration, that they were not confused by questions about the nature of the experiment or by impulses to demonstrate to us that they were unusually bright, or that their actions were not complicated by plans for what they were to do when the session was finished.

The experiment itself was a repetition of some work done many years ago by Thorndike. We changed his apparatus and method in a number of details. Our chief improvement on Thorndike's experiment was in the addition of a camera by which we could make a permanent record of certain critical movements of the cat.

Our apparatus was essentially a large box with a glass front through which the cat could be seen. In the rear was a small opening with a sliding door through which the cat was admitted to the box. In the front glass was another door by which the cat could escape if it managed to push in any direction an eight-inch pole which stood upright on the floor of the box. The cat could tilt this pole by a variety of means, by clawing, by biting, by pushing, by brushing with its tail, by backing into the post. Whenever the pole was tilted the front door opened with a click and a picture was taken of the cat. When the door opened the cat could leave the box and would find a few grams of fish in a small pan.

The cat was usually placed in the box a few hours before its regular once-a-day feeding, so that it was moderately hungry. When a fairly hungry cat is placed in such a box it may do a variety of things. It may walk forward to the glass front, paw and claw at that, sniff at outstanding objects, wander about. Being shut in the box restricts the cat's movements and makes it obviously restless. It is obviously "interested" in escape from the box in the sense that most of its responses are the sort of response that might get it past an obstacle or out of the enclosed space. It will bite and claw at the bottom of the wall, press its nose against the glass, or on rare occasions jump for the wire netting over the top of the box.

Ultimately most of the cats in some manner or other tilted the post and escaped. The cat was then replaced in the starting box, usually as soon as it had eaten a bite of fish or refused the fish. The process was then repeated until ten or twenty escapes had been made. Some twenty-five cats have now escaped from ten to eighty times each and have been photographed just as the successful movement was made and the door started to open.

The most conspicuous feature of the resulting series of photographs and of the hours of watching was that no matter what the cat's first accidental method had been, this same action tended to remain substantially the method used from that time on for that particular cat. There were many exceptions, and some cats had in the course of twenty trials used five or six different movements which operated the release. But most of these movements would be on some later occasion duplicated in remarkable detail. There was one cat which, after being shut in the box for a considerable period, took the pole in its teeth. The door opened. Thereafter in some thirty-eight trials this cat approached the pole from the same side and took it at the same point in its teeth. One cat, after being a long period in the box and growing very active and restless, backed into the pole. On the next occasion, when it had wandered to the same position from which it had backed, it backed again. Unfortunately its stern this time pointed an inch too far to one side of the pole and the backing movement did not operate the release. The cat stopped, started toward the door (the same series of movements as on the last occasion), but the door did not open. It again wandered around the cage and again, when it was facing the same point on the door, it backed. This backing continued; it was occasionally successful. But there were times when the animal would back thus for as many as forty times without escaping.

On one trial in the box this cat looked up and jumped to the top. This was repeated when the cat next found itself in the same position as that from which it last jumped. On the fifth jump it fell on the post and the door opened. On its next trial it at first backed numerous times unsuccessfully and then jumped, fell on the post, and the door opened.

One cat regularly escaped by treading on the base of the post with a hind foot; one regularly brushed the post with the base of its tail while it was turning in the box; one regularly lay down and rolled on the post; one advanced to the door, swung so that its rear was just before the post and then pushed back; one either pushed with its "forehead" or rubbed its neck on the post; one rubbed its flank. No two cats used the same means of escape. And most cats used not over two or three different movements in escape. The cat which swung and hunched the post with its stern was put into the box after several months without any experience of the box. There was no delay and within some five seconds it was leaving the box by its stereotyped method.

There is obviously a close analogy with human behavior in this conduct, because human problem solution also consists in doing one thing or another, whatever past associations would indicate, and then, when some action solves the problem, tending strongly to repeat that action when the problem again arises. We form habit solutions for our recurring difficulties in this fashion. One child has found that persistent teasing or crying will get him what he wants; another learns to manage his parents by smiling and ingratiating behavior; another stages a temper tantrum. And it is very often our first solution that fixes our habit.

To explain this requires that we first understand what a problem is. What makes the puzzle box or an unyielding parent a problem? The answer to this is that *problems are persistent stimulus situations of such a nature that they keep the animal or the person disturbed and excited until some act is hit upon which removes the "maintaining stimuli" and allows the excitement to subside.*

Such persistent and disturbing stimuli are sometimes called "drives." In a hungry animal the recurring spasms of the stomach serve to make the animal disturbed and to produce excitement. In a state of excitement stimuli which would not otherwise be responded to can get action. If a cat that has just nursed its kittens is then separated from them, the kittens, if they are not cold, will be quiet for some time. Eventually hunger begins and their stomachs are the source of volleys of impulses into their central nervous systems which produce excitement. The kittens become active and begin to crawl about. They will keep mewing and traveling indefinitely or until exhausted.

The same behavior could be produced by some artificial and external stimulus. A paper bag fastened to the cat's foot with a rubber band will similarly activate the cat, and it will become disturbed and excited and this state will continue until some one of its movements eventually removes the bag.

We are driven to action by disturbing stimuli. In human beings the number of ways in which we can be disturbed has been enormously increased by training, and we react to stimuli which would not have disturbed children. If we are in the habit of angry resentment of the noise of the airplanes from the nearby field or of late voices in the neighboring apartment, these noises will disturb us until we check them or we leave our quarters, but they may have no such effect on others. Recently a teacher in the local university went out on a boat trip with several companions. During the night he tied an empty coffee can to a string and hung it overboard where it would strike the side of the boat when the boat rocked. The anchorage was calm but passing steamers would give the boat an occasional roll and the can would strike against the side. At each series of thumps the boat owner leaped from his bunk and searched the boat, but the noise had stopped before he reached the deck. The guests were not disturbed because none of them were in the habit of investigating noises of that sort.

Some annoyances like pin pricks, cold, hunger, thirst, we are born to; some we acquire in the course of training. Many populations are little stirred by the presence of vermin that would keep a middle-class American household in a state of confusion until they were exterminated. The entomology department of a state university recently had an emergency call from a woman who had given up her house and moved to new quarters three times because of a small beetle. It inhabits all timber houses in that region of the United States, but not one person in many thousands is aware of its existence. Only by the use of a reading glass was the woman able to find the beetles about the baseboards of her home, but her life was made intolerable. As soon as her furniture had been arranged in a new house she took her glass and carefully explored the baseboards. When she had finally discovered beetles the house became unlivable.

We may thus even learn to go out of our way to find annoyances. We extend the range of instinctive biological disturbers to include a multitude of situations which, because of habits we have formed, are able to keep us wrought up until we are rid of them or, by fortunate relearning, come to disregard them.

Annoyers may compete with each other. Jail food in many of

our cities is furnished on contract and is essentially garbage, and the sight of it evokes extreme distaste. But four days of withholding, and the most squeamish prisoner becomes reconciled and eats ravenously. This method would be perfectly effective for the treatment of those minor food dislikes with which so many persons are afflicted. Here the hunger drive becomes so insistent that it overcomes years of habit. The sheriff's unfortunate boarders are like the cat in the puzzle box. Their restlessness under hunger eventually alters their habits.

The tendency to establish new habits when a "drive" or persistent stimulus continues unabated has its prime reason in the fact that when we are excited we are active, and when we are active we make rapid changes in the stimuli which affect us. Movements change not only the stimuli from muscles and joints, but also the stimuli to our eyes, ears and nose. Excitement increases the chance of new stimulation and *new response*. It results in variety as well as increase of action.

Among the new actions produced by a state of restlessness, a hunger state or a state of pain, one final series of acts is likely to do away with the disturber, the maintaining stimuli, the hunger pangs, the sliver in the finger, the beetle in the baseboard.

And here is a point very apt to be overlooked. The next time that the disturbers are present they will tend to call out, by virtue of their last association, the act that removed them. Other acts associated with them have been dissociated or unconditioned each by the next act. But after successful removal of the disturber, *it is no longer there to be associated with a new act*. The drive remains faithful to the act that removed it because that was its last association. After that no new associations could be established because the drive is gone.

If we apply this to the cat in the puzzle box, we find some order and reasonableness in the events there. When the cat pushes the post and the door opens, the sight of the open door prompts the cat to leave. But the last act before leaving was to operate the pole release and this act remains an established association with whatever stimulus pattern was acting when the pole was touched.

Replaced in the box, the cat does not walk immediately to the pole and tilt it. It must wait until in its wanderings in the box it is facing the same view as when it escaped before. The last association with that view was the successful movement.

The reader who is interested not at all in cats may be by this time very impatient. Talk of cats may have annoyed him to the point of laying down the book, or it may have failed to compete with better occupations. But this discussion was not wasted even if cats are of no interest, because the way in which these cats escaped from the box, their fixation of one of their first more or less "accidental" methods, is duplicated in human behavior.

When a man is in a state of continued anxiety, when some inner conflict keeps him active and discontented and when under these circumstances he has, with the pressure of companions, taken in a sufficient amount of alcohol to relax his tensions and bring him peace, he is in a fair way to fix this as his mode of escape from worry just as the cat has fixed whatever act it was that let it out of the box. The reason that drink tends under these circumstances to become a habit is that it brings relief, forgetfulness. And this makes so radical a change in his stimulus situation that no forgetting can occur. The next time he is in a state of jitters, the obvious association will be alcohol. No new associations are present because the jitters have not been present and *without being present cannot be associated with any new response.*

To the person who thinks in terms of pleasure and pain the habit of getting drunk remains a perpetual mystery. Why shouldn't the next morning's nausea teach him a lesson? The answer is that the next morning is so different from the state of jitters in which he began to drink that there is no strong association. To "teach him a lesson" would require that the association between jitters and drinking be replaced by associating jitters with some other response. This can not be done the next morning.

Morphine acts in much the same way. No matter what the drive or annoyance, no matter what the persistent source of excitement, whether pain or a bad conscience or a conflict of interests, morphine acts as a consummation. It relieves, not by removing the persistent stimuli, but by acting directly on the response mechanism. With restlessness gone, the morphine-taker is in the same state as an animal that has found food or any other consummation of a drive. The morphine relaxes, and the next time the state of excitement recurs, the obvious association is morphine. This was the last association with the excited state. But our interest in drug addiction must be postponed. Here it is serving only as an illustration of how habit tends to be adjusted so as to remove disturbances and annoyances.

Unfortunately the case of our cats offers no simple picture of drive. Hunger was not necessary to the behavior, and cats that had had their fill of sardines continued to escape from the box with whatever particular tricks they had used earlier in the series. All we can say is that on being placed in the strange box they were made restless until they had escaped to the familiar room where their whole manner changed. Mewing ceased. They moved about to one object after another, but with dignity and ease. There was none of the occasional vigorous clawing seen while they were confined.

In much behavior the disturbing stimuli are simple and clear. This is true of thirst, which depends on dryness in the mouth and throat; of hunger, which depends on stomach spasms. It is true of handcuffs or a jail cell where a man's freedom of movement is hampered and excitement follows, or, if all action is blocked, depression and gloom. Part of the restlessness of sex is evidently local tensions in sex organs which have the same disturbing effect that hunger has.

About hunger, sex, and other innate forms of drive whose effectiveness is originally determined by the original structure of the animal there may be organized many associated disturbers. When an animal made restless by hunger has hit upon food and eaten, the stimuli associated with eating can to some extent substitute for physiological hunger. If we have been in the habit of throwing bits of food to a hungry dog, we can induce him to go on eating long after hunger is assuaged. This secondary drive dependent on association is called appetite by some writers and distinguished from real hunger. Woodworth first made quite clear that any established habit may operate to guide later learning because it acts as a drive.

The interference with any action system under way may produce excitement. We tend to learn some new adjustment which will preserve the habit as it had been. Just as a hungry animal will associate with hunger the movement series that lead to its relief, so a person whose routine is threatened becomes restless, varies his behavior; and if some action permits him to continue his first habit, that action tends to become a part of the habit.

The father of the family who returns from work to sit in a particular chair with the evening paper is disturbed if the chair is occupied. If in his new agitation he succeeds in freeing the chair and taking it himself, his agitation disappears. Not only the father but the whole family finally adjust to his habit.

I have called on a household where the family dog behaved strangely when I had sat down. He paced about the room, returned to me time and time again. When it was explained that I was in the dog's chair and I rose, somewhat hairy from it, the dog promptly jumped up and settled down.

Let us try to put in very general and abstract terms the direction of learning and habit adjustment. The events are somewhat as follows:

1. Intense or prolonged stimuli disturb the organism and result in excitement and heightened activity.

2. The animal responds to these and other stimuli encountered with whatever responses have been previously learned.

3. Every series of movements tends to be fixed as a habit and to be repeated if once started.

4. Excitement brings increased activity and this brings stimuli in new orders. Responses tend to become more varied.

5. Each response as it occurs is associated with the drive but loses this association to the next response.

6. Eventually a response (consummatory response) removes the drive. For this in turn the drive becomes an associative cue.

Learning has now been accomplished. When next in this trouble the animal will repeat the final act. It should be noticed that the final act may be a series that requires some time to run through, provided only that it has been integrated as a serial response.

There are many sources of restlessness which are obscure. We do not know how it is that a person who is not getting enough salt in his diet is made restless and active until that deficiency is remedied. We do not know what starts the restlessness or how taking salt into the system stops it. It is quite possible that certain vitamin deficiencies act as drives and that the effect of the deficiency is to introduce restless variation in behavior until the proper food items have been discovered and eaten. We do not know just how it is that morphine adds to its habit-forming effect by so-called "abstinence symptoms." Spragg has recently given chimpanzees regular doses of morphine which were less than the amount required for sedative effect. In time the animals became dependent on their regular dose and were thrown into great agitation if it was postponed. Evidently the regular administration of the drug produced some physiological change, some bodily reaction, some adjustment to the presence of the drug, and this adjustment was sufficient to cause agitation when the drug was not present.

The addiction of the animals included the establishment of many habits of cooperation in taking the drug. The ape would be led into the room where the morphine was administered, would get upon the table, open the box that contained the syringe and present the syringe to the experimenter. On one occasion on which I was present the ape, when the experimenter delayed, reached down and pulled the experimenter's knee so that his foot rested on the table. The ape bent itself over the experimenter's leg and quietly waited for the prick of the needle.

When morphine is taken to relieve pain or distress the relief of the distress is enough to account for the establishment of a habit. Where the drug is given in non-sedative doses there must be involved a condition in which the absence of the drug gives rise to distress. When this point is reached, the drug has a sedative effect and the animal becomes addicted. The movements that result in relaxation are learned and are associated with the distress because after relaxation the distress is gone. No new associations can be made with the distress in its absence. It remains a cue for the movements which relieved it.

By a *motive* we shall mean persistent stimuli or organic conditions which create and maintain excitement. Some psychologists call such stimuli or conditions *drives*.

Common speech admits such words as jealousy, revenge, envy, pique, humiliation, profit, or gain as motives. These are motives in our sense also, though they are very obscurely described. By jealousy we indicate that impulses to be near some person, to behave toward some person with affection, are blocked by the presence of a third party. The blocking of loving action is the cause of the excitement, the motive. The resulting excitement will break established habits and new learning will occur. The goal, or the consummatory response, would be the removal of the third person from the situation. This is what the jealous person tends to learn to do.

By envy we indicate that the sight of some possession of another person stirs us to use this possession or to respond to it in some fashion. But we are restrained either by the presence of the owner or by our own training in respecting the property of others. This causes in us a conflict of action tendencies which in its turn is exciting. We tend to learn the way to the relief of this excitement, some way to possess ourselves of the object or some resignation of our interest. Envy is thus a motive because it describes a stimulus situation which is a persistent source of excitement. Avarice and greed are likewise motives. They name systems of habit concerned with the possession of money. These systems are acquired in the early use of money which has been learned in the satisfaction of other motives. But the interest in money may now be established as a habit which is independent of the original motives. The sight of money or the signs of money arouse us to possession. We are restless and unhappy if there are sources of money about us. The signs of money have become disturbers which play the same rôle as that taken by the timber beetle recently mentioned.

Many absurd things have been written recently concerning the profit motive. It has by some writers been assumed to be an innate form of drive. In so far as it means an interest in money for its own sake it is readily acquired after experiences in which money serves for the attainment of other interests; but it is not an innate interest. When "profit motive" is taken to mean any interest whatever—interest in food, in prestige, in love, in being sheltered and clothed—its significance has become too vague to make the use of the term worth while.

DESIRES, CONSCIOUS AND UNCONSCIOUS

HATE, Janet has said, is a desire for the death of someone, whereas dislike is simply a desire for his absence. Aside from the shrewd distinction here made, we may notice that this is using terms for which no amount of work with cats in a laboratory will prepare us. Desires and wishes are characteristically human and we allow them to animals only by a sort of courtesy. A dog can make efforts to eat, but it is debatable whether a dog can desire food. A caged tiger can attack a man, but it is very unlikely that the tiger could desire his death. In desires and wishes we have entered a field of behavior in which animals are handicapped. This is the field of language. Men not only adjust themselves to situations by practical action. They also talk about situations. Their talk is intimately connected with practical action, but it is a distinct form of action in itself.

When one of our laboratory cats in the puzzle box had performed the movement which normally brought its release, but had performed it with a slight difference that made the movement ineffective and the door failed to open, it was to be noticed that the cat immediately looked toward the door or moved toward the door. Sometimes the false movement of escape was followed by actually colliding with the closed door. We might describe this by saying that the cat anticipates the opening of the box.

If a dog has been stoned on a number of occasions, it may eventually respond to the sight of a man ready to throw a stone by running away. It originally ran away at the impact of the stone, but the sight of the man in throwing position accompanied that flight and has become a cue for flight. When we say that the dog anticipates that the man will throw the stone, we mean, if we stick to the facts, that the dog is ready for the throw, not that the dog puts the event into words.

Tolman has shown that a rat which is rewarded with sunflower seed at the end of a maze and has worked out a series of movements that lead it through the turns of the maze to the reward will be upset if bran mash is substituted, and this will tend to break up its habit. It has gone through the maze ready for sunflower seed and when it encounters bran mash instead, its habitual movements will be disorganized just as the movements of the cat approaching the exit are disorganized when it encounters the closed door.

The same disturbed behavior may be illustrated by a diner who lifts his cup to his lips set for tea and encounters the taste and odor of clam juice. He may be quite fond of both liquids, but to encounter one when ready for the other is disconcerting. The action of drinking tea is different from the action of drinking clam juice, and this difference is present in the very beginnings of the action.

When a human being performs an act and shows himself ready for its outcome, we say that the action was intentional. A man who falls down intentionally is a man prepared for the fall. If I tread heavily on your foot and show no preparation for your response, I may be judged to have acted without intention. If I show myself all set to run or all set to ward off your blow, I was acting intentionally. In the strict sense of the word, an intention includes not only readiness for the outcome of the action, but a verbal addition. Words are the beginnings, the initial cues, of voluntary action. We have the act "in mind" as we begin. Actually this means that we have the act in speech. We are, to borrow the pool-table phrase, "calling our shot."

A small child who has been restrained from taking in his hands the inkwell from the desk with the phrase "No, no" accompanying the restraint may sometimes be observed to reach for the inkwell, and then to say "No, no" and withdraw his hand. This is the beginning of voluntary control of action, the control of action through cues which are used by others and can be also used by the individual himself. A full intention in a man involves saying to himself the word or phrase which names the outcome of his act.

Men, Janet has remarked, must learn, like animals, to conceal the beginnings of action. The cougar must stalk his prey. In other words, he must conceal the beginnings of killing. If he did not conceal them, the victim would react to the signs of the coming event and escape. Men also learn to conceal the most significant part of the beginnings of action in speech. Men early learn to speak "to themselves" and thus not to give away intentions. Small children are incapable of this and all their words are uttered aloud. Only gradually do they learn secrecy and concealment in social situations. The two-year-old asks for the cake; the four-year-old child may have learned to think "cake" to himself and so to guide his behavior without insuring failure by giving himself away.

A *desire* or a *wish* may be defined as an action which has been initiated by its cues but which is blocked by other elements in the situation. Under such circumstances there is present what we have described as conflict. Other action systems are in evidence. And following the conflict is that state of increased tension which we have called excitement. The interference of the rest of the situation cannot amount to inhibition, or the desire is gone. The child at the tea party who eyes the tray of cake is tense with suppressed action. The action itself is the approach to the tray and the grasping of the cake. But this action system, though present, is interfered with by the presence of the mother

or by her admonition, "Not yet." If her phrase inhibited the
approach to the cake, there would be no desire present. That
this approach is not inhibited is evident in watching the child.
He may be licking his lips or clasping his hands. He is obviously
set to go. There may be partial inhibition, but some elements
of the desired action must be present if desire is present.

Among the most significant parts of the blocked action are
words which have to do with its outcome. Its name is already
formed and is a cue for the act. But this is not always the case.
Many of our actions and our readiness for their outcomes are
expressed only in muscles not concerned with speech. This is
true of all of the intentions of an animal. The cat at the mouse
hole is set for a spring, but it is not saying to itself "Mouse," or
"Ready."

When we say that we are "aware" of our own intention, it
will be found that the test of this awareness is having a word
for the act. This is the sense in which Freud and other psychoanalytic writers use the word "conscious." We judge another
person's wish or desire to be "conscious" when he can name it.
If he has not named it to himself and cannot name it to us he is
said to be driven by an unconscious wish. This is the basis for
a very important classification of wishes and desires. A wish or
a desire may be conscious or it may be unconscious. By pronouncing a wish unconscious, Freud indicates that it is *inarticulate*, that it represents the beginnings of a redintegrative
action system present without words.

Unconscious wishes and unconscious desires are continually
with us. We can rightly interpret much behavior to be dominated by wishes of which the wisher is unaware or, what is the
same thing, for which he has not words. If we find someone
meeting what he asserts to be a great misfortune with great
equanimity and ready resignation we can assert that for him it

was not a misfortune, his statement to the contrary notwithstanding.

This whole field of human behavior, the field of wish and desire, and particularly the field of unconscious desires, was almost completely neglected by academic psychologists until Freud and his followers called attention to it. We say "almost" completely neglected because there is one French writer from whom much of the psychoanalytic theory derives who has explored this field much more thoroughly than any of the psychoanalysts. This writer is Pierre Janet, whose works have been comparatively neglected in the United States because of the momentum and popular appeal of the psychoanalytic movement.

But to return to our desires. One of the early disciples of Freud who later broke his allegiance has introduced a new term into psychology to describe a characteristic way in which desires may interact. The man is Jung, and the word is *ambivalence*. By ambivalence Jung means that desires are often found in opposed pairs, both opposed desires being at the same time present in behavior. This is true, and it is a very common and interesting psychological situation with important consequences. Common sense has long recognized that love and hate are often felt at the same time for the same person, and that there is in intense love or intense hatred often evidence of this dual desire.

In fact, conflicting desires are the normal cause of excitement and emotion. If one action system inhibits another, there is no conflict. The one has simply captured the motor pathways and ruled the other out. If inhibition fails and the other member of the pair is still in evidence, offering stimuli which tend to maintain it and redintegrate it, there is conflict, excitement, and the consequences of these.

The real service of Jung's concept of ambivalence lies in the attention it draws to the fact that signs of emotion are usually signs of conflict. This is not always true, of course. Stepping on a cat's tail does not put it in a state of conflict, though it is undoubtedly excited. The statement often made by psychoanalytic writers of a few years ago that fear always indicated conflict is not justified. Excitement may be produced by intense stimuli or by simple obstacles to movement. But the notion of ambivalence throws light on a great deal of emotional behavior.

The temperance lecturer of the 'nineties derived much of the enthusiasm of his denunciation of alcohol from his own divided attitude toward it, and was prone to miss an occasional lecture because he had started on a "spree." But not all the prohibition movement is to be explained in terms of secret fondness for alcohol. Most of the opposition comes from those non-drinkers who suffer from its effects on others. The drunken husband can give his wife a horror of alcohol through the drunken acts with which it is associated.

The excitement of romantic love depends to a large extent on conflict. Malinowsky in *The Sexual Life of Savages* states that it is a somewhat rare phenomenon among the Trobriand Islanders with whom he spent several years. The reason for its absence is that there is no prohibition of sexual behavior among the adolescent members of the community—no elaborate training that establishes its impropriety. With the Trobriand Islander love is a source of prolonged excitement only when unwillingness of the partner sought or the entrance of a rival serves as the block to relief of the drive. In our own culture, as many unhappy marriages testify, the block may originate in early training which establishes strong conflicting tendencies. The type of sex instruction which was prevalent in colleges a few years ago was aimed at the attachment of repulsion and disgust to whatever was associated with sex, and there is no doubt that this instruction was often successful in establishing notions of sin and impropriety and repulsion that made the marriage of the victim doomed to failure from the start.

Jung makes the statement that when one of two conflicting desires is conscious the other is unconscious. The parent who punishes the child is aware of an interest in training it and believes that he dislikes inflicting pain. But his behavior is sometimes open to another interpretation. He looks forward to the punishment and enjoys it. Not long ago we encountered a husband who could not understand his wife's attitude when he himself was so devoted to her. He gave her many presents, took her to many entertainments, but she showed no proper gratitude. The wife's story did not deny the gifts and entertainment, but emphasized the fact that the gifts were always conspicuously different from her own expressed desires. If she showed an inclination to go to one theater her husband regularly came home with tickets for something else. So far as could be discovered, the husband had never acknowledged to himself that he was engaged in making his wife's existence as miserable as he could and still appear devoted. He appeared devoted in his own eyes.

Jung's statement that one member of any conflicting pair of desires is always conscious and the other unconscious is an exaggeration. It is quite possible to be torn between two desires and to be able to name them both. But the statement is worth very serious consideration because it is remarkably often true. To understand the reason for its frequent truth we must consider more than the individual and examine his relations to others and the part taken in those relations by speech.

There has been quoted Janet's opinion that the child only gradually develops the ability to restrict his speech to slight movements not visible to others. He learns this as part of the necessity for concealing the beginnings of his own actions in order not to give himself away and in order not to defeat his own purposes. This is fundamentally correct. The need for secrecy is the prime origin of inner speech or thinking to oneself.

Very early in life we learn to regulate our speech in the presence of others. There are things that can be thought, that is, said *sub voce*. They must not be uttered aloud because of the effects that they will have on others. What we say aloud is governed by our social relationships and by our hearers. We learn that certain types of statement lose us friends; others bring swift punishment. The child's tendency to utter whatever happens to occur to him is gradually subdued because of its effects on parents and companions. Small children often go through a period of whispering to themselves in rehearsal for their answer to a question.

But what we say to ourselves is also tremendously affected by such social relationships because what we think, the words we form without sound and with minimum apparent lip movement, all were first learned in conversation with others. There would be no words for the expression of any really private desire. All the words we can use in rational thinking are public words. Our thoughts, therefore, in so far as they are expressible in words or communicable to others, are really public in their origin and so retain this public nature. If we have a private desire there are no private words for it and, because to be conscious of a desire means to be able to state it, such private desires are essentially unconscious.

That the Freudians really use the word "unconscious" in this sense of "inarticulate" is evident from their doctrine that unconscious desires are expressed in dreams and in many of our actions and often determine our choice of words. When we take an instant dislike to someone we meet without being able to give any explanation, this is an attitude of the "unconscious." If we happen to recall the unpleasant association which is at the basis of the dislike, and can describe this in words, the "unconscious" is not involved. If a young man dreams of a death and a funeral, without acknowledging to himself or others that the corpse had several traits in common with his well-to-do uncle, the dream is an expression of an unconscious wish for the uncle's death and its results in an inheritance. If we select the key to our apartment as we reach the office door, this may be coupled with the beginnings of some action appropriate to the apartment but not to the office, and in that case could be described as the result of an unconscious wish that we were entering the apartment. The wish is unconscious in that we have not acknowledged it in so many words. Of course, the action may have no such association and may derive from the fact that it was the apartment key that we last used. When we mistake the voice over the telephone for that of a friend, this may be coupled with an already existing set to communicate with that friend. This set, in so far as it had not been recognized, or named, can be described as an unconscious wish to see the friend and this unconscious wish blamed for the error.

We may have altered our political attitude very gradually, and only become "aware" of this during some moment of crisis. By becoming aware of our change we mean that we are now able to name the new affiliation in politics. Having taken for granted that we were in sympathy with liberals in politics, we may suddenly realize that association with conservative friends has changed our politics. A young man or woman may not "realize" until long after friends have realized it that he or she has fallen in love. The affectionate behavior and attitude have been present, but the description in words had not been accepted. There is no point in making a great mystery of the unconscious or in treating it as an agent. If we are served soup and are vaguely dissatisfied with it we may, on seeing another person use the saltcellar, suddenly remark, "Oh yes, that's what it needs." Our unconscious wish for salt has become articulate.

The division of desires into conscious and articulate desires and unconscious, inarticulate desires must not be accepted as clear cut. At our best we are not very articulate and our descriptions of what we want are often ludicrously inadequate. Our description seldom coincides with the important consequence of the action whose beginning constitutes the desire. We assert that we desire a good dinner of roast beef and potatoes. The action which is thus begun is not ended when we have found a restaurant and dined on these articles of food. The biological outcome of the action occurs later when these constituents have been added to our blood streams. But this source of energy was not what we thought we wanted. If the prospective diner could be shown what his dinner will look like forty-five minutes later, he would decline to eat. The young man who was only aware of desiring the company of a pretty girl ends as the head of a suburban household. He will undoubtedly be content with this outcome, but it had little relation to what he was aware of desiring.

We may be sure that very few of our actions will terminate at the point of conscious desire. Most of them will not reach that point at all. The rôle of awareness or of naming lies in beginning the action, it does not guarantee the outcome. But that this use of words in guiding conduct is an aid to adjustment there can be no doubt. Many parents have noticed that children enter a period of better adjustment when they begin to acquire words for what they want. Before this they are compelled to cry for it if it is not within their reach. The adult who has an inadequate use of language and who is not able to name his wants is at a great disadvantage. This condition is not rare. It is a characteristic of many hysterics. Their desires are so divorced from recognition and description that they are forced to much indirection. Unnamed desires cannot be controlled. The person who has been brought to desire strongly what is disapproved of by his fellows may have learned to repress the description of his desire. He is no longer aware of it. But it may still disrupt his behavior.

In such a case a mother developed an intense jealousy of her adopted son who was a favorite with the father. She subjected him to countless annoyances and much punishment. That this was motivated by jealousy she did not recognize. It was her belief that she was doing her best to correct his manners and morals in order that he might be happy. The son was finally annoyed to the point of running away from home. He fell in with a companion who persuaded him to take part in robbing a gas station. The two were caught and given a penitentiary sentence. At the father's request a number of men joined in urging that the boy be paroled, and this was done. The boy returned home, but the mother feared that he had not learned his lesson and approached the authorities to request that the parole be set aside.

The mother's unawareness of her real attitude and wishes is in part to be blamed on the fact that such wishes are tabu. Mothers are not supposed to hate their sons and wish them put away in penitentiaries. She has accepted the tabu to the extent of not describing her wishes thus even to herself.

Language, which is the tool of thinking, is all derived from conversation with those about us. When we learn to use language we are subjected to a very thorough social control. This social control of the individual through the public origin of the very elements of his thinking, of the symbols by which the individual initiates his own actions, is what the Freudians are getting at in their notion of the super-ego. This expresses a real stage in the development of the personality. Our behavior is now subject to social influence from within us.

Many conflicts are conflicts between impulses to act and competing impulses based on the speech of others. The result is that it is the socially dictated behavior that is conscious. For it there are words. The competing impulse is inarticulate. The dark depths of the unconscious with which Freud has made us familiar are dark only in the sense that they are indescribable, or at least undescribed.

We have described a desire as an action system that has persistent or recurring stimulation and tends to be redintegrated, to go through. A conscious desire is a desire in which linguistic expression is present along with the other beginnings of the action. An unconscious desire is different from this only in that the words are missing.

X

INTERESTS

MOTIVATION has been described as persistent stimulation which energizes the organism and produces restless activity which will last until a consummatory response removes the stimulation. When some previous experience of such maintaining stimuli has attached to their pattern the specific action system which brought relief and the organism is thus set or prepared for a consummation of the tension, this is said to amount to *desire*. Such desire is to be found in the behavior of the higher animals as well as man. Even Tolman's rats evidently set out on their trip through the maze with a desire for sunflower seed, because they were obviously upset on encountering bran mash. Essential to a desire is some delay of the action. Otherwise the event can be described as a simple response to stimuli. The beginnings of the consummatory action are present, but there is some impediment to consummation. Seward and Seward point out that micturition is a reflex in an infant, but a drive (or what we have called a motive) in the older child or adult. (*Psychol. Rev.*, 1937, 44, p. 351.)

When the impeded beginnings of the action include awareness of the outcome or the naming of some feature of the outcome, the desire is said to be conscious. This means only that it is articulate. It is now communicable to others, and somewhat manageable by the individual since he may be able to manage the cue. Many of the desires of the hysteric are unconscious and therefore unmanageable.

117

A recurrent desire or group of desires is called an *interest*. A man can be said to have an interest in collecting stamps or an interest in buying a new car though there are no present indications of that interest. He may be asleep or out fishing and without any present desire. The word "interest" indicates the potential recurrence of a desire.

Like desires, interest may be conscious or unconscious. The man himself might be judged to have an interest in self-torture, an interest in bullying his employees, an interest in being conspicuous at social gatherings. Of this interest he might be himself quite unaware in that he does not name the interest and could not report its presence to another person. He would only betray it in his actions. It is quite unnecessary to speak of an unconscious mind as the source of his unconscious interest. He has but one mind, which is an abstraction describing the fact that he shows progressive adaptation to recurring troubles and change. He is not divisible into a set of minor minds.

Our conscious interests, our named interests, are built up around common experiences of the group. They are shared interests. Otherwise there would be no names by which we might recognize them or take notice of them.

These semi-public interests may have a direct biological foundation in original nature, as do interests in food, sex, freedom from pains and aches; or they may be conventional interests, interests established by training and not inborn. Frost and extreme heat are biological disturbers and tend to direct learning to their avoidance. Nearly all persons learn some way or other to allay hunger pangs. But there are other interests which depend on disturbers whose ability to disturb us is a matter of our own habits alone.

Many social customs represent such interests, and the individual learns to conform to custom in exactly the same way that he learns to satisfy hunger. The disturbing nature of hunger pangs is here replaced by the disturbing way in which people react to non-conformists. Not his own stomach but his irate neighbors furnish the excitement that compels a man to learn to wear clothing.

Modern American adult males have a strong interest in wearing trousers in public. There is no mystery about how this interest is acquired. Early training fixes it thoroughly by making the individual thoroughly uncomfortable when he is not covered. The interest may be an imperious one. It may compete successfully with other interests. Several years ago a woman bandit entered a university district pool room, lined up the patrons along the wall with the threat of a gun, took their money and then ordered them to loosen their belts and let their trousers fall to the floor. She made a successful get-away. No one started in pursuit until he had taken time to make himself presentable.

All of our biological interests are overlaid with conventions which often become stronger than the biological drive. Protection from cold is an interest with a biological foundation, but men and women will suffer a high degree of discomfort from this source in order to conform to the prevailing style of protection. Ears may be allowed to freeze rather than be covered, throats to be cold unless there is available the scarf of the current fashion.

One of the most urgent interests and one that is responsible for many breakdowns is the interest in social status or social value. This interest is established through long training. The satisfaction of many other desires depends on social recognition and prestige. Many a suicide is motivated by loss of "face."

A number of years ago, Schjelderup-Ebbe, a Norwegian psychologist, watching the behavior of hens in a poultry yard, discovered that each yard has its "pecking order" which remains fairly constant over long periods. Hen A may occasionally peck hen B, B may peck C, and C peck D; but the order is never reversed and B never takes an aggressive line with A, or C with B. The order seemed to depend on size or on the first encounter between the hens. Once established, it became a fixed habit with all the hens.

Every family and every human group also tends to establish a pecking order after long association. And position in this pecking order becomes one of the major interests so long as the order has not been fixed. Janet points out that once a stable order of social value has been established in a group there is excitement and struggle only when this order is disturbed. Cultures with rigid caste systems even including slavery may be stable. If the individual grows up to a position in the system he becomes adapted to his status and shows no discontent. The order becomes a part of his habits. In ancient Rome slaves born in that status brought much higher prices than captives from overseas. Because he was born into slavery, the status became a part of the habit system of the slave. It was enforced by punishment in early years, but the punishment succeeded in breaking up habits that were inconsistent with the status. So thoroughly did servile habits become part of the personality that Aristotle was misled into the belief that there were two races of human beings, the naturally servile and those who were naturally independent.

In a democracy youth is a period in which status is not yet fixed, and most of the troubles of youth derive from this fact. Wherever the young person goes, he is aware of being judged and rated. He notices that he is making a favorable or an unfavorable impression. Serious results which take the form of social timidity and embarrassment may follow. The consequence of an awkward movement, of a stupid remark, of the laughter of associates or of their scorn, may be to make future public appearances a torture. The normal and desirable result of embarrassment is to break up unsuccessful social habits and to teach skill in dealing with others. But this often fails to happen.

The older person, or any person with his own family and old friends, does not suffer this discomfort. His status is determined already. To that status he is adjusted by his own habits. He shows deference to some and receives it from others, unless he is at the top or at the bottom of the scale. In a static social order with a caste system this adaptation takes place early in the lives of the great majority. The cobbler's son takes it for granted that he will enter his father's trade. In a democracy where dress and speech and manner do not clearly indicate caste, there is hesitation and doubt in social behavior and a struggle for place. In many American high schools nearly one-half of the boys have ambitions to enter one of the professions. This will obviously be impossible for all but a few.

In modern Russia where a supposedly classless society prevails, it has been found desirable to introduce through state propaganda new class distinctions based on industry and skill and intelligence. These are recognized by prizes, medals, orders of merit, money rewards, and travel and other privileges. The pecking order is given a new basis in an effort to encourage public service.

A young person who has suffered some humiliation or embarrassment may adjust to this by avoiding social affairs where he is aware of being rated. If he does this, a restatement of his conscious interests is necessary. He can no longer avow the same purposes and ambitions as before because he has deserted the contest for social place in this form. He then *rationalizes* his change of attitude and makes light of social success. "Parties are silly." "Only fools would make themselves conspicuous in public." "Those people have no serious interests." The interests which have been broken up by his embarrassment give way to new interests. He is fortunate if these new interests are describable in terms which others will accept. He may acquire new interests which will eventually place him well up in the social scale and give him social value. He may turn to study, or to sports, or to painting or poetry.

If he turns to interests which are not shared by others and are not describable by any of the accepted formulas of the group, he is a lost man and an outcast. He may eventually find adjustment and peace only in retreat to an asylum, where only a few simple conformities are demanded.

Folkways and custom have a close resemblance to the constant states of the physiologist. Just as a disturbance of the temperature of the blood stream brings many adjustive mechanisms into play which restore the temperature, so departure from normal behavior in the group, through the excitement it causes others, disturbs the offending individual, breaks up his annoying habit and eventually results in behavior that does not give offense.

This social pressure does not always result in thoroughgoing conformity. It may bring only superficial conformity to group phrases and formulas. This is called *rationalization*. By that term we mean conformity in speech without a corresponding redirection of conduct.

A mother whose established social relationships are disturbed by a daughter's superior attractiveness finds and announces that she is so much concerned with having the daughter receive the best education that she will sacrifice her own comfort to send the girl away to school. Her announced interest is a rationalization, something which will not bring public disapproval of her conduct. If she had announced that she was moved to get rid of the girl so that she herself could again be the center of attention, this would have disturbing effects. Her rationalization may be adopted only for public use, and she may be able to state her real purposes very clearly to herself; or, and this is not uncommon, the desire to be rid of the girl may have no verbal expression even in the mother's inner speech.

A shift of public opinion may produce interesting shifts of interest and of rationalization. During the beginning of the World War a certain German-American was very voluble and frank in his hostility to the English and French and to American sympathizers with the Allies. When public opinion had been successfully molded in this country to partisanship on the side of the Allies and our government undertook war, open criticism was no longer possible for a German sympathizer. It led to quarrels and the threat of an internment camp. But there was a large group that was critical of the government on other grounds. The German-American became a sympathizer with the radical labor movement and showed an intensity of feeling which could not have been explained in terms of his economic status or associations. And his sympathy with the labor movement extended only to severe criticism of the government, not to any actual participation in labor disputes. His hostility to the United States government now had a different rationalization.

Interests are never completely determined by either the goad of biological drive or the goad of social disapproval. There is tremendous individual variation which depends on accidental factors in individual development. Freud has described the infant as "polymorphous-perverse." He intends this to indicate that the accidents of early life can direct the sex interest of a child toward normal and approved forms of that interest or toward any of the known perverse forms. It is assumed throughout Freud's writing that this direction is based on associative learning, but since Freud has taken no interest in the problem of how we learn, he has never made any clear statement of the principles of association. The Freudian assumption, however, that perverse interests can be established in any child through conditioning is undoubtedly justified.

The list of possible perversions is as long as one wishes to make it because no two individuals establish identical sex interests. The classes of perversion which are usually mentioned include homosexuality, or an interest in the relief of erotic drive through persons of the same sex; sadism, or an interest in inflicting pain on others which is motivated by erotic excitement; and masochism, or an interest in suffering pain with the same motivation. By fetishism is indicated the attachment of erotic interest to objects which have had an adventitious connection with erotic excitement. The fetishist may be stirred by erotic excitement and show a fascinated interest in women's hair or in women's clothing.

There is no limit to the variety of forms of erotic interest which can be established with variations of experience and associative training. In all cases the history of the interest, whether perverse or not, is like the history of the development of a taste for a particular kind of food, or the history of the cat's escape from the puzzle box. The original drive depends on the direct stimulation of erogenous areas, particularly the genitals. This causes a reflex local response in the form of a self-maintaining tension. This maintained local state is the motivating stimulus which causes restlessness and activity. The acts which lead to the reduction of the local tension retain their association with that tension. In other words, the tension becomes the conditioning stimulus for the action which brings relief.

Early experiences are of first importance because there is comparatively little chance for reconditioning. To effect reconditioning, the tension must be associated with other actions, and this cannot occur in the absence of the tension. If erotic stimulation and its relief have occurred in struggle with other persons and the infliction of pain, these acts and their results may be established as the habitual method of relief, and a sadistic interest is formed. If relief has been accomplished through acts which bring pain to the individual himself, such acts and the resulting pain may become an essential part of the relief, and an interest in self-torture has been established. This is called masochism. If relief has been accomplished through normal courtship and pleasing behavior, this will become part of the interest. In cases where relief has been accomplished through general exertion and exercise, through work of one sort or another, or through distraction, sex motivation may be "sublimated" and become the source of work, of artistic creation, of public service. The Freudians have pointed out many instances in which such sublimation retains elements which identify the behavior as reinforced by sex.

The importance of erotic motivation in the development of interests has been considerably exaggerated by Freud and his followers. To it they attribute almost all traits of personality. The fact that dogs or men who have through operation been deprived of their gonads and are incapable of the primary form of erotic motivation nevertheless develop personality traits of many sorts, indicates that more factors than sex are concerned. I am not familiar with any psychoanalytic studies of persons in this condition, though they may exist.

The late Alfred Adler has written extensively concerning the effects of forms of motivation other than sex. His notion of a "will to power" or a "masculine protest" is, of course, vaguely conceived; but his actual illustrations concern motives which originate in one's fellow men and the influence of social norms of beauty, intelligence, physical prowess and the like. We may undertake a restatement of his general theory in terms of motives as we have described them.

Social norms are established in the habits of the group. Another way of saying this is that we are adjusted by habit to the persons who surround us. If we meet one who is atypical in height, in coloring, in the size of his ears or in the number of his eyes, our behavior toward him is disturbed. If he is, for instance, far below the prevailing stature for adults we tend on this account to treat him as we treat children. But we may be thrown into confusion by his full beard and bass voice. This confusion in our treatment of him is a source of trouble to him as well as to us. Short army officers complained that the men often did not pay them the same attention and obedience that they paid to larger officers.

The short man, troubled by the way in which the public takes his stature, learns one means or another of getting relief from that trouble. He may learn to get a reputation for vicious action. The old *New York World* once published a series of pictures of New York gun men. They were typically undersized and the writer in the *World* was responsible for the statement that their average weight was close to 120 pounds. They had discovered that a gun and a reputation for using it caused others to treat them with the same respect that was shown to larger men.

The variety of effects on interests caused by deviations from social norms is infinite. In some cases the adjustment is direct and effective. There is no warping of the personality. In other cases the individual develops peculiarities that make him a serious problem. Some men go about serenely with physical defects that have seriously affected the lives and interests of others. According to Adler, our inferiorities determine our interests and ambitions. He identifies this with the adaptive processes by which a defect in a body organ, such as a kidney, produces changes in the other kidney which allow the other to take over part of the function of the disabled side. The failure of one kidney to perform its function allows the waste products in the blood stream which are eliminated in the kidneys to reach an excess which activates the remaining kidney to its limits of performance. To a sustained extra load the sound kidney responds by increasing its capacity for work, much as an exercised muscle responds by developing more capacity for work. But Adler's identification of the compensation for organ inferiorities such as a disabled kidney and the compensation for inferior social status is based on a very far-fetched analogy. The mechanisms by which the two compensations are made are different in kind. Inferior social status or social defect is compensated for by associative learning. No compensation may occur in some cases because a physical oddity may be adjusted to by the possessor's neighbors. It is only where an outlandish appearance or atypical behavior provokes neighbors to annoying behavior that we are driven to adjust to social defect.

It is annoying reception of the inferiority by others that disturbs the individual to the point of establishing new habits which compensate in the sense that they rid the individual of the annoyance. He may learn to avoid the annoying behavior of his neighbors by withdrawing from society. An aging woman who permitted a beauty specialist to inject paraffine under her skin in order to restore the roundness of her cheeks had the misfortune to have the paraffine take on numerous bulges and odd shapes which gave her a very startling appearance. When she went abroad, she had in the past been used to a certain amount of admiring attention. Now, a trip to the city or an appearance in a theater crowd caused startled glances everywhere and obvious conversation about her appearance. This was so disturbing to her that she eventually learned to avoid embarrassment by remaining strictly in her own house and venturing out for exercise only on the poorly lighted residential streets in her own neighborhood. She received no visitors and saw only a few old friends who had learned to avoid notice of her state.

In other cases of unusual appearance which has prevailed from birth on, the individual may be adjusted to the reception of the defect by the public and accept serenely his misfortune. The various forms which compensation may take will be considered further in the chapters on personality.

In many of the most serious cases the defect is not real.

Chance remarks by others have given rise to delusions of ugliness, of stupidity, of awkwardness. This is particularly likely to happen during the years just after adolescence when the youth is having difficulty in adjusting to his changed status as an adult. An overheard comment to the effect that his ears are ridiculously prominent or that his nose is too long may become associated with his general distress and social failure. In public he can think of nothing but his supposed flaw. This interferes with his ease and confidence and insures that his failures will be more certain. A few evenings spent as a "wall flower" by a girl serve to establish habits of behaving as a failure. She now does not expect attention and is not prepared for it when she gets it.

A small group of college men a number of years ago agreed to cooperate in establishing a shy and inept girl as a social favorite. They saw to it for one reason that she was invited to college affairs that were considered important and that she always had dancing partners. They treated her by agreement as though she were the reigning college favorite. Before the year was over she had developed an easy manner and a confident assumption that she was popular. These habits continued her social success after the experiment was completed and the men involved had ceased to make efforts in her behalf. They themselves had accepted her as a success. What her college career would have been if the experiment had not been made is impossible to say, of course, but it is fairly certain that she would have resigned all social ambitions and would have found interests compatible with her social ineptitude.

What truth there is in Adler's notions of the effect of an inferiority "complex" derives from the fact that one of the important sources of excitement and the reinforcement of action lies in obstacles and impediments to action. Just as fish which are not gamy offer no interest to the sportsman because they offer no difficulty and resistance, so many interests depend on opposition or obstacles for their establishment. A number of years ago at a state university there arrived a girl who had been brought up in a missionary home on an Indian reservation. Her parents had observed the strict discipline of their church. Though a number of young people in her neighborhood played cards and danced, she was not allowed these diversions. She was particularly forbidden to go to the services at the Episcopal mission which her evangelical sect looked on as a stronghold of the forces of evil. Soon after she arrived at the university she indulged in sowing a crop of very wild oats. She met once a week with some friends to spend the evening playing cards. She attended many college dances. And she would attend as many as two services each week at the Episcopal church in the university town. Her devotion to these interests is explained by the fact that she had been stirred to do all these things at home, but they had been forbidden.

If a child has access to unlimited and unrestricted supplies of sweets, its interest in them will disappear. In the chocolate factory it is not necessary to enforce rules against eating chocolates. If the new operative is allowed to eat all that she wishes, the sight and odor of chocolate are soon associated with the behavior that accompanies repletion. Chocolates cease to look edible.

A generation ago the classes in natural science in colleges in the United States attracted many of the most brilliant students in the institution. One reason for this was that there was then still much opposition to the doctrines of evolution, and taking science courses was a thrilling defiance of authority at home and in the church. Science courses lost this thrill when evolution was generally accepted in the more progressive communities. Except in the small denominational colleges in backward areas science must now depend on other motives for its appeal to students.

In its most elementary form this reinforcement of desire and interest by opposition is evident in a puppy's reactions to a rope end. If his master holds out the rope to the puppy and the puppy takes it in his teeth, the puppy's hold will last for a short time only. But if the owner pulls the rope away as the puppy is about to let go, the grip on the rope will tighten and the interest in holding it be renewed. The rattle that the baby is about to relinquish will be more tightly gripped if it is tugged at by an adult. Much annoying behavior in the schoolroom has the same origin. What had been a dull afternoon may be made lively and exciting by some infraction of the rules. Interest in the forbidden is intensified by the fact of forbidding. Unless the prohibition is so effective that it brings about complete inhibition of the prohibited action system, it adds to the value of the prohibited act.

The dictatorships in Europe are embarrassed by this intensification of interest by attempts at strict governmental control. Great efforts are being made to direct the thought and action of the general public into loyalty to the dictator and interest in national power and national prestige. This direction is, of course, managed in part by the elimination or imprisonment of disloyal citizens, but it is attempted also by propaganda and control of public speech and expression. Elaborate censorships attempt to eliminate from use the words and formulas which would interfere with the dictatorship. Equally elaborate programs in press and schools expose citizens to the slogans and catchwords which would lead to loyal cooperation. Inspired radio talks are dinned into the ears of the population. Public meetings, poster campaigns, advertising are planned for their effects on action and the control of interests. The ideal of such control would be to deprive the individual of all words in which he could so much as phrase any forbidden desire, which would put the desire beyond the reach of his voluntary action. Willing an action requires that we name the consequence of the action to ourselves. Deprived of hostile formulas, the popular will would be entirely complaisant. It is beginning to be realized that the only authority of government lies in the habits of the governed, and that if the direction of these habits can be controlled by the direction of its speech and thought, which is only secret speech, full authority is established.

XI

CONCERNING PERSONALITIES

IN THAT puzzling class of mental disorders called dementia praecox or schizophrenia one very common symptom is a condition which has been named *catatonia*. If the physician takes hold of the patient's arm and sets it in some unusual position he may then let go of the arm and it will retain its posture for a number of seconds or minutes, gradually returning to a resting position. Or the patient himself will take a position and maintain it for hours at a time. He may sit erect in his chair, looking straight forward and holding his arms along the arms of the chair. He may stand at attention. He may lie for many hours each day curled up in bed in the position which the fetus takes in the womb.

This tendency to hold some posture self-imposed or imposed by the physician, is not in the least like a simple reflex. In the first place, it is not just anyone for whom the patient will keep an imposed posture. Something depends on his relations to the physician. And a self-imposed posture can be on occasion interrupted. The patient's behavior more resembles the voluntary assumption or retention of posture than it does the postural reflexes in animals described by Magnus, the tendencies of the animal's general musculature to maintain a standing position and to restore that when it is disturbed.

One of the patients at a state hospital performed each morning his simple duty of emptying and replacing six garbage cans, and would then take the position of a soldier at attention and maintain that until an attendant touched him on the shoulder to lead him to the dining table. On one occasion a staff physician became curious to find out how the patient could be led to desert his position of his own accord. The physician brought up before the man at attention another patient, a sawhorse, a long board and a saw. He directed the second patient to saw the board along a line which had been marked on it. The second patient had no skill as a carpenter, whereas the first had been in that trade for many years before his admission to the hospital. The physician then left and concealed himself at a point where he could see what might happen. The sawyer was doing a very awkward bit of work. He departed an inch from the marked line. Suddenly the man at attention gave a glance about and stepped forward. "Here, give me that saw," he said; whereupon he took the saw, made a straight cut along the marked line, handed back the saw, and then took up again his position at attention. The position of the catatonic appears to be regulated by his accompanying ideas. It is part of the rôle which the patient conceives himself to be playing. In the case of the patient who takes passively and maintains the posture in which the physician puts him, it is as though the patient said to himself, "Oh, well, the easiest thing to do is to humor him." By his automatic compliance with the physician's evident desire to have him maintain such a posture he avoids having to enter into a struggle of purposes with another person. He maintains his aloofness from the world.

This condition of catatonia is only a rather unusual illustration of a kind of behavior manifested every day in the life of a normal person. Once we are seated in a chair, are holding a book, are looking at a passing car, are standing, the details of the posture tend to care for themselves without attention. Janet mentions in his description of the "waxy flexibility" of the catatonic that if a weight is placed on the outstretched arm of the patient, the arm does not sink under the weight but holds its position. This means that the muscular adjustment which keeps the arm in place has been quickly accommodated to the weight. The posture is not a simple maintenance of the same muscle tension, but an elaborate and accurate regulation of the position.

In other words, posture turns out to be another of the conservative states like the constant states described by physiologists. We cannot call it a constant state, because the maintenance is only temporary. A cat may lie on its back, but there are times when any interruption of its right-side-up state brings into play a complex of muscular reactions which restores it to right-side-up. If we hold a kitten by its four legs above the floor and let go, the kitten will land on its feet. This is a native or instinctive ability and requires no practice. But a man's ability to hold a posture for a time cannot be explained as inborn or instinctive because it includes much more than the ability to return to the upright position or to land on the feet. It extends to the quick restoration of almost any posture he may take, to the conservation of a tremendous variety of positions. Man undoubtedly learns to do this.

Our interest here is in the maintenance of posture as an illustration of a new variety of conservative state that tends to be restored when it is disturbed. Another conservative state is established in any habit, for any habitual action which meets slight distortion or interference tends to carry through. Habits exhibit a regulation which tends to the similar execution of a movement even when this requires differing degrees of muscular contraction. Lifting a weight adjusts muscular tensions to the resistance of the weight. We walk up hill and down, though very different muscular contractions are demanded. When the sun shines on a man the one thing he does not do is to warm up. He remains below 99 degrees Fahrenheit. When a book is placed on the outstretched arm of the catatonic the one thing the arm tends not to do is to sink under the pressure. When the door we are opening sticks, our energy of movement tends to accommodate itself and with an extra pull we open the door. The extra resistance does not balk the action.

Desires and interests also exhibit this tendency to self-maintenance. The very interference which makes a desire or a wish tends to produce emotional reinforcement and to bring about new methods of gratification. But over a period of time, habits, desires, interests all tend to change. A man who has served a ten-year prison term leaves the prison gates a new man. Some of his habits have been replaced by prison habits. He is likely to show his experience in his prison gait. His speech will have the flavor and slang of prison life. Some of his habits will, of course, be unaffected. His abilities to skate, to play checkers, to use a typewriter will show little change. In order to forget these skills he would have had to establish new associations with their cues, and prison life has given no opportunity for that. The prisoner has lost many of his former interests and acquired others. His affection for his family may have changed. The resentments with which he entered prison may have been intensified or lost. Prison conversation has altered his speech and his thinking. The abnormal isolation of the sexes in prison causes many of the inmates to emerge from their term of confinement homosexuals if there has been opportunity to exercise that habit, or given to forms of self-relief, or impotent.

In all this are we to say that the man has a new *personality*? He has kept the legal identity of the body. The law looks on him as the same man. His fingerprints are still recognizable. He may or may not answer to the same name by which he entered. But we must admit that in many respects he is a different person.

How can we define *personality* so as to allow for its development and change through experience? It is obvious that a man may change in many ways that do not change his personality. Whether he is standing or sitting, he is the same personality. He does not lose his personality during sleep or while he is eating or reading a book. These are changes in him which are occasioned by transient stimuli, but they do not represent changes in his personality.

As a tentative definition we shall adopt the following: A *man's personality at any given time consists of those modes of his behavior which we judge will show comparatively strong resistance to change.* This definition has its good points. It allows for change in personality traits and for degrees of resistance to change. Of one man we may say that his affection for his wife is part of his personality. It will survive adversity. Of another's love affair we may judge that it does not enter into his personality because it would not survive a quarrel or the sight of a new pretty face. One man's generosity is part of his personality. In another man an equally generous action we regard as an accident of circumstance. He happened to be in funds when the appeal was made, or he was slightly intoxicated, or he was interested in making an impression on some onlooker who happened to be present. The first man's generosity we regard as more deep-seated because it would have been shown even in the face of handicaps.

Life is defensive change which leaves the essential identity of the living creature intact. The organism changes in order to avoid changing. Mental adaptation means that the organism not only reacts defensively but changes its type of reaction. If it is periodically disturbed by some repeated stimulus, its reaction to this stimulus gradually improves its form and the disturbance no longer disturbs. On a long sea voyage in fog we are at first much upset each time the foghorn is blown. As time continues we are less and less upset until our reaction is finally only a small fraction of what it was. To recurring hunger pangs we react with excited and energetic movement. The time comes when we go quietly and efficiently to lunch instead of crying and threshing about in our cribs. This view of the nature of mind is substantially that adopted by Rignano in his *Psychology of Reasoning* and by Humphrey in his *The Nature of Learning*.

Adaptation of any sort leaves the animal the same in certain essentials but different by virtue of its reaction. In mental behavior this process is one of endless change. The animal that learns becomes gradually very different from what it was. After an adaptation through the establishment of a new habit, the new habit is part of the animal. And, what is of particular importance, it is the new animal, habit and all, that tends to be conserved in the next adaptation. If we change our residence to another country and another diet, we alter our food habits and our food interests. But these in their turn will be hard to change. If we return to the country of our birth we must become readapted to our native food. Recently two Canadians who had been born in Normandy returned home to spend their last years in the village of their birth. They had looked forward to this for forty years in Canada and had always regarded themselves as French people, not Canadians. Two months in the native village was all that they could tolerate. They had become habituated to new comforts and new ways. The old could no longer be borne.

Habits and interests are conservative forms of behavior. They tend to resist change. Many of the outstanding features of mental ill health owe their distressing nature to this tendency to resist change. The outstanding characteristic of a phobia is its conservative nature. Compulsions, fixed ideas, hysterical paralyses and anesthesias all prove difficult to retrain. The difficulty of a neurotic is often that he cannot forget. His habits are conservative and skillful management is required to break them up.

If we mean by personality the more conservative modes of reaction, we exclude those minor shifting habits by which we adapt from hour to hour and day to day to our constantly shifting environment. A change of residence means that we must change our habits in walking home after work, or must change our habits to accommodate the new arrangement of the apartment rooms. The new sink and its appurtenances may be in a position the reverse of the old. These transient habits are not part of the personality.

We will obviously include in the personality our well-organized interests because these are lifelong characteristics of behavior. The interests of many eminent scientists can be traced to childhood activities and a mother who responded to the collecting of bugs with kind enthusiasm or to a prepossession with numbers with proper attention. We will include those interests centered about sex which Freud has called to the attention of psychologists because these are extremely stable and conservative features of behavior when they are once established as habits. It is very unlikely that an adult homosexual will through retraining be able to change the direction of his interest. We will include many of the traits which Adler describes, the directions of ambition which have been molded through our social experiences. The sons of ministers are found beyond all expectation in *Who's Who*. It is possible that association with a higher-income group which does not involve belonging to that group establishes interests and devotion to success which would be more often lacking in the children of the propertied classes or the children of the working class who have no contacts with greater wealth.

One type of conservative behavior has not been mentioned. It has a peculiarly important place in the integration and direction of life activity. This is the tendency to accept a character or rôle and to act out that rôle, the tendency to play a character.

In small children this is often obvious and laughable. One day the small boy announces, "I'm a tiger," and for the rest of the morning he goes about on all fours, growls, bites, and insists that he is eating meat on the living-room rug. He asks occasionally about the habits of tigers, what they like and what they dislike, and these suggestions are carried out in his own way. The interest in taking a rôle is not confined to children. It is almost universal among adults. We recognize a description of ourselves, acknowledge our attributes or our membership in a class, and appropriate behavior follows the thought. Knowing the meaning of any word indicates the attachment of that word to appropriate actions. A boy who thinks of himself as a student tends to behave as a student and to reject incompatible behavior. He dresses the part as well as acts it. A man who has been mentioned in the local newspaper as a prominent citizen may be changed for the rest of his life by that chance paragraph. He now begins to reject actions which are not the actions of a prominent citizen. He now buys his theater ticket for an orchestra seat because prominent citizens do not sit in the gallery. At the haberdasher's a new verbal formula enters into his choice of clothing. Is this a suitable hat for such a person as he is?

Napoleon once remarked that the way to rule the French was through glory. He meant that by conferring orders of nobility and honors on the right persons he could control their behavior in his own interests. A French member of an academy has this membership indicated on his calling card. From the time of his admission to the academy his behavior is no longer that of a non-member. He bears himself in public as a member should. By means of commissions in the Naval Reserve which carry their titles, the reserve officer is directed in his behavior. This becomes part of his rôle. He thinks of himself as a naval officer. In a democracy the hereditary titles which do so much to affect the part which a man thinks of himself as playing are lacking. Some of the omission is supplied by organizations which give a precarious right to titles and uniform. Elks, Moose, Shriners, Knights of this or that, are altered by their membership in these societies. The Elk behaves as an Elk, the Lion as a Lion. Or we make what we can of titles like judge, colonel, professor.

A man's verbal symbol for the character he is playing is a strong directive force in many of his activities. If he is a father, if he is a policeman, if he is a member of a union, if he is a Democrat, if he is a valet, his acceptance of the description serves to introduce a consistency into his actions which is often the guiding clue to his personality. The rôle is often one of the most fundamental personality traits.

The stage and motion pictures are responsible for the rôles which many persons have assumed. Most high schools in the United States have dozens of Garbos obvious to the most casual passer-by. Small boys listen to "educational programs" on the radio and go about for days making machine gun noises and putting a tough swagger into their walk. All children take such rôles, and nearly all adults. A group of students in a university conspired to fasten a rôle on an unsuspecting and unintelligent fellow student. They persuaded him that he had the "makings" of a great orator and that he should begin with a career in student politics. He accepted the rôle at once, and his manner became ponderous and deliberate and patronizing. His speech took on longer periods and formal phrases. He accepted the pretended deference shown his opinions as a matter of course.

The character assumed is not always heroic. A boy who is called a coward by his associates may find himself acting out that description. The girl who overhears someone referring to her as ugly may think of herself as ugly and begin to plan her life to fit her part. She may accept her ugliness as *beauté du diable.* Much of the docility of a slave originates in his acceptance of the character. As a result of this acceptance his behavior is the behavior appropriate to a slave. In many instances in college an outstandingly intelligent student has been led to think of himself as stupid and refuses to attempt tasks that call for brains. A person who has been publicly charged with theft may begin to accept that description and its consequent behavior. Parents who use epithets in correcting their children, who accuse them of lying, stealing, cheating, and the like, may seriously affect the rôles which the child builds for himself in the course of time. It is often a mistake to have named the offense.

In the psychoses the assumption of a character is often a conspicuous part of the patient's behavior. The patient may accept the rôle in the manner of the small boy who plays tiger. Only a part of his behavior is made consistent with his kingship or deity. For the rest of the time he does not rebel at washing dishes or performing other menial tasks about the hospital. It is not so much that he believes himself a king as that he wants to play at being a king. He will often acknowledge the pretense, but continue with it.

Many nervous breakdowns have their origin in such rôles. The man who thinks of himself as an open-handed host loses his income and his social adjustment is thrown completely out of gear by his persistence in the rôle. He continues to be generous and spends more than he can afford. A small girl may play at housekeeping and her older sister may marry under the influence of the same rôle. To have a household means being married. If the marriage is a failure and the husband does not play the part that would be necessary for maintaining the rôle, the wife may continue to pretend in public that all is well, that she is happily married and has a pleasant home. She must keep the recognition of the true state of affairs from the public because she is keeping it from herself. She is still playing that she is happily married and doing her best to disregard the unpleasant interludes with the husband's non-cooperation. If the public becomes aware of the failure of the marriage it will be necessary for her also to recognize that failure or to withdraw from the public. Only in retreat or in an asylum can we be successful in maintaining a rôle against a public rejection of that rôle. Disgrace, which is often so intolerable as to lead to suicide, always consists in the public rejection of a character part which we have adopted. Disgrace seldom threatens physical harm or serious physical discomfort. An astonishing number of men in public life have failed to survive a public rejection of their rôle. The exposure of a politician as accepting a bribe may leave him broken in spirit.

The adoption of a rôle may be tremendously reinforced by the inclusion of a dress or uniform. The individual is made doubly aware of his rôle, and the behavior of others is made to conform to his character. At the university efforts to control campus traffic by placing janitors in their working clothes or in ordinary civilian dress at critical intersections during rush hours were quite unsuccessful. A janitor blowing a whistle was just a janitor blowing a whistle. When the janitors were put into traffic officers' uniforms their difficulties disappeared. Reacting to the public's new behavior, the janitors themselves took on a new dignity from the experience of being obeyed, and showed a new confidence. Previously the very manner in which they blew their whistles betrayed that they were prepared to be disregarded.

A failure of any action dictates the next acts. The boxer who fails to have his guard up meets his opponent's blow and reacts to that. On the next threat he is on the defensive. The boxer is said to have lost confidence because he is acting like a man who has been hit. The salesman who is refused by a number of prospective customers in succession is prepared for refusal and not for success. He tends to behave at the beginning of the interview as he was caused to behave at the termination of the last. This anticipatory character of associative response is a very common characteristic. Many of the stimuli which have accompanied the final response to a refusal to buy or to being hit by the other boxer are present at the beginning of the next meeting. Their last associations are with the conduct of failure, and they now evoke that conduct earlier in the meeting. Confidence is merely a habit of success formed by experience with success.

In many serious cases of maladjustment the essential difficulty is the acceptance of the rôle of failure or the rôle of invalidism. Most persons are roughly accurate in their evaluation of their own capacities. This is based on experience. A large group of teachers interested in knowing something of the nature of an intelligence test was given such a test. It was announced that those who wished to place their names on the test blank for identification could do so and obtain their grades. More than two-thirds of those whose names were written on their blanks received grades above the average of the group. We have a rather shrewd notion of where we stand in skill or in intelligence when compared with our acquaintances, and it is the unusual person who seriously underestimates his capacities.

When the adopted rôle is beyond the individual's capacity, the difficulties of maintaining it may lead to breakdown. Some rôles are much easier to maintain than others. Janet mentions that one of the most satisfactory character parts is that of the sub-officer or lieutenant. The leader and the chief executive have responsibilities and difficulties in maintaining their authority. The second in command does not share this responsibility, but does share in the prestige of his leader. The place of the leader may be taken by an organization. The member of an extensive group shares in the prestige of the group. His own purposes and interests have the sympathy of other members. The group is a defense against the sense of loneliness which is a continuous source of fear and anxiety to some persons without such affiliations. This dependence on the close sympathy and support of other people is a natural result of early experience in the family which has been a refuge in times of stress. Many secret societies depend for their appeal on this feeling of insecurity which many persons develop when they have grown up and left the family protection. The other members of the society are pledged by awesome oaths to aid and comfort fellow members in distress. A common neurotic symptom is the feeling of being terribly alone, of having no one in whom confidence can be placed, no one who will exert himself in the neurotic's behalf without any thought of reward. Many of the neurotic's exaggerated demands upon those about him, much of his domineering or exasperating behavior, much of his quarrelsomeness, his protestations of affection, his protestations of worthlessness are really directed at verifying the fact that there are others on whom he can depend. He may need to reassure himself every day that there is someone who will remain devoted to him in spite of abuse.

Innumerable clubs and associations, religious cults and political groups offer the individual this comforting addition to his rôle or character part. The amateur radio enthusiast, the stamp collector, the horse-collar manufacturer, the realtor, the Townsendite, the spiritualist, the beauty parlor operative, the embittered communist or the frightened Fascist derives tremendous comfort and a feeling of security in knowing that he is not alone but is a member of a group or of a "movement." Nearly all religions offer such fellowship.

The individual who does not identify himself with numbers of others is likely to be at a loss concerning the part he is to play. If he has no loyalties his life is threatened with a loss of meaning and value. What is there that is really worth doing or worth being? In many cases the sudden acquiring of an enthusiastic loyalty has brought on the cure of neurotic symptoms, and an individual who lacked confidence and decision has suddenly become sure of himself and able to look the world in the eye. Faith in some cause serves to bring unity and consistency to behavior. We are quite correct when we undertake to describe a personality by first listing the individual's loyalties and affiliations. These may give an individual life most of the meaning that can be found in it. A man is an enthusiastic liberal or a die-hard Tory or a radical in politics. He is a Presbyterian or a Baptist or a Roman Catholic. He is devoted to his children, or absorbed in his business which takes precedence over any transient interest he may develop in reading or in sport. The acknowledged interests which guide his behavior are made consistent with his rôle.

In that major act of self-negation which consists in self-destruction, there may be expressed an almost infinite variety of desires, but it is safe to say that in the large majority of cases the underlying difficulty is a divergence of rôle and status. The disappointed victim has accepted and adopted a valuation of himself that does not fit the position which others force upon him. He has not received the just deserts of his rôle. His virtues and his work are unappreciated. Between continuing his rôle and accepting the impaired value which others set upon him there is an irreconcilable conflict. He has often tried desperately to make good in his character part, and by work or an appeal to sympathy to enlist support for his own notion of his merit and his deserts. These efforts have failed. It is probable that many suicides are determined when the victim gains his first insight and understanding of the discrepancy between his rôle and his actual status. It is also probable that many suicides are only an extension of the appeal to the sympathy of others. Fantasy has before the event pictured the changed attitudes of friends and relatives when the death is made known, the regrets which these others will feel at their failure to appreciate the suicide, the new understanding which the world will have of the suicide's earnestness and the new appreciation of his ideals. Most suicides are preceded by threats at self-destruction and follow only when these threats have failed to bring family or friends or the public to time, have failed to compel others to accept the victim's adopted rôle. Mark Twain's adolescent boy daydreaming of his sweetheart's grief and despair as she stands by his grave and places gently on it a tear-stained rose is an excellent description of the adoption of the rôle of the dead hero. The dead hero has lost his identity as a living organism, but still remains a character part that can be played.

Our accepted rôle, which is our articulate self and which is the thread of consistency that runs through our conscious acts, is our most vulnerable point. It is therefore the point at which we are most subject to attack and most sensitive to attack. Even small children learn to take advantage of this and to "call names" as an easier substitute for the use of fists. The adult who is stirred to anger by the interference of another readily becomes articulate concerning the other's social value and traits. Allport and Odbert have collected some 17,953 terms which are in use to describe persons. These make up about four and one-half per cent of our English vocabulary. Just what proportion of them carry an unfavorable aura of meaning is hard to determine, but it is considerable. These make telling weapons in disputes between individuals.

We have used the word "personality" to indicate those more conservative habit systems which behavior exhibits. Among the most important of those conservative habit systems is the set of verbal cues for action which in each individual makes up his notion of himself. It is the guiding effect of these acknowledged cues which gives the life of the individual social consistency and meaning.

THE DESCRIPTION OF PERSONALITIES

WHEN a parent or a spouse consults a psychologist about a member of the family the complaint is almost never that the ailing member is unpredictable. It is usually the very predictability of some habit or some attitude that forces the consultation. The mother knows only too well that her small boy will continue to bite his nails, or quarrel with his sister, or show a devilish ingenuity in avoiding his lessons. Families learn so well the manners and ways of the rest of the household that the routine of the dinner table, the daily argument over the use of the car, the inevitable shirking of duty by one child, or the self-effacing performance of duty by another brings very few surprises. We learn to know our friends so well that we can prophesy concerning them.

As compared with a friend or a fellow member of the family, a textbook in psychology can give very little information about what any particular person will do in various circumstances. Science labors at a great disadvantage in predicting the behavior of individuals because the best source of that prediction is the past behavior of the individual in question. A textbook of psychology cannot be burdened with several million biographies kept up to date. But this would be necessary in order to foretell what Jones or Brown will do in this or that set of circumstances. Science must be confined to very general rules applicable to individual cases, but science cannot be bothered with the application. This must be left to the person who knows the case and its history. Nowhere is science at a greater disadvantage in prediction than in the description and understanding of personality.

There are in existence a few highly efficient systems of predicting individual behavior in terms of the more stable traits, but these systems have not been worked out by psychologists. One of them is used by credit men in the business world. If a merchant arrives in a city intending to set up in business, the firms that supply him fixtures and stock must decide whether or not to extend him credit. In other words, they must determine one of his personality traits, his dependability or his tendency to pay his debts. Their decision is made on the basis of information furnished by a credit bureau. The information consists in his past record in his former location. If the report from the firms with which he has done business in the past is to the effect that he paid his debts promptly, this is accepted as a fair sample of his behavior in the situation of a debtor and may lead to an extension of credit in his new location. If the report is adverse and mentions that three former creditors report that he avoided pay and only one states that he paid without threat of suit, he will be refused credit.

This is an actual measure of a personality trait. It is so dependable that large sums are daily risked on the basis of this measure. There is one other department of community life in which a similar estimate of a personality trait is made. That is in the police headquarters. A criminal record is a strong indication against a citizen. If an applicant has a record of two convictions for embezzlement, or the would-be truck driver has been several times arrested for driving while drunk or for reckless driving, we are properly loath to give him a job. Slocombe and others have found that proneness to accident in motormen tends to be a rather stable trait, and that about fifty per cent of the accidents in a large city transportation system involve only about twenty per cent of the drivers. It is the same men who keep on having one accident after another.

When we try to measure personality traits by an actual long-time record of an individual's behavior in the situations in which we are interested, we are on firm ground. Habits and interest are subject to change, but they are also strongly conservative and change occurs only when there has been some radical change in the situation. We are quite justified in judging men by their past records. We shall sometimes be mistaken, because there may be gradual inner evolution in a man's conduct, and sudden conversions which depend on shifts of dominance in a conflict are not unknown. An intense love may turn to hate because the two were both present all along, although affection prevailed in overt behavior. But we are generally fairly safe in judging an individual's future by his past. Repetitiousness is one of the outstanding features of conduct. The lazy scholar tends to remain a lazy scholar. The nail-biter continues to bite his nails. The erring husband continues to make errors until senility changes the pattern of his ways.

But this fairly easy and certain prediction on the basis of past record is of no use when the question is asked, "What can be done to change this person, to rid him of an annoying habit or of a distressing attitude?" His past now gives no information because it has no record of his behavior under altered conditions. Only the observation of other persons who have been subjected to some form of interference will answer this question. It is in this case that the psychologist's information about the nature of learning and his observation of other persons prove of some use. He may have discovered that nail-biters who have been sent to a manicurist for a number of regular visits give up their bad habit. The cue for the action may have been the feeling of the rough edge of the nail and the removal of this cue may stop the habit, particularly when the nail is now strongly associated with the visit to the manicure and a new attitude toward nails. The psychologist may not have the intimate and prolonged acquaintance that makes its possible to foretell behavior in detail, but he has a larger equipment of observation and record of many persons in typical situations. If he can recognize and classify types of persons, he has an opportunity to make rules for such types. He may discover that self-centered or introverted individuals are more subject to neurasthenic crises, or that the extrovert is more subject to the development of hysteric symptoms. He may find that one type of treatment has more chance of success with extroverts than with introverts.

But in order to make such discoveries and to formulate such rules, the psychologist must first know what he means by these types of personality. He must define introverts and extroverts in such a way that cases of introversion and extroversion are recognizable and verifiable. He must, if it is possible, develop measures of these traits, in order that degrees of introversion and extroversion may be recognized. Before he can assert that sending a child to a nursery school will tend to increase the child's interest in and response to other persons, to make him more extroverted, the psychologist must have some device for measuring extroversion. Otherwise he cannot check his assertion or be sure that it was the result of observation in the first place.

To provide these definitions of personality traits and the necessary means of measuring such traits an enormous amount of work has been done by psychologists during the past fifteen years. This work took its start from the partial success of intelligence tests. The first widespread use of intelligence tests was with the draft army during the late war. Nearly two million soldiers were given some type of test which aimed to measure something variously conceived as a congenital ability to learn, a congenital ability to adjust to novel situations, or a general factor or ingredient in abilities and skills of all sorts.

If we have had a long-standing acquaintance with an individual we know his extent of success and failure in many undertakings. We know how he thrived in the schoolroom, in business, in social life; we know whether or not he is "tool wise" or clumsy with tools. The intelligence test was an effort to measure a general ability which entered into all these successes or failures. It could obviously not be based on the past record of the individual. It was confined to a short sample of his behavior, thirty minutes to two hours. This sample was expected to furnish the basis for predicting his success in many types of undertaking which had not yet come within his experience, types of undertaking for which the learning had yet to be done. Intelligence tests consisted of setting the person to be measured certain problems, or asking him for various bits of information which he might have previously acquired. It was hoped that by standardizing the problems and questions and scoring them "objectively" and without the possibility of bias, the resulting score would be a valuable measure of the individual's abilities and would serve to predict how he would adjust to many situations.

These hopes were in some measure realized. But psychologists have become much less sure of what they are measuring in such tests. During the history of the development of intelligence tests it was always necessary to have some independent measure of intelligence as a basis for judging the value of a test. The persons available for testing were school children, soldiers, and children who had been brought to psychological clinics for advice and help. In the case of the school children only was there available a ready "criterion" of intelligence. This consisted in the grades which teachers had assigned the children on the basis of their school work, or in the opinion of teachers who had been acquainted with a group of children for a period and were confident that they could give a roughly accurate estimate of their intelligence. Items in intelligence tests which failed to predict these two criteria were discarded, and the intelligence test was built up about the prediction of school success.

It was promptly discovered that certain other things could not be predicted. Large firms which introduced intelligence tests in the selection of their salesmen found that there was little or no correspondence between an intelligence score and the ability to sell merchandise. Other firms discovered that such tests were of little use in the selection of executives, because success as an executive was not predicted by intelligence score. The army found rather little actual use for the results of the tests. They were in general predictive of success in activities which closely resembled the schoolroom situation. Men who made high scores were more apt to make high grades in the final examinations of army training courses if these examinations were conducted with paper and pencil. But intelligence scores did not predict "power of command" or a large variety of other qualities which the army was interested in knowing. Resourcefulness would probably be indicated almost not at all by such scores.

In general it was found that the brief sample of a person's behavior which made up a test was a fairly good indication of his future performance in very similar situations. Test scores are good indicators of future test scores; they are somewhat poorer indicators of pencil and paper examination results. They are not at all indicators of future performance with tools or with driving a car, or of success in dealing with people.

With the methods of the intelligence testers many psychologists set out to measure a long list of personality traits. Among these are introversion-extroversion, ascendence-submission, proneness to neurotic behavior, leadership, honesty, humor, the ability to "mix" with others, suggestibility, perseverance, conservatism and radicalism, and many others. The results of this testing program have been so far very disappointing. My own experience was concerned mainly with introversion-extroversion.

These terms were introduced by the Swiss psychoanalyst, Jung, and have been adopted by many psychologists. By introversion, Jung means a tendency to be responsive to the "inner world," to turn the "libido" inward "towards one's own personality." The extrovert is oriented toward the outer world.

This is, of course, an extremely vague description. Its vagueness makes it free from attack on any ground except the ground of ambiguity. Before any scientific use can be made of the notion of extroversion or introversion these terms must have meanings which will enable one to judge of the presence or absence of the trait.

In an effort to examine such a possible trait of the personality I undertook a number of years ago to define a number of extro-introvert characteristics more concretely and to measure these. One of these possible characteristics is the extent to which a person tends to share the word-associations of his neighbors. Jung himself was the originator of an experiment in which this could be measured. A number of words (in our own experiment on introversion-extroversion this was 100) is read to the subjects of the experiment and the subjects are instructed to respond to each word with the first word that comes to mind. The stimulus word may be "head." One person may respond to this, "tail," or "foot," or "face." The list of one hundred words was thus read to several hundred people in small groups. They wrote their own responses. The words were read so rapidly that there was little opportunity to reject one response and choose another. The responses of about one hundred persons were then examined and listed. The most common answer was found. Persons who gave this most common answer were scored one point.

In responses to the hundred words there was one girl who forty-seven times used the word which had been most often used by the rest. There was also one who used such a common response only once. The rest of the subjects ranged between, averaging twenty-one common words. Each person now had what we took to be a measure of his tendency to respond as others about him responded, supposedly an extrovert trait.

We attempted another measure of a possible extrovert trait, the extent to which students were acquainted with current local student affairs. An examination was prepared which we called a "gossip test." The items all referred to such information as the name of the reigning popular orchestra, the names of the captains of the university teams, the location of certain eating houses or places of amusement, the affairs of the undergraduate class organizations, etc. Some students turned out to be acquainted with all this information. Others were ignorant of practically all such campus affairs. We assumed that a wide acquaintance with such items of campus gossip would be an extrovert trait, and that ignorance of this type of campus gossip would indicate the recluse, the student who was out of touch with his fellows. The grade in the "gossip test" stood as a measure of this possible tendency to seclusiveness.

We also had the same students rank their instructors in the order of their teaching ability. We supposed that this might measure introversion-extroversion on the ground that the student whose ranking of his instructors agreed with the pooled opinion of the whole group was presumably more alive to the opinions about him than the student who was in radical disagreement with this opinion.

To these measures we added a test designed by Laird, the Colgate Personal Inventory, which was alleged to measure introversion-extroversion. This test consisted of a number of personal questions based on an old inventory published by Woodworth during the war. The questions concerned such items as the extent to which the person tested felt embarrassment in speaking in public, the extent to which he believed that others did not understand him or were unfair to him.

There turned out to be no correspondence between the scores of students in any two of the tests. If these were introvert or extrovert traits there was no tendency for them to agree with each other. The person who was in close touch with campus affairs was not necessarily the person who gave many responses in common with the others in the Jung association test. Sharing the group's opinion of instructors did not indicate that one would be scored an extrovert on the Colgate test or that he would share the answers of his fellows in the Jung association test.

We concluded that people are not consistently "turned inward" or "turned outward" in their interests; that introversion, like intelligence, appears to break up into a number of traits on close examination. The traits which we had presumably measured, a tendency to exhibit common associations, a tendency to notice what went on about the university, a tendency to adopt the opinion of teachers which was most commonly expressed by other students would themselves break up into more specific patterns of response if closely examined. We would find that our "gossip test" did not measure acquaintance with all forms of campus information to be gleaned in talk with other students, but acquaintance with particular topics, or the conversation of particular groups. When the instructions for the Jung association test were changed to make it appear desirable that one should respond often with the common words, students who had before responded with highly individual words now increased their number of common words. There was little agreement with previous scores. We were not measuring just a tendency to extrovert responses, but we were measuring the effects of our instructions. Agreement with the common judgment of teachers might be the product either of a tendency to repeat overheard opinions or of a tendency to make shrewd observations for oneself.

A boy was some time ago brought to a clinic for advice. Ten months before he had been getting on very well with his family. They shared his confidence. His interests were known and approved. Rather suddenly the situation changed. He became secretive about his movements and silent in the family circle except for grudging and evasive answers to questions. His school work was neglected. Obviously he was occupied with thoughts and daydreams which had very little to do with family affairs.

At the clinic skillful questioning developed the fact that he had fallen in with a gang of boys of his own age who had first established a rendezvous where they met frequently, and had then drifted into forms of sex behavior which would be obviously tabu in all of the families. To this interest was added occasional pilfering of items which would be acceptable to the gang. An observer of the boy's conduct at home would have pronounced him now an introvert, whereas he had been a year before a decided extrovert. But an observer of his conduct with the gang would have formed no such opinion. With the other boys he was distinctly extroverted, if by that we may mean that he talked freely with them and was very responsive to the outer world of the other boys. *It was not his personality that had become introverted, it was only his relation to his family that had changed.*

We have the same difficulty in the use of such a trait as "honesty." Observation and tests will show very little prediction of honest or dishonest behavior in one type of situation from honest or dishonest behavior in another. A schoolboy's reliability in money affairs will prove to depend largely on the situation. In one situation experience has led him to be scrupulous. In another, he may have had no such training. And his behavior with money will have little connection with his honesty in taking examinations, or his accuracy of statement in recounting his adventures. Honesty depends on previous training in the situation now confronted.

A number of years ago in an argument with G. H. Allport I urged that psychologists would be forced to give up the search for general traits of personality and their measurement. Allport pointed out that to be consistent in supporting my view that we were concerned only with specific habits and not with general traits, it would be necessary for me to refuse to characterize anyone as industrious, or as more industrious than another. I should be compelled to abstain from all general statements about people to the effect that they were intelligent, genial, honest, self-centered, domineering, courageous. It would be necessary for me, instead of pronouncing that my friend X had courage, to specify that he dived without urging from a thirty-foot platform, that he had on two occasions resisted successfully attempts to hold him up, that he had expressed publicly opinions that were very unpopular among his acquaintances. It would also be necessary for me to mention that my friend could not bring himself to face an operation which he agreed was essential for the restoration of his health, and that he was always thrown into a state of panic in a dispute with a traffic officer. If there are no general traits, I should be incorrect in recommending a laboratory assistant as resourceful or as industrious. I should be limited to naming the amount of work that he had done on certain special tasks or to describing the problem to which he had found his own solution.

In this argument it is obvious that Allport was more nearly correct than I. We continuously make judgments that one person has less stamina than another, that one person is more neurotic than another, that he is less timid, less vindictive, more contentious, more generous than another. Allport's own attempts to measure the tendency to ascendence or submission illustrate the very legitimate sense in which we may use descriptions in terms of general traits of the personality. For the measurement of ascendence-submission Allport uses a list of forty or fifty situations. These are described. One is a restaurant and the coffee is served him cold. What does he do? Does he summon the waiter and ask to have the cup returned and replaced with hot coffee? Does he murmur something to his fellow diner? Does he remain silent and only feel put upon? On the subject's answers to such questions he is assigned a score indicating his position on a scale of ascendence-submission.

The theory behind the use of a score in such a test is this: the situations described in the test represent a wide sampling of common situations. The person who responded to a large number of these situations in a submissive manner is more likely to respond in a submissive manner to other common situations than is a person who was submissive in only a few of the cases of the sample. We can very properly refer to the first man as submissive, or assert that he is more submissive than the second man. There is, of course, the objection that what we have sampled is a response with a pencil on paper, not a response to a traffic officer or to an aggressive salesman in the flesh. Until observation establishes that we can trust a sample of behavior taken from responses to written statements to predict what will happen in actual life, we must be rather tentative in our use of Allport's ascendence-submission score. But that there is some validity in it is indicated by its substantial agreement with a very different measure of our aggressiveness, namely, the opinions of our friends.

Even when tests for general traits of the personality have been developed and their validity established, there will continue to be difficulties in their use. General traits, being abstractions, do not have the usefulness of the knowledge which comes by long acquaintance with an individual. Suppose that we have devised a test for courage which has sampled the individual's response to one hundred situations in which he may act courageously or with cowardice. Suppose also that we have found that his verbal reactions to the descriptions of these situations do really predict his reactions in the face of actual danger, which is possible though not very probable. We shall still confront the fact that a "courage score" does not indicate just what our subject will do in any special situation. Two men may make the same score, and not agree in responding courageously to any two situations.

In other words, such a general rating in courage would not be of any great use in predicting behavior. It will not indicate whether a man would go to the rescue of a drowning person. An accurate prediction of that requires some knowledge of his behavior in a similar situation in the past. A general score in honesty will not indicate the forms of honest behavior to be expected. Only by the division of honest behavior into more special fields will we get a more precise notion of what to expect. Honesty at cards, honesty in sales talk, honesty in the payment of debts, honesty in describing the fish that got away, constitute such special fields, and to the extent that they are more specific they will exhibit more consistent behavior.

Criminal records betray this high degree of specificity. A criminal is not just a criminal. He is a pickpocket, a confidence man, or a safe-blower, or a grocery-store thief. A confidence man is not just a confidence man. He has his specific habits which enable the police to recognize him from the particular form of confidence game that he practices. The grocery-store burglar is not just a grocery-store burglar. He is a grocery-store burglar who always enters by the rear door and is known by the items which he takes. With a man's record before us we can do much more than say that a man is a criminal. We can say that he is given to snatching purses from women after nightfall, or that he drives up to a gas station and gets out of his car while the at-

tendant is filling the tank, approaches the attendant from the
rear and commands him to put up his hands. Criminality is not
a general trait of personality, but a specific interest and a group
of specific habits.

The question whether personality traits are general or specific
may be answered thus: the behavior of an individual is determined by a mass of specific habit responses to specific cues
according to associations established in the past. Long training
in a polite household or among honest associates may establish
many responses of a given type, responses which we classify as
politeness or honesty; and something resembling a general
characteristic may appear as a result of such training. Where a
person can be described as industrious, introverted, shy, neurotic, impulsive, deceitful, we are dealing with habit families or
large groups of habits which have been established through
multitudes of experiences. Such traits are like skills, which require the learning of many diverse habits. And in such traits we
shall find subdivision possible. A man may have established
many habits of neatness in his office and betray no tendency to
be neat at home. A girl may spend hours on her dress and person, and may regularly leave her room in disorder. The joiner
may keep his shop and tools in remarkable order, but regularly
go unshaven and unkempt. Are such people neat, or are they
disorderly?

Even the intelligence which psychologists have been measuring for many years now tends to appear better described as a
group of more specific traits, and there is a strong movement
toward substituting tests for more special aptitudes in the place
of general intelligence tests. What were confidently accepted
fifteen years ago as tests of general intelligence are now recognized to be tests of school aptitude. The notion of general intelligence is useful particularly in indicating those extreme cases
in which individuals prove inept in a large sampling of abilities

or those equally rare instances in which many abilities are present in high degree. For the great majority who are high in a few abilities or aptitudes, low in a few, and average in many, special measures of these special abilities are required.

The same remarks apply to introversion and extroversion. The schizophrenic patient in the hospital has lost interest in his social environment. Death and misfortune in his family no longer disturb him. He cares little for the opinion of those about him. He may profitably be described as highly introverted. In my own experiments with college students this general introversion was not present. Most students have some companions with whom they talk freely and to whom they are responsive. Most students also find themselves in some surroundings less responsive and less free. The great majority of college students cannot be described as introverted or extroverted. They must be understood in connection with their associates. Some are mute in the classroom but expansive with their own special crowd. Others express themselves readily in classes but are shy and retiring at college social affairs. In the insane hospital the manic-depressive patient in his more elated states may be very properly described as extremely extroverted. He is keenly aware of all that goes on about him and this responsiveness to external events may be so exaggerated that he does not stay with a topic of conversation even long enough to finish his sentence. Something that he sees or hears will interrupt his train of ideas and send him off on a different tack. His conversation may be unintelligible because of this flight of ideas.

All the personality traits in which we are interested concern relations to other persons. Aggressiveness and shyness, dominance and submission, truthfulness, loyalty, cooperativeness, obviously depend on the human environment as well as on the individual. It is not surprising that we fail to discover more than a few extreme cases in which such attitudes toward other persons apply to all other persons. Any college teacher is frequently astonished to discover that the rather diffident student who has attended his classes for a year has first mate's papers or has spent two seasons cooking in a logging camp or has been managing a fleet of trucks during his college career. His diffidence is not a trait of his personality as a whole, but a rather specific response to the classroom situation.

Allport is correct. General traits of personality exist and are theoretically measurable. But their description and measurement are beset with much difficulty and have not yet been satisfactorily achieved by psychologists. We are compelled to recognize such general traits, but we should always be cautious in dealing with them.

XIII

THE SELF AND VOLUNTARY ACTION

A SNEEZE is a typical involuntary act. No one remarks to himself that this is a good time to sneeze and then sneezes. Its convulsive movements we recognize as a "seizure." It interrupts our planned conduct with a totally irrelevant action. W. D. Wallis (pp. 130-131) remarks on the customs which have grown up about sneezing in various cultures. The bystander exclaims, "Gesundheit," or "Prosit," or "Votre santé," or "God be with you." Wallis explains this as a survival of an animistic belief that the soul may depart in a sneeze; but, however such customs arose, they cannot now be mere survivals. Their present support is probably the recognition that the action is not under control. It is not the act of the sneezer.

The involuntary nature of the act lies in the fact that the actor cannot initiate the action by giving himself its cue. He merely feels the warning tickle and proceeds to sneeze. Nor can he, on this warning signal, give himself a cue for an inhibiting action. Only when the agent can determine that an act will or will not take place by a cue for its occurrence or a cue for its inhibition is the act under voluntary control. The most important of such cues are words, and the importance of words derives from the fact that acts which are attached to words can be initiated by conversation—the conversation of others, or the inner speech of the agent himself.

In some actions the close bond between word and movement is very easy to observe. To say "six" and write "five" at the same moment is almost impossible; but to say "five" and write the digit as we say it is easy. It is equally difficult to pronounce to oneself a word and at the same instant type another word. This can be done after much practice, just as the ability to type the original word on pronouncing it was acquired. It is not only writing that is thus connected with speech. The meaning of any word lies in the responses attached to that word as cues. The word is associated with the appropriate action. Most persons will find it impossible to "think" a tone below their actual singing register. This is because such "thinking" demands a muscular set of which they are incapable.

The older psychology recognized this connection between ideas and movement and called it "ideomotor action." But the failure of the older psychology to recognize that verbal thinking is really subdued speech and that an idea is a stimulus because it includes muscular activity which affects muscle sense organs kept this psychology from recognizing that the idea is itself action and that in ideomotor activity the verbal action is just a part of the beginning of the whole act. In children this connection between speech and action is much more apparent because they have not learned to suppress speech to minimal movements and they are often unable to perform an act without first saying the word, or to say the word without performing the act.

In adults the act as well as the word may be checked and appear only when delicate measurements of action currents in the muscles are made. A subject who is told to "think" of moving his finger but to refrain from moving it will show no overt movement, but the muscles of the finger will betray the electrical changes that accompany slight contraction. All thinking began in action. All thought words began in spoken words. The action has become subdued, suppressed, minimal. Thurstone in his *The Nature of Intelligence* argues that the capacity for this suppression of action to mere traces of the former muscular contraction is an essential of intelligence.

Most of our actual movements, of course, are started without the assistance of words. The telephone bell rings and we rise to go to the instrument to answer. A friend waves at us and we wave in return. We leave the front door and walk to the curb, enter the car, push the starter button, release the brake, operate the clutch and are off. What we do next depends on what we see and hear and, what is more important, on what we are doing at the time. One movement is the cue for another because each movement is a stimulus pattern as well as a response. A cup of coffee offered to a man driving a car through the city traffic will not stir him to respond as he would at the breakfast table. The movements of driving control behavior and eliminate the possibility of a normal response to the proffered cup.

Words are themselves movements and enter into this control. Many of our actions are performed to an accompaniment of words like Guatemalan weaving in which the weaver's motions are accompanied by song, and patterns are memorized through the song accompaniment. Most of the training given a soldier is training in word-action associations to insure that his action can be ruled ultimately by the army high command through verbal orders. Uniform response to many words is necessary in an army, or the units of that army would not be interchangeable.

What is it about an action that makes us call that action voluntary? What do we mean by self-control of action? We recognize that the disciplined soldier's response to a command may not be a voluntary act and that it may approach an automatic obedience. It is an act with a verbal cue, but something more is required if the act is to deserve the name "voluntary." In the first place voluntary action is limited to situations in which there is a choice. This means that at least two action systems must be in some sense ready to go. There must be stimuli present for two incompatible acts. We choose between going and staying, between saying yes and saying no, between turning right and turning left, between taking up the food or leaving it.

Luria in his *The Nature of Human Conflicts* has called attention to the fact that when a small child is confronted with a choice he tends to go immediately into action. If several pieces of cake are offered him on a plate he reaches out at once, but his action will probably be confused. He reaches for the piece at which he is looking. As his hand closes over it, it is no longer visible but some other piece is. He touches the other also. His action shows a confused mixture of taking and rejecting. A tracing of his hand movement shows an irregular path, zigzagging back and forth among the pieces on the dish.

An adult behaves very differently. Offered the same platter, he does not immediately reach out. There is a pause and at the end of the pause a single, direct, efficient movement captures the largest piece and removes it from the plate. I have watched visitors in the Hyde Park Zoo teasing an orang-utan by offering it more pieces of fruit than it could manage. One in its mouth, one in the right hand and one in the left filled all the available storage places and the offer of yet another orange would put the ape into a state of great agitation. The orang was not capable of choosing, of taking some and disregarding others.

One of the essentials of true voluntary action is that an individual shall respond to a choice by a pause, an interval of no overt activity. Both actions are held in check. This is followed by the execution of one act or the other, but not by a confusion of the two.

Janet gives an illustration from the behavior of a dog. If the dog has been trained to retrieve a ball we may throw it time after time and the ball will be expertly overtaken and brought back. But if we suddenly throw a handful of balls instead of one, the dog will be thrown into confusion like the confusion of the ape at being offered too many oranges or the confusion of the child on being offered several pieces of cake.

What is it that takes place in this pause which precedes a voluntary choice? Luria is convinced that the pause is somehow occupied with speech. This is undoubtedly correct. The adult has this advantage over child, ape and dog. The adult can, when action is blocked by conflicting action, have the advantage of increased central inhibition which keeps the two acts somewhat in check and prevents an immediate confused response. The adult has also the advantage of verbal direction. The words which are a part of the beginnings of both acts have their own preliminary competition for control. No person can murmur to himself two words at once, and the conflict between the rival action systems must be resolved in its verbal beginnings before there is an actual conflict in the muscles used for the overt actions.

An adult who is confronted with a plate of cakes can look them over and name their properties. He can think or say to himself, "Larger," or "More frosting," or "That," or "Enough." These are the germs of action and direct his movements. If an adult is placed in the position of the orang and is offered more articles than he can accommodate, he can say to himself, "That's all," and turn away. If he is placed in the position of the dog with a confusing number of objects before him he can say, "The far one," or "The blue one," or "That one over there," and select from among the number. This does not mean, of course, that any adult does not occasionally behave like child, ape, or dog.

There is something more than the pause to be observed in a voluntary choice. Many years ago Stevenson Smith and I attached a pneumograph to a number of subjects and had them sit before a table. On the table were two objects, and the in-

structions were to pick up one or the other of these objects but
not immediately. The tracing of the breathing as recorded by
the pneumograph showed that for a little while after the instructions were given breathing was regular. Then, after a pause,
there would be a brief holding of the breath and this was often
followed by a choice. The subject would reach out and take one
or the other of the objects. It is our belief that this holding of
the breath served to build up a state of excitement and general
tension and that this state of excitement is essential to the
breaking up of the deadlock in action. In excitement the state of
equilibrium is less stable, and one act or the other may prevail.
We had in our instructions given no cue as to which object was
to be taken up. The subject could not reach for both at once.
The tendency to reach for one inhibits the tendency to reach
for the other until some muttered word guides action in the
direction of its object.

If all incompatible action systems when stimulated together
had the outcome of an unambiguous triumph of one system or
the other, life would be extremely simple. Hesitation and indecision would not exist. There would be no such thing as deliberate choice. With stimuli for approach and stimuli for avoidance both present, one action or the other would prevail by
virtue of priority or superior number of cues or facilitation from
the current posture. Something like this simplification of life
exists among domestic fowls. Two hens approaching at the same
time a hole in the wire netting that is just large enough for one
do not have the troubles that two human beings manifest in
like circumstances if they have been politely reared. Nor is a
hen often reduced to inaction when it is in trouble. If corn is
sprinkled out of the hen's reach through the netting of the
poultry yard, the hen does not stand still and think it over. It
goes into immediate action. The action may be quite ineffective
and may consist of rushing up and down her side of the fence,

but there will be little sign of interference between movements. What she does she does thoroughly and without reserve. Most of her doubts have to do only with approaching and not approaching.

In the higher animals and in man there are obvious signs that competing actions are not thus unambiguously and easily settled. Inhibition is not complete, and rival action systems enter into competition in muscles as well as in the central nervous system. Opposing muscles may both be tensed and the interference between two systems may appear as actual interference of one set of muscles with the action of another. Some of this must, of course, be true also of the actions of the hen; otherwise she could execute no controlled movements.

When rival or incompatible action systems are both stimulated and there is no complete inhibition of one by the other, the result is *conflict*. Conflict is a failure of inhibition. And the normal result of conflict is an emotional reinforcement of the energy of action. This reinforcement derives in part from the fact that any resistance to the contraction of a muscle stimulates the muscle's proprioceptors to volleys of nerve impulses which traverse the central system and return to the muscle and to other muscles. We have spoken of this as a "reverberation" of nervous impulses and its effect is a general increase in the tonus of sections of the body musculature. Holding the breath has this same exciting effect. The increase in general muscle tonus carries with it all the physiological devices for the facilitation of muscular contraction—an increased heart beat to provide for circulation, increased respiration to provide for oxygen and the elimination of carbon dioxide, adrenine from the glands above the kidneys which counteracts the effects of fatigue in muscles and releases blood sugar from the liver, and the spread of the chemical mediator, sympathin, which is produced at the ends of the sympathetic nerves or in the effectors they serve and which reinforces the effects of adrenine and the sympathetic system. A state of conflict, therefore, is normally a state of excitement. The system of reinforcement of action is delicately adjusted to meet the requirements of increased action.

These states of conflict are almost continuous in waking experience and sometimes pervade sleep. The man in the orchestra seat who squirms and fidgets is only betraying incipient starts at leaving the hall to see that his car was not parked by a fire hydrant. The man sitting by his own fireside is not reading the paper with his usual resting calm. His wife's request that he speak to his heir about coming home more directly from school has not been complied with, but the beginnings of compliance are there in sufficient strength to disturb his reading. These are trivial conflicts, and they have only passing effects. There are other states of indecision which may have more serious results.

In man the mutual interference of rival action systems can more readily be reduced to slight and tentative movements than it can in animals. The presence of the two interfering systems may not be at all evident to the eye of an observer, but only to the electrical recording of faint muscular tensions. The work of Max on minimal speech movements in the lips of normal persons and in the fingers of deaf-mutes has been mentioned. Thurstone's suggestion that the capacity for checking action to minimal expression is the outstanding characteristic of intelligence has also been mentioned. With this goes a capacity for using these minimal movements as reminders and cues for other minimal movements and for action. A man can swim while sitting quietly on the bank of a stream. He can harpoon a fish while lying in his tepee. He can sail a schooner in the South Seas while eating his lunch in an automat. He can, that is, go through some of the movements of these actions. His performance may not be evident to the man in the chair beside him, but it is there none the less. These reduced actions constitute thinking. In the adult man the blocking of one action by another initiates a period of such minimal movement. His trial and error solutions of problems commit him to nothing until some one of his tentative actions finds itself unimpeded and develops into a line of conduct. He has made a choice.

Man has another advantage over the animals in a type of musculature and muscular activity which is almost his monopoly. He has an elaborate set of muscles which are not used in getting about from one place to another or in manipulating things about him. These are the muscles involved in speech. Their actions do not interfere with the rest of behavior. And through training in his culture the activities of these muscles have become associated with man's grosser actions. He has learned to name his movements and the naming has become a part of the budding movement.

The connection between excitement and the ability to resolve a choice has had many pages devoted to it by Janet. His long experience with mental disorders leads him to the belief that this is the central difficulty in functional mental disease. He gives convincing evidence that the inability to make decisions is the chief characteristic of neurotic patients.

Janet does not explain this inability in terms of excitement and muscular tension but in terms of mental *force* or energy whose physical basis he does not undertake to explain. Most neurotic disorders are, in his opinion, characterized by inadequate *force*. And the main symptom of this inadequacy is the inability of the patient to make decisions or to perform what Janet calls acts of higher order as distinguished from acts of automatic habit. Such patients he calls *déprimées*.

It is my own belief that Janet's *force mentale* is closely related to the muscular excitement which serves for the reinforcement of action. The depressed person is a person in whom the somatic conditions for vigorous action are not present. It is common knowledge that decisions are much more difficult to make when we are fatigued or weak from illness. In a normal person the very occurrence of a conflict serves to produce the excitement which makes the situation unstable, introduces new elements into it and so resolves the conflict. In fatigue or illness or in the neuroses this excitement fails to reach the point necessary for overcoming the block.

It is in the realm of voluntary action that nervous disorders have their most striking effects. The sufferer becomes incapable of making decisions, and continues in a state of continuous but inadequate excitement which is prolonged until symptoms of actual exhaustion appear. And many a nervous disorder has its cause in a difficult decision. If the patient could only make up his mind whether to go into bankruptcy or not, whether to leave home for a career or not, whether to marry or not, whether to get a divorce or not, he would not break down. Or a series of difficult decisions may end in breakdown because the effects of difficult choices are cumulative. Most of the students who "go to pieces" in their study have behind them a broken home which made them face continual decision between father and mother, or a difficult attachment in which they could not decide whether to continue or to break off, or a revolt against parental control which would not resolve either into compliance or a refusal to obey. The inability to make minor decisions may be caused by a major indecision. The sufferer cannot make up his mind about the simple choices of everyday life. The exhaustion brought on by his main problem makes everything a problem. Indecision may extend into the far past and into the future. He worries over whether or not to cross the bridge long before he reaches it, while he is confronting it, and long after he has crossed he continues to worry over whether he should have crossed.

One woman recently expressed an absorbing indecision over

the question whether or not she should have married the man she did ten years before. This would not worry a person in normal health. The past event would be reacted to by a normal person just as he would react to spilled milk. There are a number of things that can be done when one stumbles over the threshold of the grocery store and drops his quart of milk on the cement walk. He can stop and mop it up, or he can walk away and pretend that it was not his milk that fell. The milk obviously cannot be unspilled. In reality things are bad or good only to the extent that something can be done about them. One of the most characteristic marks of mental failure is worry over the past or the inevitable.

An attempt to conceal something from those about us is a state of conflict. Our natural movements and speech would betray us. These we keep in check. Luria found that murderers examined in Moscow just after their arrest reacted to the necessity of making a choice in the manner of children. They tended to go into immediate confused action instead of showing the normal period of inaction and the resultant organized movement. Students who were waiting for their trial before a commission that annually expelled those whose political opinions were not satisfactory to the Soviet régime were in the same condition. When they confronted a simple choice in the laboratory they showed confusion in their movements. The brief period in which the conflict is settled verbally was in their case missing. It is clear that states of excitement tend to disturb voluntary action and to deprive an adult of his ability to hold movement in check for that important pause during which his conflict is settled by the results of competition among the verbal "starters" of movement. Extreme excitement so reinforces action that the conflict is fought out among the gross bodily movements which are concerned, not among the slight initial movements or among the verbal cues which are the most important of these initial movements.

We are now in a position to describe the general nature of voluntary action. Its first essential is a state of conflict or interference between two action systems. Among the beginnings of both actions are words, and the conflict must be resolved here first. During the period of hesitation verbal associations may reinforce one formula or the other. This is what we usually call thinking. The verbal conflict being resolved, the prevailing formula will initiate its appropriate action. The limits of voluntary action are set by previously established word-action associations. We can will to do only those actions which we have previously done and named while doing them. An action is truly voluntary only when it can be begun or can be checked by verbal cues.

A generation ago psychologists used to talk a great deal of what they called *suggestion*. By this they meant the control of the behavior of another person through verbal cues. The effects of hypnosis, the effects of advertising, the effects of propaganda were all explained as due to suggestion. McDougall described suggestion as an "instinctive tendency" in men. Men are naturally suggestible. This is not incorrect, because all men do show themselves amenable to suggestion. But if we are interested in knowing how any individual man will respond to any particular suggestion we must know much more than that suggestibility is a general human trait. We must know whether, in this particular man, his act has been attached to this particular verbal cue.

Suggestibility is the result of learning a language. When we acquire any language, such acquisition lies in associating the sounds of the language with action. The use of suggestion is merely the use of these acquired cues in the direction and control of the behavior of our neighbors. There is no essential difference between causing a man to perform some act by suggestion and causing him to perform that act by request. It is evident that the basis of social cooperation lies in the attachment of action systems to language. Through this attachment it becomes possible to adjust our behavior to the behavior of other persons.

By far the most interesting use of words in the control of action is in the control of one's own action, in other words, self-control. We recognize that an act is our own when it is thus directed. The sneeze is not our own act but an "outside" interruption in our action because it is not controlled by verbal cues. We cannot say to ourselves "No" and inhibit the sneeze. A small child who is just beginning to develop voluntary control over some of his acts may be observed to reach after something forbidden and then say "No" and check the action. He has been restrained at first by some other means, by taking his hand, by pulling him away, by slight punishment, or by a startling exclamation from an older person. The older person's "No" accompanies this and has been repeated by the child as he checks his act. "No" has become a signal for the check and the act is now under the child's control in the sense that by its presence or absence the act is determined.

We describe a person as *responsible* when his behavior can be thus guided by verbal cues. If he does not respond to requests, arguments, threats of punishment and other forms of verbal interference by his neighbors he is not responsible. Children acquire responsibility as they acquire the control of action through language.

In the language of Freud this has been recognized by calling the young infant an "id," the Latin for "it." This is to indicate that no true self-direction has yet appeared in its behavior. After the infant has had experiences with pain and noxious stimuli and with the relief of various forms of drive, he may have desires. He is no longer merely restless from stomach activity in hunger. He has anticipations of food, is prepared for eating and can be said now to have a desire for food. The acquisition of specific desires gives direction to what were previously blind urges, mere states of disturbed activity which were maintained by local tensions in the stomach, from sticking pins, from cold or too great heat. Freud would now say that the child had developed an ego.

After the child has learned to talk and desires have been complicated by the addition of words and these can serve to reinforce or deflect action, Freud speaks of the super-ego. Action is now affected by the opinions and the praise and blame of others. All language is learned from others and is primarily the expression of the interests and desires of others. A conscience is merely an equipment of verbal habits which operate in the control of behavior. The social nature of conscience originates in the social nature of language. The voice of conscience is the public voice, or such part of the public voice as has become established as verbal habit in the individual. These two Freudian terms, *ego* and *super-ego*, describe very real characteristics in the development of a personality.

When a verbal formula serves to guide conduct toward the achievement of that formula, and serves to inhibit action that would be inconsistent with the end result described or named in the formula, action is said to be self-controlled. A purpose is a verbal statement of some end result of action. The verbal statement may be a response to a drive. After a child has had experience in getting food and in naming it, the name may be aroused by hunger and the appropriate action may be aroused by the name. Or the behavior appropriate to eating may be aroused directly by the use of the name by the child's mother.

Later the word serves through associated behavior to guide the child to food, to inhibit distracting action and to keep him to his purpose. The word may become the core of the purpose. By it action is integrated. A person who lacks self-control is a person whose plans do not serve to guide action to the achievement of those plans. A man who announces that he has stopped drinking but finds the announcement ineffectual lacks self-control. We call him "weak-willed" when his verbal statement of his desires does not lead to their consummation.

There is a common form of delusion in which the sufferer believes that others are continually directing his behavior. An old longshoreman once called on me to complain that an obscene phrase kept repeating itself in his mind. He was not responsible for this, he said. It was the work of a woman whose lecture he had attended three weeks before. She was in some mysterious way causing him to repeat over and over the obnoxious words. He visited me to ask whether I believed that shooting the woman would stop the phrase from occupying his thoughts.

His conviction that he was not responsible for the phrase is based on the fact that his resolves to avoid it came to nothing. In spite of good resolutions, even as a result of good resolutions, he continued to repeat to himself his unwanted formula. He could say to himself "No" or "Think about something else," but the phrase kept on. It was quite natural that he should then attribute it to someone else. It is people who utter phrases, and since it was not he who chose this, it must have been chosen by someone else. The longshoreman was unfamiliar with the psychological explanation in terms of habit. He did not realize that even his good resolutions, because they were once followed by the forbidden words, had become cues for those words. I have known two radio operators who were similarly annoyed by radio messages which they heard everywhere, in bed, at mealtime, or on shore. The messages were, of course, only their own habits. Practice in following the Morse code heard on their instruments had associated words with the code and ultimately led them to perceive the code even when it had no outer source. One of the operators had worked out for himself an explanation. He was getting messages through the gold fillings in his teeth.

I have heard the author of the scenario for an elaborate pageant assert that not he but the Holy Ghost was responsible for the words. When writing and speech appear to carry themselves on without verbal anticipation of their direction and topics, this delusion of outside control often arises. The speech is not planned in advance and so is taken to be appearing "of itself" or through the plans of another. The college lecturer who has been repeating almost verbatim the same lectures for fifteen years has no delusion that his speech is inspired. He is aware that past associations have established his sequence of words, and he is able occasionally to "think forward," that is, to name his next topic.

The frequent phrase "as if inspired" is a recognition of this common perception of not choosing one's thoughts or utterances. We are "as if inspired" when we are surprised by our own words and have not been ready for what we are saying. An experience of my own will serve to illustrate this inspiration. I found myself one afternoon writing on a topic in psychology with a facility which was very different from my usual hesitant and unhappy state when writing. For a brief and pleasant moment I was convinced that I had become a writer. Not until I had finished the short paper and sat thinking of myself with a new admiration did I suddenly realize that what I had written was a repetition of my lecture delivered just before sitting down at the desk, and that the writing had been facile enough but had no other merits.

The most striking instances of such inspired production are found in automatic writing in which the subject's attention is centered on something else than his pencil and paper—on, for instance, a conversation with another person. The writing carries itself on with word chains and associative sequences previously established, but the subject does not look at the writing and does not notice the cues or plan what is to be written in advance. It is therefore said to be unconscious, and it is not later remembered. It lacks the corrective of reading and planning and often contains enough of indiscretion and impropriety to make such writers wary of demonstrating their "gift" before strangers.

The Freudians are quite accurate in holding that such unconscious expression betrays underlying desires and wishes that would be checked if they were given full attention. The sources of the writing are the same as the sources of ordinary speech and are directed by stimuli. The desires expressed are not in the strict sense unconscious, because they are in their own way articulate, and strictly unconscious desires are inarticulate. But the expression of such desires in automatic writing is inarticulate in the sense that the writing is not being reacted to at the time with verbal comment and is not being guided with speech.

Janet's analysis of the notion of *power* throws a considerable light on these cases of delusions of outside control. Human actions, he says, are distinguished from other events by the fact that they are foreshadowed by the speech of the actor. The actor talks about what he is going to do, names the consequences of his action. This talk directs his action and serves to hold him to his announced purposes. But we learn early in life that there are great differences among men in their tendencies to carry out announced intentions. In some, what is announced is then performed. In others, plans and announced intentions are very poor indicators of the future. We learn to discount their promises.

Our notion of power derives from this tendency of announced purposes to be carried out. A weak person is a person whose purposes fail to be achieved. A strong person is one whose intentions are excellent warnings of the event. We extend this notion of power, first learned in connection with people, to physical events. A powerful stream of water is a stream that carries everything in its own direction. A weak flow is a flow that is deflected by obstacles. This metaphor has become a basic idea in science and enters into the notions of momentum and energy, but it derives from experience with our fellow men.

Delusions of impotence are founded on experience with plans that do not mature. So are correct beliefs of impotence. We recognize ourselves as weaker than another when the other's plan and not ours comes to realization. The delusion of being governed by an outside force or another person may be the result of having our actions come out as another person might wish, though he may not have expressed that wish.

Several years ago a young woman, a student in college, was brought to a psychologist by her mother. She had developed a conviction that she had lost all power to act and that all of her acts were really acts of God. She was not a free agent. The history of this conviction was that she had two years before read a devotional book which recommended that all decisions be taken to the Deity in prayer. She had cultivated a habit of doing this, and even trivial decisions were made by this device. When a friend whom she had met on the street asked her to go to see a motion picture she would tell the friend that she would give her decision later. Arrived home, she sat down in the easy chair in her own room which she used for this purpose and prayed over the question. Eventually she felt sure either that it would be right to go, or that it would be wrong to go. Once the decision was made she would consistently abide by it.

She had the misfortune in college to fall in with a group of irreverent students who made light of her method and convinced her that her religious foundation for the method was mistaken. She decided that God could not really have been concerned over such trivial matters as she had been praying about. She ceased to retire to her room and seek advice. But this brought on trouble. She had no other method of deciding questions and she was brought to the psychologist in a lamentable state. A simple question might start her to trembling and she would be unable to answer. It was pointed out to her that whatever the state of her religious belief, the method that she had been using had been efficacious. There could be no doubt that she could make her decisions by its use. She was persuaded to return home and decide whether or not she would accept the psychologist's general advice and cooperate with him, using her familiar means of making the decision. She did so and returned to report that the familiar event had taken place. She had felt suddenly convinced that she should take the psychologist's advice. After this she was gradually brought to widen the circumstances under which she could arrive at decisions, and she recovered from her neurotic symptoms.

There are tribes of American Indians who made and still make a practice of sleeping on important decisions. During the night a dream will occur which will be interpreted as favoring one course of action or another. The sleeper has entered sleep with his state of indecision, which means with a conflict of tensions, of action systems which impede each other. It is no doubt these tensions that lead to the dream and the dream solution is effected in much the same manner that ordinary waking solutions are effected. The dream depends less on verbal associations, and the decision of the dream is subject to possible reinterpretation in the morning.

Indecision or the failure to resolve a conflict lies behind nearly all neurotic behavior. The indecision may be the primary cause of the neurosis but it is often a secondary cause, the primary being a physical inadequacy which has robbed the patient of his ability to make ready decisions. Fatigue and many physiological disorders may make impossible that access of energy which serves in the normal person to break the *impasse* and to establish a new habit which solves the problem.

To assist the making of decisions when the situation does not clearly indicate one course of action or another, men have had recourse to many devices. Some of these have become social institutions like consulting the oracle, or drawing lots, or tossing a coin, or opening the Bible at random. The gambler facing the question of whether to place his money on the red or the black, or on one number rather than another, cannot by any amount of thinking make a correct decision because there is no correct decision. A game of chance is a game in which there can be no basis for choice before the event. The outcome is deliberately made to depend on no known causes. This is what we call chance. Gamblers, however, must decide; and the result is that they allow themselves to be guided by irrelevant associations such as a dream of a number, a number seen on a street car, a stray remark of a child, by any straw that will help to turn the balance of opposed actions one way or another. Gambling derives its whole thrill from these states of indecision in which both choices are strongly reinforced because either may be the lucky one.

Like the individual with delusions of being controlled by another person or a spirit, the gambler tends to attribute the outcome to "Lady Luck" or to a jinx. We do not call this a delusion because it is so common and widespread. The man who believes that luck is against him has arrived at that notion by the same processes that are used by the man who believes that certain persons whom he calls "They" are out to defeat his intentions. His intentions are obviously defeated; that is real enough. All he has to do is to blame this defeat on some hostile agent, and not on his own ineptitude, and his delusion is established. We are surrounded from birth with opposition from other persons. We become used to interpreting opposition as the result of an intention, even if the person or agent with the hostile intention remains unidentified.

Chronic indecision which characterizes many neurotics is annoying to associates and strong pressure is brought upon the undecided person to make up his mind. Individuals sometimes learn to escape this pressure by pretending to make decisions, but actually continuing in the state of anxiety that attends indecision. They may learn to announce false decisions with a very emphatic manner, to look in public the picture of the strong, silent man. In dealing with the public, in commanding troops, even in training a child or a dog, indecision has fatal results and must not be shown even if it exists. The administrator learns to appear fixed in his verdict. He learns this because he will be in hot water so long as it appears that he can be made to change his mind. A certain judge has succeeded in learning to make prompt decisions even if these are after inadequate deliberation, but he has been unable for a month to decide on the position of his new office desk, which stays in the middle of the room where it was left by the truckmen.

Personality has been defined as the more conservative and stable systems of habit, desire and interest. These tend to be self-protecting; and when they are threatened, the disturbance resulting normally results in the restoration of the threatened interest. A decision is our own when it is determined by these deep-lying habit systems which make up the self, when the result of the decision conserves our established interests. When we are frightened or bluffed or annoyed into a decision that sacrifices these deeper interests we are said not to have acted as free agents. The freedom of the will lies in this self-determination and in the conservation of personality against threatened change.

If we try to define the manner in which we use the words "I" and "me" or "myself," this definition must be in terms of the articulate rôle which we have accepted, or the traits and properties which are accepted by the speaker. An act that is not his own is an act that does not derive from the set of verbal cues that attaches to his rôle. What is the relation to this self to the unconscious or inarticulate desires that enter into behavior? How is the self concerned in conflict and in the making of decisions? The answer to this question requires some examination of the manner in which unconscious or inarticulate desires enter into conflict with the verbal guidance of behavior which is self-control.

When a desire is blocked not by a simple obstacle or by the lack of means for its execution but by another desire, one desire or the other is often unconscious. This fact Jung has indicated in his concept of *ambivalence*. The conflict is responsible for emotional excitement. This makes it often possible to infer the conflict from the presence of the excitement. It has been often pointed out that that obnoxious person, the super-patriot, is usually of alien origin. The exaggerated fervor with which he expresses his sentiments and the zeal with which he denounces what he takes to be disloyalty derive from his own inner conflict. He is divided against himself, and may be quite unaware of that division. Only his super-patriotism ever gets into speech. His old loyalties to another cause and his first hostilities toward his adopted country have been repressed. A new line of speech has supplanted them. But these old loyalties and hostilities have not disappeared from his behavior and they account for his energy. It has also been frequently noted that the recent convert to a religion has an enthusiasm which is lacking in the man who was brought up to that belief. The ecstatic zeal which is shown in denouncing sin derives not so much from the harmful effects of sin as from its attraction to the denouncer. The savagery of civil war and the lasting quality of the hate in which it results derive from the conflict between hostile desires and lifelong habits of friendly cooperation with the other side. If we are torn between killing our former neighbor and offering him protection, whichever course wins the conflict is likely to be vigorously pursued and attended with much emotion.

One of the effects of ambivalence is *overcorrection*. It is not the person brought up to an easy and natural use of the prevailing fashions in grammar and diction who is offended by "errors" in speech, but the person who has only recently acquired the habits of good usage and who is, if he does not speak carefully, likely to relapse. Often the first knowledge of the psychological consultant that the person seeking advice has formed homosexual interests is the extreme horror which is expressed toward such a perversion. The patient often believes that his unfortunate preoccupation with that topic represents aversion only. The middle-aged man who finds himself in a state of shock over the immodest fashions prevailing on civic beaches has failed to notice that the generation of young people wearing those costumes are habituated to them and his own fascinated regard is duplicated only among men of his own age who were brought up among other styles.

We are indebted to Freud for a realization of the extent and the importance of inarticulate desires in everyday conduct as well as in disorders of behavior. Many an automobile collision is the result of a passing impulse in one of the drivers to teach the other a lesson, but this impulse is seldom acknowledged or remembered after the accident and may have been quite inarticulate at the time. It is always inarticulate in court. Many a horrendous wedding gift is broken during the first years of marriage, though the act was not deliberate and intended. Many an appointment is forgotten without the forgetter's acknowledgment even to himself that he was divided in his attitude toward keeping it. It is probably true that we are more likely to leave behind us our umbrella or our overcoat or our book in the house of someone whom we like to visit than in the house of someone whom we dislike. A number of years ago the magazine *Time* published a letter from an indignant subscriber, a minister whose bishop had made a speech. In reporting the speech *Time* had, he asserted, gone beyond the bounds of decent journalism in interjecting occasionally the word "applesauce" in italics. In reply, the editors called the indignant subscriber's attention to the fact that he had misread the word. It was printed as "applause." When the high school girl who is about to go to her first dance mistakes various familiar neighborhood noises for the sound of the door-bell we recognize that her perception is determined by an action system all set to go. She may appear to be reading, but the muscles which will carry her to the door are in a state of readiness to act. Of this she may not be explicitly aware. So long as she does not notice her state and recognize her preparation for the door-bell she may be said to be dominated by an unconscious motive. The broken wedding present may have been the victim of just such a state. Its unwilling owner may have even on some previous occasion made a slight rehearsal of the act of throwing it to the floor. As she now picks it up, this action is carried out, at least to the extent of interfering with the housewifely movements of dusting.

In many cases of conflict which lead to behavior difficulties the conflict would not survive if both of the conflicting systems were articulate. The conflict would be settled in the realm of discourse, either discourse with others or that inner discourse which is called reflection. The rivalry of the two systems could be talked out. Any college adviser finds himself often handicapped by the fact that the person seeking advice does not know what he wants or, thinking he knows, is leaving out of the discussion some strong desire that must eventually be reconciled with his articulate wishes before a solution can be reached. A young woman calls frequently to ask whether or not she should marry a certain young man. Her question as she states it concerns how she is to know that she really loves him. This problem she argues continually with herself. There are times when he seems to her as handsome as the reigning movie hero; but there are times when he does not. It is tempting to advise her that anyone to whom the young man in question ever looked like a movie hero must be genuinely blinded by love, but it eventually appears that her real question has not been asked. She was thinking in the terms in which it is conventional to view a possible marriage, the terms of the magazine love story. But her real doubts did not concern the state of her affections at all. The occasional surmise that it might be better to marry Mr. X or Mr. Y eventually betrayed the fact that her hesitation concerned the young man's business chances and the probability that he would be a devoted husband. She was quite ready to turn her attention elsewhere if a higher probability of security offered. It would, of course, be absurd to suggest that this desire for security and protection, which was her main interest, was unconscious. But the articulate expression of it was completely repressed when she sought advice, and there was reason to believe that she was not herself really recognizing it and weighing it in her attempts at a decision. When it was finally recognized she had little hesitation in deciding to wait, at least until more returns on her friend's earning power had come in.

Another young woman suffered a nervous breakdown. She had six months before quarreled with her fiancé and he had several days later married another girl. This was not the cause of the breakdown, though it was the beginning of the critical situation that led eventually to disaster. Several months after the marriage the young woman began to meet regularly her ex-fiancé at the sessions of an organization to which they both belonged. The wife did not attend. There was always an opportunity for the exchange of a few words between them. The actual cause of the breakdown was that, without fully realizing the nature of her desire, her dreams and fantasies tended to concern being with him and included an occasional expressed anxiety about the wife's health. It would, she thought, be a great misfortune for the young man to be married to an invalid. The wife was actually in excellent health and the signs of illness which the young woman talked about amounted to nothing more than having observed that the wife had a little less color than when she was married. The disappointed girl did not realize that all of her thoughts of the future were concerned with vague and irrational fancies of a return of her fiancé. When she was led to put this in so many words and to talk over the whole situation, the conflict was resolved. She realized when she confronted squarely the possibilities that there was no chance of supplanting the wife. Once her decision was made she ceased to attend the meetings which kept alive her interest, and turned to her work. Her neurotic symptoms disappeared.

It is probable that if the fiancé had been lost through death rather than through another marriage there would have been no breakdown. The very inevitability of death would have insured against a maintained conflict. Death would have made the decision. It was not the loss of the man but the struggle with herself that proved exhausting. She was unable to resolve her conflict by her own efforts because she was unaware of it and did not recognize the desire involved. Once it was recognized it could be the object of discussion and verbal associations might eliminate it as a possible course of action. What she unconsciously wanted would simply not work out.

The technique of psychoanalysis purports to uncover such unconscious desires and by making them articulate bring about a resolution of a troublesome conflict. Many persons have discovered for themselves the relief that can be found in a trustworthy and sympathetic listener. The relief comes not from the advice that may be received, but from the control over behavior that is established when desires and aversions are recognized and made articulate. They can then for the first time enter into plans and their effects on behavior are no longer blind and erratic. Their possibilities can be canvassed; they can be given a place and a date; their attendant consequences may be suggested by a verbal description when the inarticulate desire would have failed to carry any warning.

Our inarticulate desires are in a sense outside the limits of the self. They belong to the personality and may be lasting and conservative features of the personality. But they are not part of the articulate rôle or of the individual's accepted notion of himself. They drive him to action that conflicts with his acknowledged interests and purposes. When they are expressed in his actions we say that he forgets himself or we advise him to remember who he is. In forgetting himself he is forgetting his accepted attributes, his age, his rank, his fatherhood, the duties of his office, his former promises, or some other of those named elements that go to make up his acknowledged verbal description.

XIV

THE ORIGINS OF PERSONALITY

IT IS to the brilliant and original mind of Sigmund Freud that we owe a new realization of the dependence of adult interests and desires, particularly of unconscious interests and desires, on the experiences of early childhood. Even those of us who are severely critical of Freudian theory must grant that Freud has revolutionized psychology and extended its field to cover human motives and human interests which had been entirely neglected by the academic psychology of the universities. There is no doubt that the need for observing the proprieties in teaching young people had limited academic psychology to the features of behavior to which impoliteness and impropriety could not possibly attach—to the study of color vision, pitch discrimination, investigations of the distance apart that two points on the skin must be in order to be recognized as two and not one. In the analysis of sensations, sensations of impolite origin were never mentioned.

It happens that Freud's new doctrines appeared just as psychologists were being disturbed from another source. G. Stanley Hall and Edward Thorndike were beginning to search in the field of psychology for a new understanding of children in order to answer the problems of teaching. This new interest in child behavior, which was by Thorndike extended to an interest in how learning takes place, made the next generation of psychologists very much aware of Freud and his doctrines, and these are being gradually taken into the field of academic psychology.

The interests of psychologists in Freudian theory were also forced by the tremendous popular vogue of psychoanalysis and its writings. This vogue is responsible for the neglect in America of another even more profitable source of information about human behavior. This other source is the work of the French psychologist, Pierre Janet, to whom frequent reference has been made in this book. Janet was the successor of Charcot at the clinic for nervous and mental diseases at Salpétrière in the environs of Paris. Like Freud, Janet built his theories of human nature on an experience with actual persons and not on teaching college students or through work in a college laboratory. The work of Janet has some great advantages over that of Freud and his followers. It was developed not as a cult but as a science. By this is meant that it was continuously offered the academic world in lectures and in publications. The work of the psychoanalysts was presented largely to medical practitioners and has never been reduced to clear statement. Psychoanalysis has been conducted as a secret cult with the continuous assertion that only its initiates could be expected to understand it. This character was imposed on it by its founder who has been extremely intolerant of criticism and has, each time one of his followers disagreed with him in any detail, expelled him from the fellowship. Jung and Adler began as disciples of Freud but suffered this expulsion as soon as they developed ideas of their own.

Psychoanalysis thus failed to take advantage of one of the first aids to science, free criticism. Being a means of livelihood, psychoanalysis tended to develop its orthodoxy and has been slow to correct errors of method. Psychoanalysis has had another handicap which has lessened its claim to be scientific. It is first of all a method of treating patients and not a theory of the mind. As a method of treatment it depends on rendering its theory clear to the patient. An understanding of his own case is taken to be essential for a cure. But neurotic patients as a class have had no training in science and are not particularly given to intellectual interests. Consequently the explanations of Freudian doctrine have had to be aimed at a naive public. This explains both their strong popular appeal and their unscientific nature at the same time. In order to make Freudian theories appeal to the general public they have been couched in dramatic terms. The figures of the Freudian drama are personified forces. The id, the ego, the super-ego are all persons with likes and dislikes of their own, wishes of their own, and with mutual hostilities. The Freudian account of the development of the personality took naturally to description in mythological terms because these were readily accepted by the patients.

To the man in the street dramatic explanations are perfectly good explanations. From childhood on he is familiar with persons; and if the ego is a person, that makes everything clear. But such explanation is to scientific psychology what the four winds of the Greek mythology are to meteorology. The north wind is Boreas. He blows when he wants to blow and destroys when he has been offended. The super-ego, says Freud (*New Introductory Lectures*, p. 87), "enjoys a certain independence, pursues its own ends, and is independent of the ego as regards the energy at its disposal." In melancholia it "abuses, humiliates, and ill-treats" the ego. It threatens and reproaches. "When one watches," he says, "the efforts of the ego to satisfy them all [external world, super-ego, and id], to obey them all simultaneously, one cannot regret having personified the ego, and established it as a separate being" (p. 108).

This lamentable handicap in beginning its account of the personality with a set of mythological fictions insured popular interest and at the same time a scientific distrust of the Freudian psychology. In spite of this handicap, the mass of new information and the new field of study which the Freudians have introduced compel the statement that a revolution has occurred.

Titchener, who was the foremost psychologist in the United States thirty years ago, was rigidly scientific in his methods, but he was occupied with problems that were interesting only to a handful of people.

In the account of the development of personality which follows, Freudian theory is not the guiding thread. We shall, instead, attempt to explain the origins of a number of personality traits in terms of associative learning. It will be noticed that many of the problems raised were first mentioned by Freud.

It is quite legitimate to begin our account with the event of birth. This does not mean that learning has not occurred before birth. There is great plausibility in E. B. Holt's contention that learning commences with the first movements of the infant's muscles. By the time that the infant is born many associative responses have been established. A touch on the·palm has become a signal for "making a fist." Whenever the flexors of the fingers contracted, this resulted in a touch on the palm and the touch has become the associative cue for contraction of the flexors. More important, it is probable that the tendency for any pattern of muscular contraction to maintain itself is beginning to be established before birth. Each time a muscle contracts, the spindle-shaped sense organs lying among the muscle fibers are stimulated and this stimulation becomes associated with the contraction of the muscle. A circular reflex is established.

Although this prenatal learning is important in the life of each individual it has much less interest than the rapid establishment of habit that begins with birth. The prenatal environment of nearly all children is much the same. The position in the womb and the type of movements made are much alike. Temperature is nearly constant. The fetus is protected from light and sound and from sharp contacts. It is with the episode of birth that experiences begin which sharply differentiate personalities.

Otto Rank, Freud's associate in the clinic in Vienna, has put forward an elaborate hypothesis concerning the effects of birth on personality. According to Rank, the very experience of being born leaves its mark on the natures of all persons. On that occasion the child leaves the protection of the womb, a sudden and tremendous change in his complacent and quiet life. The passage to the outer world bombards him with stimuli. He is put into a state of acute distress and, according to Rank, he is filled with a desire to return to his safe haven. In later years whenever the world is too much for him, this desire for return comes over him and is a strong unconscious interest. This interest may be, Rank would say, the explanation for the withdrawal of the schizophrenic patient from the world and its affairs, which desire often ends in his lying in bed and refusing to attend to what goes on around him. Kempf has published in his *Psychopathology* pictures of such patients who are not only withdrawn from the world but who lie in the posture of the unborn infant in the womb. The desire for a return is supposed to underlie all our later behavior, and a long list of actions and thoughts are supposed to symbolize the desire.

Of all this I am extremely sceptical. The reason for my scepticism is that I do not believe that a desire for return to the womb could possibly be established except through an experience of such a return. The new-born infant may become hungry, but this is not a desire for food. It is only that his stomach is the seat of stimuli which produce restless movement and excitement. A desire for food would eventually be established by experiences in which taking food brings the relief of hunger and causes hunger to disappear. Hunger may after such experiences be an associative cue for the specific acts of taking food, for lip movements as in nursing, for swallowing, for saliva flow, and the like. These can be observed in a hungry baby after it has taken food many times, and these anticipatory movements constitute a desire for food.

But there is no behavior of return which could form the basis of a desire to return to the womb. No baby has ever been observed to try to scramble back. We must put this theory down as one of those flights of fancy which have been indulged in as a result, not of observing babies, but of imagining how we adults might feel and act under the circumstances. The evidence for such a desire has been drawn from the analyst's interpretation of adult dreams and other symbols.

That the experience of birth is an exciting one there is no doubt. Even this we are, however, likely to exaggerate because new-born infants are remarkably insensitive to pain, and minor operations without an anesthetic can be performed on them without resulting in excitement or struggle. This is probably due not to failure of nerve conduction or of the sense organ to initiate sensory impulses, but to the lack of integrated habits of response which would be released by pain stimuli.

From birth on the infant enters a social world. This centers about the mother. For the mother herself the baby becomes a more or less absorbing interest. In establishing himself as the mother's chief interest the baby does his share. He cries when hungry or when intensely stimulated by cold or other sources of discomfort. Crying is probably the automatic result of excitement. It serves to disturb the mother and to direct her behavior. If she takes him up and he finds her breast and nurses, the crying will stop. It will stop if hunger was its cause, because the flow of milk into the stomach inhibits hunger spasms. If the cause was cold or a pain, crying will go on until the mother at length does something to relieve him and in this way her habits of care are established. In the human mother tradition and social pressure contribute their own share of direction. In the chimpanzee mother of a first-born child, habits and skills roughly adequate to maintain the infant will be established without any tradition or social direction.

In this establishment of skillful care there are, of course, many other cooperating reflexes. The mother in nursing the child is, for her part, relieved of the pressure of milk. Holding and fondling the infant, rhythmic movements, serve to relax both mother and child. These therefore tend to become part of the habits of both. Freud asserts that the beginnings of antagonism toward the mother, that antagonism which is necessary if the child is to turn elsewhere for affection when he matures, arise from the cessation of nursing. He assumes that the child is insatiable and resents the end of feeding. This is perhaps another unjustified generalization. The insatiable appetites of children are not conspicuous in most cases and often the difficulty is in getting the child to take enough milk. Before such a generalization is made it will be necessary to find whether regularly satiated infants fail to develop as great an antagonism for the mother as do those not satiated. The Freudian evidence again comes not even from the direct statements of adults concerning their own nursing, for this has been forgotten, but from interpretations by the analyst of various symbolic elements of dreams.

It is not open to question, however, that the infant's experience with the mother has a profound effect on its development of interests. The mother becomes the means by which most of the infant's disturbers are removed. Getting her attention becomes the one means of relief from nearly all difficulties. The mother becomes the child's chief interest and his habits of getting her attention and habits of cooperating with her in satisfying his needs become stable on their own account. The child becomes interested in the mother for her own sake.

That there are sexual components in this interest is probably true. In handling and fondling the child there is bound to be some stimulation of those areas particularly about the genitals that give rise to tension in sex organs. This tension in its turn serves to distract from other troubling stimuli, to reduce annoyance from other sources and so to establish habits, even though the tension itself is not relieved through erogenous zone stimulation. Ignorant nurses frequently use the stimulation of the genitals to quiet a child and the effect of this stimulation is much like the effect of an old-fashioned sugar teat placed in the mouth.

But to hold that the child's interest in the mother is in early years mainly sexual or that it is incestuous as the Freudian theory demands is merely another case of judging the matter not from observing children but from interpreting the behavior of adults.

On the treatment of the child by the mother and later by the rest of his family will depend many of the larger habit systems which are established. Just as the cat in the puzzle box learns one method or another of escape and keeps on with this method until it is broken up either by the accidental interference of new behavior, or by changing the apparatus so that the method will not work, so the habit methods used by the child for the satisfaction of his stimulating "urges" or the specific forms of his desires will be shaped by the conditions that he meets in the family. If, for instance, his mother is able and inclined to rush to his aid whenever he whimpers, whimpering may become his settled method of getting what he wants. If she is busy and cannot respond to every sound of distress, he will learn to solve many kinds of situations by his own efforts. Horton and I had one cat which never escaped from our box within the time limits that our affairs would allow us to wait. It, unlike most of the others, was a family pet in a household where mewing at a door was enough to bring a member of the family to its aid. During the course of several sessions this cat merely sat looking at us and mewing instead of ranging about the box. We suspect that its home training was the cause of its difference from the other cats.

If a child lives with a family amenable to argument, he may establish this as a settled means of satisfying the desires which depend on his family's permission or help. If he lives with a father, his early years spent with a person so much more powerful and more wise than he is may establish habits of deference or of hero worship which outlast his growing up. The time eventually arrives when the father-hero may be displaced. The boy may find that others are not so much in awe of his father as he is. Being present when the father is humble toward the traffic officer or is reproved by his employer, the boy may substitute new attitudes for his hero worship. Or if father and mother quarrel and the boy is forced to take the mother's side, the childhood attitude toward his father may be replaced by hostility, indifference, or contempt. But the habit of hero worship may be only "side-tracked" and not broken up. The father no longer evokes childish awe because conflicting responses have prevailed in the father's presence. The older set of worshipful habits is, except for its former cue, the father, still intact and may be attached to new cues. The boy finds a new hero.

That such boyish habits are taken advantage of by nationalistic movements and by religion is obvious. The *fatherland* can have sons only if the sons are prepared by their relations with the real father to take that rôle. The fatherhood of God began in the fatherhood of the father. An attitude of hero worship organized about the father may be inherited by a group leader or by a national hero. Men take naturally to being led because they have adjusted themselves to the presence of a parent who is, compared to the small son, very wise and very strong.

When the father is stern and domineering and the son physically energetic and strong there may be revolt. This will happen if the father's exercise of authority has not been of a sort to cause adaptation. The exaction of complete obedience leaves no room for revolt. It is only when authority is capriciously exercised that it will stir rage and resentment. If this has occurred, this body of habits may be reflected in adult years. The boy may never outgrow a smoldering resentment of authority. He becomes a natural revolutionist. When parental authority is exercised continuously, consistently and effectively, the result is uncomplaining obedience. We adjust ourselves eventually to any consistent régime, no matter how harsh. When authority is only occasionally exercised, the son has no opportunity to form habits of obedience. This happens when the father notices the boy only when he is stirred by the boy's interference with his own plans or habits.

The modern girl often wonders how the young women of a few generations ago could bear to submit to the authority of a husband. The answer is that the family of those days was built upon authority by the father which was seldom questioned, and the obedience which the girl gave her father was readily attached to the husband, and with little resentment.

The girl's situation in an American family is somewhat different from that of the boy. She is not so encouraged to develop independence by the pressure of social opinion. A dependent boy is said to be "tied to his mother's apron strings." It would not occur to us to use that phrase of a girl because her greater dependence on the mother is taken for granted in our culture. But the same conflict appears in the relations of the girl to her mother. If the girl is not successfully "weaned" from her mother-habits and grows to maturity still dependent on the mother, we may find signs of the conflict which failed to establish self-reliance still present. There will be much emotionality in her relations with her mother. These will be the mixture of love and hate which illustrates Jungian ambivalence. In many cases the girl's resentment may have become inarticulate because verbal conformity to the dependent rôle has been forced upon her.

In our own ostensibly democratic culture there are fundamental differences in the early direction of personality that depend on economic status or on social status. A laboring father who returns to his family tired and who eats in silence and then rests, interfering with the children's behavior only when they threaten his own peace, will have an effect on sons and daughters very different from that of a father who has leisure to take more part in family life. The nature of this effect will be understood if we bear in mind the nature of learning. The child will acquire the ways in which he is forced to behave. We learn to do in any circumstances what we were caused to do in those circumstances. The boy who is left to his own devices establishes those devices as his habits of response.

That components of sex drive have an important share in directing interests from birth on was not clearly recognized by psychologists before Freud. G. Stanley Hall and his followers assumed that sex interest depended on the physiological changes which take place at puberty. But the capacity for erectile tissue to be put in a state of tension by tactile stimulation of the genitals and possibly by other means is present at birth. The capacity for more or less sudden relief and relaxation through the completion of the sex act is not attained until adolescence. The effect of erotic stimulation in small children is to arouse a somewhat self-maintaining state in the genitals which acts as a distraction and will reduce general excitement and crying. This relaxing effect depends on continued stimulation and the habit-forming nature of such stimulation undoubtedly is a consequence of the relaxation. This operates just as does the relaxing effect of food in the stomach after hunger. The genitals when stimulated respond with local tension which will cause restlessness if stimulation is discontinued. Restlessness tends to insure the eventual association of the act of stimulation with local tension. Most children acquire some interest in thus stimulating themselves.

Much the same description apparently fits the activity of nursing. Babies may be quieted by the movements of nursing, and the thumb or the old-fashioned "comforter" may be habit-forming. Thumb-sucking is a mild, continuous satisfaction, but it does not have the dramatic and conclusive satisfaction of taking food which definitely puts an end to activity. Stimulation of the genitals in children resembles this closely. Fatigue or sleep will eventually bring a gradual end to the activity, and such self-stimulation does not fix as definite and specific habits as does the actual consummation which is possible after adolescence.

There are obvious cases in which sex enters into the attitude toward mother or father. It is, however, very doubtful that this occurs when mother or father does not cooperate in the establishment of a desire and interest by offering the necessary stimuli. The actual nature of mother and father "fixations" is more dependent on the rôles taken by the parents in the child's general activity, in their interference and assistance in relief from all forms of drive including pins, thirst, and ice cream cones as well as sex.

The variety of combinations into which the reinforcement of erotic drive may enter is endless. When relief has occurred almost any adventitious accompaniments which were being noticed at the time may become fixed elements of the interest. Items of clothing may acquire values which are peculiar to the individual. The sweetheart's possessions or apparel may acquire sex-reinforced values. The attachment of erotic interest to objects which are commonly neutral is called by Freud *fetishism*, and the object a fetish. It is not an exaggeration to say that love has as many forms as there are lovers. Because of the circumstances attending its earlier experiences one person associates erotic feeling with domination and the attending inarticulate thoughts furnish later daydreams of the exercise of power, of being surrounded by slaves who approach to do homage; one dreams of performing services for others, of winning praise and admiration for devoted care; another imagines himself pitied for his sufferings and admired for his fortitude in bearing them. These dreams are the beginnings of action and may lead to corresponding behavior. When two persons are both committed by the accidents of their past to the association of devoted service with sentimental emotion, and when they marry on this basis, they may find marriage a difficult state. Neither has a willing object for his devotion.

The family constitutes the most important part of the environment of the majority of children. Each family that does not break up in divorce must establish its set of habit attitudes and its family customs. To these the individual members adapt themselves. If one child is deaf, the others learn to speak more loudly when addressing it, or to neglect the deaf child. Parents form habitual attitudes of devotion or of fault-finding. To these the children's habits become adjusted. If a family has one or more "difficult" members, the family is likely to develop another member who is a peacemaker. Families in which all members tend strongly to take the initiative produce so many annoying and disturbing situations that some of the members will be made to accommodate themselves to the lead of others.

The habits developed in the family are the basis of personality traits in the adult. A prominent American writer has complained bitterly in print of the callous disregard of literary genius in the United States, though he has by both public and critics been given what an impartial observer would call his full share of attention. He spent his childhood and youth as an only child of very intelligent parents whose ambitions and devotion centered about him. All his school triumphs were the occasion for rejoicing and praise at home, and he became so habituated to the absorbed attention that greeted his achievements that when he struck out to earn his own living by his pen, the lack of appreciation caused real suffering.

Families often adapt to a difficult or ailing child by flattery and praise which at first will tide the child over depression and discouragement. To the flattery the child soon becomes adapted and it must be increased and exaggerated to have its effect, until finally not even the overstatement and fulsome praise will bring relief, and the lack of it will bring acute distress.

It is obviously impossible to classify the varieties of adjustment to be found in man because these include all the vagaries of taste in interest that actual persons exhibit. What understanding we may have of the origins of the personality derives from our knowledge of the nature of learning. Each person will establish as habits the behavior that prevailed on the occasion of his first solution of new situations. As a rule these early habits will change only when they later prove unsatisfactory, which is another way of saying that the first solution later failed to bring relief and continued trial and error behavior, or, preferably, trial and success, has substituted a new solution. The last solution is now the course of action associated with the trouble.

Learning or habit adjustment takes place when we confront disturbing situations. The readjustment of habits continues until a solution is reached, which means only that the disturbance is removed. The habit solution is now a component of the personality. But it must be noticed that such habit solutions are specific to the situation. One such experience will not establish a personality trait like honesty. Children learn to be generally truthful only when they have had thousands of experiences in which a false report has gotten them into trouble and a truthful amendment of the report has gotten them out. One unfortunate experience with lying does not establish a habit of telling the truth in all situations, but only in situations which closely resemble the one experienced. Truthful descriptions of events in speech are no more natural and can no more be taught by one experience than can accurate drawings of a landscape. Truthfulness and honesty are skills which require long training.

These virtues and other virtues appear as traits of character or personality when a child is brought up in a family with traditions and attitudes which act as continual correctives in the child's behavior. Such general traits involve thousands of different associative habits. It is incorrect to speak of truth-telling as "a habit." A consistent tendency to tell the truth includes thousands of habits. We speak of a habit of self-reliance; but self-reliance depends also on the situation, and when we find a child who proves self-reliant in a large number of situations we may be assured that he has learned this attitude in a large number of experiences. But since the membership of the family includes the same persons over long periods and these persons are subject to habit, each child has opportunity to be exposed to an indefinite number of situations in which he may have been left to his own devices, or to an indefinite number of situations in which an overzealous mother regularly interfered and took charge.

Since personality is a man's form of adjustment to the situations in which he has found himself, it is obvious that physique and character have close relations. The tall man and the short man must acquire different habits when they live in the same environment. Physical strength allows very different adjustments to one's fellows from those which are forced upon the weakling. Illness compels changes in habits and interests. Inadequacies in the mechanisms for emotional reinforcement of action lead to forms of neurotic behavior which will have the attention of a special chapter. Man has an astonishing capacity for adapting to handicaps. Mental health and a high degree of serenity are possible in blindness, deafness, the loss of arms or legs, confinement to bed. Many forms of adversity, continuous hunger, inadequate shelter and clothing, chronic pain, may all be met without breakdown of mental health. The beggar is often happier than the king. On the other hand, breakdown and unhappiness are often met with in persons who have, so far as the bystander can observe, no sources of real discomfort or objective causes of distress. In such cases, the real difficulty is with the personality itself. The underlying systems of habit which make up the personality and which are strongly resistant to change have fatal defects and unresolved conflicts.

XV

DELUSION AND BELIEF

PRACTICAL men have always recognized the general truth of Freud's doctrine that thought and belief are directed by wishes. Recently in England a criminal case attracted much attention among lawyers. A man was allowed to plead guilty to a charge of murder in the first degree. Many hold that this should not be permitted and the reason for holding this is the assumption that no man would in his right mind admit a crime punishable by hanging, no matter how true the charge. We do not even expect the motorist arrested after an accident to admit that he was exceeding the speed limit.

We regard it as natural for undertakers to be convinced that burial at sea is wrong, for communists to believe that differences in ability are the result of differences in training, while German nationalists find the reason for such differences in racial origins. We expect the owners of factories to believe that a high tariff is necessary for national well-being, unless their chief business is export, in which case they believe that there should be reciprocity. Most car owners believe that their cars are better than others. Most parents believe that their children are virtuous, honest and intelligent. Some beliefs, however, go beyond what we regard as natural. There are limits to the rule of desire over belief. The poor man who believes that he is the king of England or that he is worth many millions is obviously carried further than the rest of us by his desires.

The limit which such beliefs transgress is set by what we hold to be evident truth. We may ourselves believe that we can write or that we are rather good at the piano. Such beliefs are tolerated because the truth is not easily discovered, especially if we refrain from publishing or from playing in public.

When we ask what is a practical test of this truth which sets the limits of right belief we find that the answer lies in the acceptability of the belief to our fellow men. There is no other final test of truth, even the truths of mathematics and of science. Money, as Dewey has remarked, is good if people will take it, no matter what its metallic constituents are or what is printed upon it. Several years ago an explorer traveling through Central America passed through one district in which only United States half dollars were acceptable in return for his supplies. Another district refused to recognize these and demanded iron coins which a long-dead dictator had issued. In a third district only Mexican silver was regarded as genuine money.

Statements resemble money in that it is their acceptability that is their mark of truth. Statements are human actions. Our friend who believes that he is the king of England would be the king of England if the English accepted his statement. This is the only basis for kingship as well as for truth.

We find, then, a number of beliefs embodied in statements which are not acceptable to us and to others. We call these false. If we judge that they will be readily given up by their makers when they are found to be not acceptable to others, we call such statements mistaken. If the holder of a belief or the maker of a statement refuses to give it up in spite of its inacceptable nature, we say that the belief is a delusion. A delusion is a false belief which is held in spite of evidence that would cause the rest of us to give it up. The wishful character of our beliefs is thus held in restraint. We believe many things which are not in line with our desires because they are part of the body of general current beliefs. They are common knowledge or go by common consent.

Delusions differ from our true beliefs only in that they are not subject to this restraint of public opinion. Both true beliefs and delusions are forms of adaptive behavior, but delusions are not adapted to the attitudes and convictions of those about us. Viewed as adaptations to unusual situations, delusions will be found as reasonable and as predictable as true beliefs. Janet has described numbers of patients who have developed a very common type of delusion, the conviction that they are dreaming and that the physician and the hospital are merely parts of their dream. Janet's explanation of this common delusion is well conceived. Feelings of unreality or convictions that one's surroundings are those of a dream are based on very real features of the situation. By "reality" we mean those features of our situation which we must taken into account. Things and events are real in so far as they affect our behavior and compel us to adapt to them. The outstanding characteristic of those persons who suffer from feelings of unreality is a state of depression. In this state many of the reactions which they would normally make to their surroundings are suppressed. One such patient explained to Janet that if he were real and not a dream figure she herself would have been moved to rise from her bed and welcome him, to take his hat and coat and dispose of them for him. Feeling herself stirred to do none of these things, she knew that he was only a dream. His reality or non-reality is judged on the basis of her own response, which is the same that she would give to a passing visual image or to a dream. The overcoat is intangible or not touchable because she herself is not stirred to touch it.

This feeling of unreality is very common in states of depression. Such states closely resemble dream states in the incompleteness of our response, but in depression this incompleteness is caused not by sleep but by the depression of action. The delusion of dreaming is based on actuality, not the surrounding actualities but the real nature of the patient's behavior.

Another common form of delusion, the delusion of persecution, is likewise founded on reality. The deluded belief is only a very natural misinterpretation of surrounding actualities. Such a belief was recently developed by a college student who later had to be sent to a mental hospital. This student had begun to affect a peculiar walk. Many young people do this in connection with temporary rôles which they have adopted, and swagger or strut occasionally. But this student walked in such a way that his body moved in a straight line, which gave his progress an odd slinking appearance. Small boys playing marbles on one occasion gave him one look as he passed and without hesitation picked up their marbles hastily and fell into step behind him. The student began to notice that people eyed him covertly and that there were occasional glances and whisperings when he entered a room with strangers.

There are several ways in which we may respond to such a reception. It is always disturbing to be whispered about because it breaks up our social habits. How does one approach or begin a conversation with someone who has just been muttering something about you to his friends? We are at a loss, and being at a loss means being confused and excited. In rare cases our disturbance may lead to taking stock of ourselves and analyzing the cause of the odd behavior in others. We may correct the behavior that attracted unfavorable notice. Or we may, and this is more likely to occur, withdraw from the company which has caused us such distress.

But this is not a complete solution. The disturbed state we may carry away with us and it is necessary to find some way out which will restore our calm. What we carry away from the room is an upset of our self-esteem. We are led to doubt our social acceptability because others have refused to behave toward us as our rôle would demand. But this rôle or character which is under attack is a conservative state. Like any redintegrative set of habits, it tends to be restored when it is interrupted. We tend to find a solution that will leave us with the same character, the same social value. We are in the habit of thinking of ourselves as important, as dignified, friendly and gracious. These habitual ways of thinking of ourselves do not readily give way to an unfortunate reception by others.

We eventually discover a solution which allows us to continue thinking of ourselves as dignified, gracious and friendly. The solution is that someone has been spreading malicious gossip about us. We do not know who it is, but the effects are evident. We arrive at a delusion that persons unknown, whom we call vaguely "they," have spread the reports that cause people to look at us askance. This solution allows our self-esteem to remain as it was. When we are asked by others to explain our new avoidance of public appearances we give these reports as a reason. We suggest new details as they occur to us. Eventually we have worked out a systematized delusion of persecution.

All of this happened to the college student. He would now tell any available listener about his mysterious enemies. Asked why they were not more in evidence he must, if he is to hold his new belief, make it acceptable to others and he invents new reasons and new evidence. The mysterious enemies remain in the background because they are afraid to come out in the open. He tries to enlist sympathy by showing that his friends also are threatened. Nearly every person who deals with such cases is occasionally warned that he himself is in danger, because this will make him an interested listener and place him on the right side.

As the persecuted college student developed his delusion it eventually took another form. Too often he had been asked why anyone should take the elaborate trouble to persecute him that his enemies took. This question threatens his delusion and the delusion has become a conservative state. He finds an explanation. These enemies are really jealous of him because he is the actual governor of the state. The enemies fear his power and so remain secret. They fight against his public recognition because it would interfere with their own criminal operations. This leaves his self-opinion not only protected but enhanced.

In all this we may recognize the way in which our minds work. Our most common response to criticism is not to correct the fault which gives rise to it or to change our self-rating to fit hostile opinion. We hit upon some easier solution, like the cat in the puzzle box, and maintain our self-complacency. We discover that our critics are ignorant, inept and malicious. We continue to believe that we are good salesmen or good mechanics or good teachers.

I once had occasion to visit a patient in a mental hospital with a member of the staff who has since then died. The patient spent the time talking of his persecutors who had ruined his business. This had in fact collapsed because of his own poor judgment. Not content with ruining his business, his enemies had had him adjudged insane and committed to the institution. "Their" motives were jealousy of his ability and of his business prospects.

As the staff member and I returned to the hospital office, the physician gave me an elaborate explanation of his own status. He had worked at another hospital for ten years and had been generally acknowledged to be the best man on the staff. When the superintendent died, my acquaintance and the rest of the staff fully expected that the acquaintance would succeed to the post. But evidently his superior abilities had aroused jealousy because the trustees had obviously been told some slanderous tales of his conduct and had appointed an outsider. He did not know just what the tales were, but believed that they concerned his private morals. How else could the action of the trustees be explained?

We recognize in this very familiar and natural behavior. And we may suspect that the staff physician's "hunch" that the slander concerned his private morals merely incorporated certain anxieties which he had had for some time over possible disclosures of actual missteps. Human beings are not very inventive, and it is certain that our thoughts and acts are all based in our own past experiences. Our friend's derelictions may have gone no further than desire, but they were undoubtedly the foundation of his belief in the reporting of scandal to the trustees.

Delusions, we observe, are not a strange form of conduct found only in certain persons whom we call insane. They are only inacceptable and annoying beliefs which are rather obstinately held against argument and evidence. They are formed just as all beliefs are formed, and they are defended just as other beliefs are defended. All beliefs, whether true or false, are guided by our wishes. In delusion the condition of the patient makes them less amenable to correction and criticism than they would be in a normal person. The resistance of delusions to correction and criticism may originate in the strength of the drive behind the wish, or it may originate in physical conditions which make the deluded person less responsive to other persons and their opinions. It may derive from actual deterioration in the central nervous system which deprives the belief of inhibiting associations. The mother who is easily convinced by a spiritualist medium that her recently dead child appears regularly to communicate with her we can understand. Her emotional state, her preoccupation with memories of the child cooperate to make her accept the medium's statement that it is the child's voice that she hears. The schizophrenic patient has become so apathetic toward other persons that he is not concerned with their criticism. He plays a character and does not care whether or not others accept it. The paretic whose central nervous system is invaded by destructive lesions does not recall the associations which would inhibit his belief. His annoyance with the medical staff or the attendants of the hosptal may lead to fancies that he is better and more powerful than any of them. He has immense wealth and high social position. He does not clearly recall anything that would disprove this.

We have described the basis of delusions of unreality in physical depression. Janet points out that a state of depression may lead to delusions that our surroundings are useless, ugly, uninteresting, or very remote, or to delusions of invisibility or the delusion that we are dead or that our friends are walking corpses. These delusions are all the natural consequences of the depression of action. If we are not stirred to make use of an object, the object is useless. If we are quite unconcerned by the presence of a person, he is to us no longer real. We do not have to take him into account; at least our depression leads us to disregard him. If we find ourselves without desire, this state resembles death and may be taken for death.

One very common type of delusion consists in the belief that other persons can read our thoughts. This also is based on actual experience. All persons have learned to conceal the beginnings of many of their actions, and inner speech is in part the result of this concealment. We learn not to "give away" our intentions by expressing them aloud. We learn not to express our opinion of the other guests at the dinner as we did at the age of four. We learn to conceal our desire to leave the gathering and to wait for an excuse that will be acceptable. With many persons secrecy becomes of tremendous importance because of some major immoral desire whose expression would lead to catastrophe.

But a person who is overwrought often betrays his intentions without the use of speech. And when he finds that others have recognized what he has thought only to himself, he is convinced that the other person can read his thoughts. This fear is often expressed to a psychologist.

Many delusions illustrate what the Freudians call *projection*, which denotes the assignment to other persons of traits, usually desires, which we are aware of in ourselves. The envious person attributes his envy to others. The unfaithful husband believes his wife unfaithful. The college student who regularly cheats in examinations believes that practically all students cheat. These beliefs, like many delusions, do not represent the beginnings of action. They are not programs of conduct so much as attempts to regularize the individual's own thoughts. They are rationalizations which settle conflicts at the verbal level. By believing that all other students cheat at examinations, the cheating student can avoid thinking of himself as open to special criticism.

Many delusions have to do merely with the adoption of a rôle that is a poor fit to actual circumstances. As a boy I knew a small-town Negro who made enough to live on by doing odd jobs. Whenever there was a parade with a band he armed himself with a piece of broomstick and marched ahead of the band, keeping time with his baton. Eventually he ceased to need a real band and could be seen occasionally leading a parade that had its only existence in his own actions. He had adopted a rôle. But the adoption of a delusional rôle of this kind is often very little more than what occurs in the play of children.

Janet describes in his "Alexander" a recruit who could not adjust to the army routine, to commands and to discipline. He developed a violent anger and was sent to an institution for care. There he eventually adopted the rôle of commander in chief of the army. He promptly became tractable. There was nothing further to resent when he was himself in command. By disregarding the failure of other persons to carry out his commands, by playing the rôle like a child among tolerant adults, he could spend his time playing general, murmuring his commands to himself.

A delusion may be the result of an inability to adapt to change or the maintenance of old habits and manners after misfortune has made these absurd. The lady who has lost the family fortune may develop delusions that she is still the mistress of a large household. The servants have just stepped out rather than left. Or the death of a loved member of the family may leave an unstable one who refuses to acknowledge that death and believes that the absence is only temporary. Practical conduct may be amended to fit the altered circumstances but these are not faced in thought or in word.

When a delusion has been argued with friends it is generally built up and strengthened by the argument. This is, of course, the normal effect of argument on convictions in general. New reasons are discovered for the belief, and what was at first a transient opinion which might have been readily given up is now a *systematized delusion* and there is a ready reply to every objection. Giving up a systematized faith which has been through association woven into many lines of thought is much more difficult than giving up an unsystematized delusion. Attack on the delusion is upsetting and one way or another is discovered in which the delusion can be maintained. The delusion is now a strong conviction and will be defended with great fervor.

It is, of course, our more indefensible beliefs that are held with such emotion. Jung's notion of ambivalence describes this fact very well. A belief that is not open to attack from others and has not been threatened in argument is held without heat. It is our doubtful opinions to which we apply the word "doubtless." Doubt itself is a conflict and establishes a state of uneasiness in which new behavior may appear and our mind be made up.

The easiest and most natural solution when any of our opin-

ions is questioned is to find some way to discount the hostile
evidence and maintain the belief. Systematized delusions, which
would require the upsetting of many associated opinions and the
breaking of many verbal habit formulas, are illustrations of that
conservatism that is part of the nature of living creatures and the
nature of mind. Under attack the belief may be altered and
amended, but will remain fundamentally the same. The unsystematized delusion or the unsystematized belief may have only
a very superficial existence and represent merely a verbal habit.
It may be the result of repeating something which has been
overheard. Such beliefs will be less hard to change than if we
were required to change associated action systems at the same
time.

Many delusions have their more important determining conditions in depression or exhaustion. These often disappear with
astonishing ease when physical health is recovered. The man
who has several days before been convinced that he is being
poisoned or that he is made of stone, now speaks with just slight
embarrassment of the silly ideas which he had been defending.
The delusion may have survived stormy argument during the
illness. The reason for the quick recovery is that the delusion
was associated with the whole situation of fatigue or depression
and there is very little about a state of health to sustain the delusional ideas. The association of beliefs with general physical
states is well recognized. When we are depressed we think only
of depressing topics or see only the depressing side. If someone comments that June is the best month of the year, the depressed person reflects that now the days begin to grow shorter
and winter will soon be upon us.

Delusions are false beliefs, but it is evident that the psychological determiners of false beliefs are the same as the psychological determiners of true beliefs.

XVI

ADJUSTMENT THROUGH THE
REINFORCEMENT OF ACTION

WHEN every human act can be viewed as a readjustment following a disturbance, a classification of the forms of adjustment is obviously difficult. We have already indicated one classification. We have distinguished the direct reactions which all living organisms make when disturbed, and those progressive or improving adjustments to recurring disturbances which have been called evidence of mind. We have left to the physiologist the description of those reactions which do not change with experience. The mechanisms by which constant states are automatically defended are the subject matter of physiology. The psychologist is interested in those defensive reactions which change with experience.

In this process of learning by experience we may consider another division into two classes. It will be profitable to consider separately the effects of excitement and the effects of depression. This distinction is worth while making because excitement and depression have characteristically different effects on what tends to be learned.

The normal course of learning when a man is disturbed by hunger, by pain, by interference with an integrated habit, or by the conflict of two interfering action systems is first of all an access of energy in his movements. These are more vigorous because the physiological mechanisms for the reinforcement of action have been active, and respiration, circulation, the supplies of blood sugar and oxygen have been increased. Adrenine has counteracted the effects of fatigue in muscle tissue. The increased capacity of the muscles for action means that stimuli which would not have produced movement before the state of excitement will now have an effect. The excited man not only moves more vigorously than he would if calm, he makes more movements. We describe him as restless, uneasy, distressed, jumpy, nervous, irritable.

But the new movements affect seriously the stimulation which the man is receiving. And these new stimuli in their turn increase the variety of movement. As a result of this energizing and varying of his action, the excited man may hit on some action or some line of action which removes the original source of the excitement. He finds food and hunger is allayed, or he finds shelter from the cold and is no longer distressed by it. Or the interrupted habit whose interruption has produced uneasiness is modified and proceeds to its completion. Or the excitement upsets the balance between two conflicting action systems and one or the other of them displaces its rival, and calm is restored.

The final course of action is now associated with the disturbing situation; and on the next occasion, or after a series of encounters with the source of the disturbance, this source is responded to by the act which removed it, and it is no longer able to produce excitement. It produces only movement.

It would be a mistake to believe that because excitement is a normal factor in producing readjustment of habit, the more excitement, the better off is the excited person. Excitement may have very undesirable results when it is extreme. The exaggeration of movement which is caused by excitement may break up useful habits as well as useless ones. The boxer who gets into a rage loses his skill and his more acute perceptions of what his opponent is doing. In violent excitement men become in a sense blind and deaf. This is not because eyes and ears do not function, but because the stimuli from his own violent movements dominate his responses. The external situation is disregarded. In its extreme form this constitutes a temper tantrum.

Tantrums may bring such disregard of outer stimuli that the usual effect of excitement in introducing variety and breaking up habits may be absent. The tantrum may become highly stereotyped. I have known a head sawyer in a lumber mill who would fly into a rage and fling the tool with which he was working far into the bush, to spend a half day later searching for it on his hands and knees. Children's temper tantrums are likewise often stereotyped. One child holds his breath until his color changes. Another lies on the floor and screams.

Left to themselves, of course, such tantrums blow over. No child ever holds his breath to the point of asphyxiation. There comes a time when the impulse to breathe may inhibit any conflicting muscle set. When the tantrum has subsided and the annoying situation which gave rise to it remains the same, new associations are established. In the future this annoyance will no longer produce a tantrum. Inhibitory conditioning is established because now the annoying situation leads to the behavior which followed the tantrum. If, however, the tantrum has been successful and the child has, for instance, overcome his mother's obstinacy, he will repeat the tantrum when he is annoyed in the future. The annoyance has disappeared and the child cannot be retrained when he is calm. Only on the next appearance of the annoyance can his action be led into other channels.

The tantrum which includes violent action dissipates itself eventually by using up the energy that has been mobilized through exciting emotion. Muscular activity not only uses up the fresh sources of energy but produces fatigue in the muscles and this brings an end to the disturbance. There are many varieties of actual behavior during the event, and these depend on the accidental circumstances of early tantrums.

Such tantrums may survive childhood and continue to appear in the adult. They usually undergo considerable modification. Bankers and plumbing foremen do not lie on the floor and scream. But the essentials of the tantrum may survive and include the storm of excitement which makes the enraged person oblivious of his effect on bystanders. He is for the moment almost completely dominated by stimuli from within himself.

There is no clear boundary between adult tantrums and panic, which is also a condition in which extreme excitement renders the individual less responsive to details of his external situation because he is completely occupied with his internal stimuli. The only distinction which can be made lies in the type of behavior which we expect to accompany the excitement. In panic we look for withdrawal and avoidance. We describe the seizure as rage or as temper when tendencies to avoidance are not in evidence.

Every psychologist is asked many times what can be done for the panic which is called stage-fright. Part of the answer must be that the excitement which is the basis of stage-fright is essential for stage success. If public appearances were not exciting, few actors or orators or performers would learn the skill that makes them eventually successful. The spirit and enthusiasm of the performance depend on stage-fright.

This form of panic which reduces so many neophytes to a pitiable state before a performance has its origin in the confusion and conflict that are introduced into behavior by an audience. We have all formed habits of response toward people who are looking at us. But our training has not included addressing our response toward no one in particular. When we are confronted with many hearers and onlookers any tendency to address one of them is inhibited by tendencies to respond to others. We are thrown into somewhat the same confusion that the dog shows it a handful of sticks is thrown instead of one. We also have many habits developed about the situation of being watched. Attention to what we are doing and to the watcher is not possible. If our attention is on the watcher, our performance is interfered with and at the first sign of confusion in our performance we are thrown into panic.

There is very little dependable advice which can be given to a person who is about to make his first public appearance and who is in a panic. He may sometimes be helped by directing him to confine his attention so far as he can to certain familiar elements of his situation. He can be given some reassurance concerning the symptoms of stage-fright itself in order to prepare him for them and keep him from the fear that his symptoms will disturb the audience as much as they do him, or the fear that the unfamiliar symptoms indicate that he is seriously ill. The only advice which is essential is that he should carry on at all costs. The panic cannot last indefinitely. Like the temper tantrum it will eventually wear itself out; and if he is still performing, he will be rapidly acquiring the ability to perform without panic. If he is interested in being able to speak in public, he must expose himself to that situation on many occasions.

It is possible to minimize stage-fright by the method of negative adaptation. In first appearances he should be so practiced that his performance will not readily be thrown into confusion. Many persons have been so gradually introduced into public appearances that they have been able to adapt themselves by degrees and have never suffered extreme panic. But unless the situation of addressing a crowd continues to be in some degree exciting, there is no possibility that they will become outstanding speakers or performers. Many of the greatest actors have acknowledged that something approaching panic has continued to attend their first appearances in a new play all their lives.

Excitement is required not only for the energy and the enthusiasm of a performance but also for the improvement in performance which can result only through the breaking up of old habits. Without continuing enthusiasm any actor "gets in a rut." It is essentially stage-fright which keeps him from going stale.

Much light on the direction of learning and interest for which emotional reinforcement is responsible is found in the differences between youth and age. If we confined our observations to the play of small children we should conclude that they tend strongly to learn whatever brings them thrills. Bright lights and action, noise and movement appeal strongly to them. The firecracker, the figure eight at the amusement park, swings, shouting all have lost their fascination for the middle-aged. Small boys who have been swung by the heels put themselves in readiness for more. Even if their parents could find someone large enough to do this service for the parents, they would avoid rather than encourage it.

Part of this difference between youth and age is not dependent on differences in physiological capacity for excitement but is the result of experience. The prospect of a cruise in a small boat loses its thrill after a number of trips with poor food, hard bunks, and no sleep over the week-end. The adult who has experienced this a number of times associates boating with his reactions to its discomforts. He associates travel with its hardships and expense, love with its more lasting consequences.

The old are disillusioned. But there is a physiological difference between youth and age that has even more effect. In youth there is a higher degree of residual tonus in muscles. The facial expression in old age loses its eagerness. Smiles are more fleeting. There is far less of that random surplus of movement which children display. The older person who goes for a walk walks to his destination. The child who has accompanied him has filled the walk with many small side trips, or has varied the walk with skipping and hopping and an occasional run. Not only does the old person have less chronic tension in muscles and less ready reserves of energy, he fatigues more quickly and does not respond so readily to rest. In fatigue movement itself becomes painful and is a source of uneasiness. We learn to avoid fatiguing exertion as we learn to escape any disturber.

In youth there is quick recovery from fatigue. In age exhaustion is more lasting and because it is more lasting there is an increased chance for the associations established to include reactions to fatigue. A youth and an old man both venture on their first skiing experience. A morning on skis may tire both, the youth probably less than the older man. There is a rest for lunch. The youth is recovered. The older man's state is one that establishes a close association between starting out and the avoidance of effort caused by his fatigue. Starting out has no discouraging associations for the youth because he has never started out tired. When the older man surveys the proposed course up the snow slopes of the mountain and back, it occurs to him that he is already at their destination.

Primary directors of learning are the constant states of the physiologist. There is a continuous variation of heart beat adapted to furnish an adequate circulation of blood, and a constant adaptation of breathing to insure adequate oxygen supply. When the efficiency of the heart is lessened as it is in old or even middle age, the added demands on heart and lungs bring painful distress which operates as an annoyance and which persists until behavior is altered to give relief. But relief comes only through lessened effort. The older person learns eventually to avoid beginning activities that get him into such states of distress. He conserves his efforts and this conservation is organized into a systematic interest which affects all his behavior.

During the war, the War Department eventually ruled to admit to officers' training camps only men under thirty-one. The reason for this decision, I am told, was that experience had shown that the older men both in camp and at the front were so occupied in looking after their own comfort and in saving themselves from exertion that they had no surplus time and energy for the prosecution of the war.

In the difference between youth and age there is more than disillusionment and readier fatigue. It is very probable that the physiological mechanisms underlying excitement are more effective in youth. Excitement is less readily produced in age and is less effective in reinforcing action. Affection in the aged lacks emotional reinforcement and tends to be limited to habitual lines of expression. It is perhaps regrettable, but it is a fact that as we grow older we become less and less capable of affection. The self-sacrifice which old persons often make lies rather in sacrificing interests which are growing less interesting. It does not ordinarily lead to expending energy in others' behalf. Interests are gradually restricted to food and comfort and to the maintenance of old ways and habits.

In this present account of the effects of excitement on learning there is an apparent contradiction. How can it be true that excitement leads to the breaking up of habit and a readjustment which minimizes disturbance, and at the same time be true that young people in good health tend strongly to go in for thrilling and exciting occupations, beating on tin pans, teasing the puppy, riding indefinitely on the merry-go-round, or, a few years later, for fast driving, skiing, motor-boat racing, quarrelsome parties at night clubs? Even older people do not avoid thrills, though they begin to restrict them to a passive rôle, to the rôle of spectator. Gambling, business competition, politics, struggles for fame and for publicity involve less physical exertion from participants than the amusements of the young. The audience at the fight, the theater, the concert gets some of the excitement without much expenditure of energy.

Excitement appears to be an interest in itself, not merely a physiological device for learning how not to be disturbed. The lack of excitement, dull times when we have nothing to do, states of boredom and ennui are, especially during youth, hard to bear in themselves. All of us would find a life in which our wishes were immediately gratified quite intolerable. We spend our efforts struggling for relief from motivating stimuli, only to find that continued freedom from these annoyers leaves us annoyed at their lack.

At the University of Pennsylvania pharmacological laboratory many years ago the dogs just received for experimental work were kept for several days in a receiving cage. They were then dipped to rid them of fleas and placed in a second cage. Any impartial observer who took time to observe the condition of the dogs in the two cages, those with fleas and those without, would have judged the first to be the more contented. The undipped dogs had a twenty-four-hour occupation at which they worked with interest and zeal. The dogs in the flealess area paced the cage, howled, and gave many signs of distress. They suffered from acute boredom.

There are several reasons for the strong tendency of young, healthy animals or persons to seek excitement. One of these is that our physiological economy is adapted to struggle and a certain expenditure of energy. An easy life leads not only to soft muscles and fat but to deterioration. The restlessness shown by caged animals as well as by members of the human leisure class is probably a regulatory mechanism for keeping the organism fit. The undriven organism has a surplus of energy which must find outlet. There are, of course, wide limits of adaptation. We can become habituated either to very little exercise or to hard work. But it requires habituation to stand a life of no exertion without restlessness. If we are habituated to regular work, periods of enforced inactivity are annoying.

Excitement is thus a relief from boredom which is a form of distress in normal health. There is a second reason why men appear to seek excitement. This is the fact that it is the more intense stimuli which are regularly responded to, to the neglect of others. Only after selective training and conditioned inhibition can we disregard the noise of traffic for a conversation, or the flames in the fireplace for our book. Children prefer noisy toys because these dominate their response, being comparatively intense stimuli. Responses accompanied by excitement are reinforced, and so the actions we perform when excited are the ones we establish as habits. The front page of the newspaper may carry two stories, one the organization of a peace society and the other an act threatening war. It will be the account of violence which we read. This carries thrills attached to it by associative learning, or caused by the conflict of tendencies which is aroused in us as we read. War news can nearly always crowd peace news from the front page. Only after a war has been long pursued and we are used to its headlines can rumors of a peace compete.

With repetition, excitement and enthusiasm gradually yield to habit and routine. Much of the sustained thrill of children's play derives from the fact that they are continuously encountering situations for which they have established no routine habits, situations which include conflicts of action systems. Romantic love, in so far as we mean by that a state of excitement and emotional stir, gives place in marriage to calm acceptance and a household routine. The husband or wife of several years' standing who exhibits the symptoms manifest during courtship—the heightened pulse, agitation, loss of appetite, inability to keep the mind on a task—would be a subject for interference by friends or for consultation with a psychiatrist. This does not mean that a normal marriage diminishes the attachment of each to the other. It means that the attachment is now expressed in habits without conflict. We might find a storm of excitement outclassing any that took place during courtship if the marriage were threatened by serious illness or by a new attachment of one of the pair. Husband and wife are now tied by habit and common interests rather than by unappeased desire. Desire may be in evidence only when they are separated because it depends on obstacles and interference.

Besides the restlessness of boredom and the dominant nature of intense stimulation, there is a third basis for the apparent tendency to seek thrills. This lies in the fact that a chronic problem or a chronic state of indecision may furnish not quite enough excitement to bring on a solution and that the introduction of excitement from some new source may be the cure for the difficulty. This is particularly true in those persons whose physiological sources of reinforcement are below normal. They may learn to seek excitement to relieve them from their troubles. To such cases the next chapter will be devoted.

XVII

EFFECTS OF INADEQUATE REINFORCEMENT

A TIRED child, if kept awake, is cross and difficult. He loses interest in his play and turns from one thing to another. Nothing satisfies him. He cannot make up his mind what he wants to do or wants others to do. In the adult some of the features of this behavior may be overlaid with social habits, and the tired grown-up may show the effects of his fatigue only by withdrawing from the conversation or from the company. If he does not withdraw he is likely to show irritability and impatience. He is occasionally at a loss for a word and his speech is less well controlled. He gives offense when he should have held his tongue. This interference with normal control of action is taken advantage of by police third-degree methods, and the suspect who has been kept awake and under strain for a prolonged time "gives himself away." He cannot maintain the careful control of his speech that is necessary for concealment. One large city police system is rumored to use a device for bringing on a state of confused exhaustion with minimum delay. The suspect is made to place a heavy iron ball in a frame and to lie down with his head beneath it. By pushing hard with one foot on a small lever he can keep the ball from falling. Unknown to him, a light rubber ball resembling the iron one is substituted. Under the strain of apprehension of the fall of the iron the person under interrogation becomes confused and may break down and confess.

Fatigue damages our conduct because it makes action painful

and distracts and interferes with the inner behavior that we call thought. Muscles that have been overexercised do not respond as usual to stimuli and action becomes incoordinated. But fatigue has another effect which is superimposed upon its interference with behavior. In extreme fatigue, particularly in fatigue that comes after prolonged excitement, the physiological mechanisms for reinforcing action can no longer produce their normal effects. Adrenine, for instance, will counteract fatigue effects in muscle, but there is a limit to this counteraction. The reserve sources of energy in muscle are not inexhaustible, and when the emergency action of the sympathetic nervous system and the adrenal glands has been in effect for some time the limit of reserve sources of energy is reached. Muscle does not continue to recover indefinitely from the effects of fatigue under the action of adrenine.

We are forced to conclude from their behavior that there are many persons in whom there exist inadequacies of the physiological provisions for the emotional reinforcement of action. The reason for believing this is that many people, without being fatigued as a result of exertion, exhibit all the symptoms of fatigue, particularly as fatigue affects behavior. A very large proportion of those persons who are vaguely described as "neurotic" are chronically in this state, and there are periods in the life of nearly all individuals when the same symptoms of inadequate reinforcement are in evidence.

No writer has approached Janet in the description of the depressed neurotic. His phrase, *déprimées*, used in naming this condition has been mentioned, as also his theory that such persons are lacking in some *force mentale* or mental energy. Janet refuses to speculate concerning the physical basis of this mental energy. But an examination of recent work in physiology will show a considerable body of information concerning the bodily changes which energize muscular activity. Janet's treatment is in line with the former tendency to speak of mind and body as though they made up separate entities. A recent series of fourteen short papers written for the *Medical Record* by E. J. Kempf gives a brilliant review of the available information on emotional changes and their rôle in increasing or decreasing the energy of movement. The capacity of somatic muscles for action or for maintaining attitude and posture depends on the circulatory system, the lungs and respiratory muscles, the constitution of the blood and the effects of the sympathetic nervous system and adrenal glands. In good health these structures maintain the capacity of muscles to respond at emergency rates. Through the blood stream are supplied hormones, cortin, insulin, adrenine, thyroxin, and blood sugar, oxygen, and heat to the effectors. Through the sympathetic nerves Cannon has shown effects of acceleration on the heart beat, vasomotor changes affecting blood pressure, increased blood sugar from the liver, the inhibition of digestive secretions and of the peristalsis of digestion, sweating, the secretion of adrenine, widening of the pupils of the eye, the erection of body hairs, and other bodily changes. The bodily changes which may accompany panic include a weakened pulse, weakened muscular contraction, a cold skin, dizziness, the relaxation of bladder and anal sphincters.

Inadequacies in any of the functions which energize action have characteristic effects on behavior. These effects may not be in evidence except when the individual confronts an emergency. The most conspicuous effect of inadequate reinforcement of action is that when the man is in difficulty, when he encounters obstacles to the satisfaction of some motive, when he is in a state of conflict, some of the mechanisms of excitement appear, but these are not adequate to enable him to break through the difficulty or to resolve the conflict. With inadequate emotional reinforcement of action a man becomes irritated, restless, anxious, but he does not develop the degree of rage that would be necessary to change his course of action and to solve the problem. A dilemma keeps him worried but does not anger him to the point of upsetting his equilibrium and delivering his action to one or the other of the rival systems.

The most damaging feature of inadequate emotional reinforcement is that in difficult situations the tension of body muscles is increased but not increased enough to cause the situation to break one way or another. And the continued tension has in the meantime the effect of producing exhaustion, interfering with rest and sleep, so that the situation involves a vicious circle. The victim of the original defect in physiological reinforcement may be thrown by a minor problem or a minor indecision into a state whose effect is to increase greatly his inability to make a decision. The indecision causes a state of tension; the tension produces fatigue; and the fatigue lessens the chances for decision. The addition of fatigue to the condition may bring a general collapse of adjustment which we call a nervous breakdown. This is misnamed, because the condition is not based on changes in nerve tissue, which may be functioning properly, nor is it in the last analysis a real breakdown because the final collapse has a real utility in protecting the victim from actual damage to his physical structure.

Probably any man could be placed in a situation which would bring on such collapse. Some situations are intolerable for any human beings. Central American prisons in the old days, solitary confinement in verminous dungeons, torture, cumulative misfortune can put any man in the condition which we describe as nervous breakdown. But there are great differences in what different individuals can tolerate. A student in apparent good health may break down under a state of conflict induced by pressure from her divorced and mutually hostile parents. A business employee previously in good mental health may break down when discovery of irregularities in his books threatens and he must decide whether to make a confession or continue rather futile attempts to cover up his wrongdoing. A wife not previously neurotic may break down when facing the question whether to divorce a drunken husband or to try to continue living with him. Many army officers developed neuroses under heavy responsibilities which demanded decisions that they could not make. An animal in the laboratory will break down with many like symptoms when confronted with a too difficult discrimination.

Anrep at University College, London, trained dogs to enter a door on which there was displayed a circle and to find food behind the door. A companion door had on it the figure of an ellipse, and if the dog attempted to enter this door he received a strong shock. The dogs learned readily to enter the door with the circle and to leave strictly alone the door with the ellipse. Anrep then made the ellipse more and more nearly circular until finally every dog came to a state of indecision sufficient to cause nervous breakdown. Such dogs were agitated, showed bad temper, tremors, and had lost the ability to discriminate between the original figures. Approach to food and avoidance of shock both tended to be associated with the circle.

Being in a state of indecision may thus bring on in healthy dogs or healthy men a condition which resembles the chronic state of the neurotic. Inadequate emotional reinforcement may thus have a somatic basis in physical disability or be the effect of situation.

Some of the more conspicuous effects of inadequate emotional reinforcement we may undertake to describe. The outstanding effect has been already mentioned. This is the loss of the ability to resolve conflict and indecision. The victim of the inadequacy of reinforcement fails to develop the degree of rage or fear that would change his habits to meet his difficulty. He remains in a condition of worry and anxiety. This indecision may extend to trivial choices. He is placed in a state of equilibrium when confronted with a choice. In the more acute cases when action is severely depressed, the victim may be unable to dress because he cannot decide whether to put on his right shoe first or his left. The word "aboulia" is used to indicate this lack of ability to make a voluntary decision.

One major indecision may produce a continued state of tension which in its turn so exhausts the victim that he becomes incapable of making minor and trivial decisions. Many persons are familiar with this experience and have, while some important choice was pending, known that state of inadequate reinforcement which, like extreme fatigue, causes us to hesitate long over many unimportant matters.

States of indecision apply particularly to the commencement of an action. If an action is under way it has an advantage and is not subject to conflict. But when a radical new move is confronted, conflict is particularly in evidence. Whether or not to marry, whether to attend this college or that, whether or not to resign one place to take another, present major choices. The beginning of any action involves some conflict because it means a radical change of attitude. The depressed person finds it enormously difficult to write a letter. And it is the beginning of the action that is hard. The letter itself may be a very simple affair, once it is begun, but he finds it impossible to make himself begin it now. Presumably all those persons a little over a decade ago who placed over their desk the printed motto, "Do it now," were to be classed among our cases of inadequate emotional reinforcement. If it were not that many actions end themselves, the ending of action would be as hard as the beginning. But eventually we reach our destination or the end of the line and there is nothing to do but leave the car. Neurotics find it sometimes as hard to end a visit as to begin it, or as hard to leave their book as it was to take it up. Any radical change of action involves some conflict.

The most usual and outstanding effect of inadequacy is to limit the circle of one's interests. These tend to be restricted to essentials because of the distress accompanying physical effort. The interests usually first affected are those that we call ordinarily unselfish interests. This term is not well applied because all interests are within the possible range of the "self." The inadequate person becomes *egocentric*. His conversation tends strongly to deal only with his own person and history. If he reads a book it is only a possible bearing on his own immediate needs that will be noticed. Any topic mentioned by another is turned immediately into a reference to himself. If he makes gifts we notice that their value is carefully estimated for maximum effect with minimum outlay. The return gift is the real aim of the action. He learns to count the cost of every service to others, and to consider its effect. He wishes to be loved for himself alone. By this he only means that he hopes for devoted service from others, service which will not depend on any return from him.

The egocentric person may indulge in teasing and hurting those close to him. His gratification lies in the reassurance that their devotion will survive the test. He may be given to extreme self-depreciation and the appearance of modesty. But an examination of his modesty and his low self-estimate betrays that it is expressed under circumstances calculated to stir others to polite disagreement. He elicits compliments by his humble statements. He develops that form of functional deafness that makes it necessary always to repeat a compliment paid him. By this means he hears it twice instead of once.

Such egocentrism is in the great majority of cases based on actual physical weakness and deficient physical energy. It is a necessary habit adjustment to inadequacy. For generous action or for wide-ranging interests the egocentric has no surplus. His ventures into these fields have caused distress and overexertion, and distress has resulted in new habits of conserving strength.

This is not to say that there would be a perfect correspondence with physical strength and generous behavior or wide interests. To such an association there would be two exceptions. In some cases of extreme physical weakness and invalidism egocentrism has not conspicuously appeared because regular and dependable care by others has not compelled the invalid to learn to conserve effort. In other cases we must make a distinction between physical strength and adequacy of emotional reinforcement. Well-developed muscles and a high degree of physical strength may accompany inadequacies of the emergency mechanisms for reinforcing action. A man who can lift a fairly heavy load may not be equal to resolving conflicts with which a person much weaker would have little difficulty.

A neurotic trait closely associated with egocentrism is *seclusiveness*. No other adjustments offer such difficulty as the decision of conflicting response toward persons. To the stable features of our environment we become quickly adapted. To the new arrangement of furniture in our household we soon accommodate our habits. We learn to enter the new car without continuing to take divots from our scalps. We learn our way about the new city, or the operation of a new type of apartment elevator. These objects continue to behave in the same ways. Our environment of persons is less stable, and in spite of the repetitiousness of human habit, there is more change and variety in persons. The exhausting effect of visitors on patients in the sickroom demonstrates that even a short conversation has its difficulties.

The individual who is depressed or who has inadequate emotional reinforcement may learn to avoid the disturbing effect of other persons by withdrawing from their society, or at least from the society of those toward whom he has no fixed habitual attitudes which have proved to avoid stress and tension. He confines his meetings so far as possible to old friends or to his family. These have through long association been adjusted to with routine habits. He knows "how to take them." He learns to avoid situations which involve meeting new persons or meeting people toward whom his attitude might involve conflict. He cannot call upon the friend in whose family there has been a recent death, because the death will be uppermost in the thoughts of both, and they have never discussed death. He would not know what to say. Inadequacy may lead to retirement to the country.

The inadequate person may find escape from chronic distress in *fantasy*. Daydreams, romantic literature, the motion picture serve to restore serenity to a troubled spirit because they offer distractions which erase the tensions of conflict and indecision, and at the same time these diversions do not involve one in action or confront him with decisions that must be made. We can forget our troubles (if they are not extreme) in the mystery story or the romantic novel or the theater. No rôle is forced upon us and no possibility of failure can disturb us when we are taking the passive attitude of an observer. Exciting emotion may be stirred, but it is here adequate to a situation which demands almost nothing from us. The depressed person learns addiction to these diversions just as the morphine-taker has learned his addiction, or for the same reason that thumb-sucking is habit forming. Morphine by its physiological effect on the nervous system and thumb-sucking by its distracting power both serve to relieve tension and anxiety. After some experiences of this relief the particular form of tension or anxiety remains associated with the diverting occupation because that was their last association. Even chronic pain may be forgotten at the ball game or at any spectacle which will claim our attention. Diversions are occupations which serve to eliminate the action systems which are entering into conflict and which are responsible for distress.

Another neurotic trait is a general fearsomeness. This may attach to almost anything that is not familiar and not met with fixed habits already established. Just as the neurotic tends to avoid meeting new people, so he tends also to avoid new places, new foods, new ways, new tools. The fact that he has not previously eaten salmon or oysters or kidney stew leads him to refuse these dishes and to cling to his familiar diet. New things find him unprepared. They offer surprises, and surprise is exhausting. Being thrilled is an exhausting experience for many persons. It puts them into a condition of distress and tension. The same thrilling quality which leads those in good health who have adequate reinforcement to choose adventure rather than safety makes adventure to be avoided at all costs by the inadequate.

Paradoxically it is to be noted that many neurotics develop along with their timidity an occasional recklessness. Janet describes two women who had been regular visitors at his clinic, troubled with a complex of neurotic symptoms originating in inadequate *force mentale*. The records of both showed a long period of absence from the clinic during which the patient was in each case fairly normal in behavior. He discovered that this interval had been filled with regular thefts from Parisian department stores; and when the patients were eventually caught and the thefts settled for, both women had returns of their neurotic symptoms. These two cases illustrate a common tendency in cases of neurotic inadequacy. The problems and decisions of their daily routine were too much for them. Chronic indecision probably based on some defect in physiological reinforcement of action contributed to that deficiency and insured the continuance of neurotic behavior. But the danger and risk of stealing articles from the stores was sufficient to put into effect their mechanisms of reinforcement, to give them enough thrill and excitement to render them, for the time being, like normal persons.

Many returned soldiers after the great war exhibited this same curious tendency. Returned to their homes, they suffered from depression and were unable to readjust themselves to an unexciting civilian routine. They discovered that there were occupations which would offer sufficient thrill to return them to the condition of normal persons. Bootlegging, aviation, mercenary service with foreign nations at war, even highway robbery and safe-cracking all enlisted some of these "shell-shocked" veterans who were sufficiently stimulated by their new activities to remove their indecision and break distressing habits. On the tonic excitement of adventure or of evil doing they could again face the world.

Many neurotics learn by trial some means or other of raising their action level to what is demanded for a normal life. There is no doubt that many criminals find that the excitement they derive from the risks of their trade is necessary to them. Without it they slump. Depressed persons may discover that gambling, quarreling, speeding, slandering their neighbors, arson, the stimulation of big city life, or erotic adventure is a means of reaching that normal level of tonus and excitement which is necessary if they are not to develop symptoms of neurosis. Many neurotics have a respite and return to normal living and the ability to make decisions when there is an emergency. When the emergency is over they relapse into neurotic disorder. Stimulation which calls into play the organism's varied mechanisms for excitement disturbs the balance of indecision and resolves conflicts.

It was Haldane who described an analogous situation in physiology. He found that certain occupational disorders caused by breathing fine dust could be remedied by breathing coarse dust as well. The finer particles had not activated the cilia which remove dust from the lungs. The coarser dust put the cilia into action and the fine dust was removed with the coarse. Similarly the slight chilling of an area of the body surface may cause sneezing which would not have followed a cold shower. The more extensive chilling would have excited a vasomotor defense against the situation, contracting skin blood vessels and preventing chilling.

It is highly probable that alcoholism and drug addiction are based on neurotic inadequacy. Through their depressant effects on action both alcohol and morphine act as consummations for nearly every form of drive or annoyance. Because they bring relief, they are habit forming. But the depressed neurotic suffers from chronic tensions for which he cannot find relief by other means. A chance experience or two with a relaxing drug tends in him to fix a habit. Among the dipsomaniacs who are periodic drinkers there are reported many homosexuals. Their perverse interest finding itself blocked through social restraint builds up cumulative states of tension for which they have established no relief. Drinking to excess may leave them dangerously ill, but at the same time it leaves them weak and relaxed. As they recover they build up again over a period of weeks or months a new state of tension. This is associated with drinking from the last experience. In the meantime while they are in a fairly normal condition there is no opportunity for retraining because this requires the presence of the associative cue for drinking, the tension whose relief had been found in alcohol.

The most common source of physical inadequacy for action is, of course, fatigue. The contraction of any skeletal muscle is achieved by burning up the blood sugar in the muscle, with a consequent reduction in the oxygen of the tissue as well as of the sugar. Exercised muscle which has been desiccated and analyzed shows the products of this consumption of sugar, which include carbon dioxide, lactic acid, and others. If these are produced in the muscle more rapidly than the blood stream can carry them away for elimination there is an increasing fatigue of the muscle, a lowering of the capacity for work.

Recent investigation has disclosed that the nervous impulse, when it arrives at a junction between nerve cells or at the muscle, occasions a local production of a chemical mediator and that this is effective in causing the muscle to contract. In skeletal muscles this mediator is acetylcholine, which is highly unstable and rapidly disappears. In the smooth muscles of the stomach and intestine and other viscera the mediator released by nervous impulses is of a more stable nature and can be carried in the blood stream to stimulate distant muscles and glands. Cannon and Rosenblueth have summarized this work in their *Autonomic Neuro-Effector Systems.* It has been established that the phenomenon of fatigue involves primarily the nerve-muscle connection. A nerve-muscle preparation may be stimulated to the point at which it gives little or no response. But continued stimulation of the nerve can be shown to be causing nerve impulses as usual, and direct stimulation of the muscle by electric shock causes the muscle to respond without much sign of fatigue. The fatigue or the diminished capacity for work must lie in conditions prevailing at the point of connection between nerve and muscle, and it is quite possible that it is a failure of the chemical mediator.

There must exist, of course, true muscular fatigue, caused by the effect of oxygen and sugar deficiency and excess of carbon dioxide and lactic acid on the muscle tissue's ability to contract. There must also exist a true nervous fatigue, or a diminished capacity of the nerve trunk to conduct. But both of these would occur only at a point of exhaustion far greater than is necessary to produce neuromuscular fatigue or the inability of the nerve to excite the muscle fiber to contraction. Failure of the chemical mediator after continued action might also account for a central-nervous-system fatigue in which the transmission of impulses from one neuron to the next is interfered with. These two forms of fatigue, affecting the nerve-muscle connection and the nerve-nerve connections, would account for the well-known effects of protracted attention and mental work, and for the relative freedom of routine habit from fatigue.

Added to these physical varieties of fatigue which depend on chemical changes in exercised muscle there is another variety which is responsible for some of the sensations of fatigue. This probably has its origin in the stimulation by carbon dioxide and lactic acid excess of the sense organs in the muscles. These stimuli, being annoying or painful, act as drives whose consummation or relief is brought about by conserving effort. A distaste for exertion is added to the incapacity for exertion.

The fatigue which has its source in the sensory impulses from the exercised muscle is sometimes referred to as subjective fatigue and is not necessarily in close agreement with physical fatigue, which is defined as the lessened capacity for work in the muscle tissue itself or in the mechanism for exciting muscle. "Feeling tired" depends on the response to the stimulation of muscle sense organs. Physical fatigue may be present but not "felt" because distraction prevents the individual from "acting tired." Every person has had the experience of ending some activity and immediately noticing fatigue which had not been noticed while the activity was in progress.

It is also possible to "feel" tired when there is no actual fatigue state in the muscle and presumably no fatigue products to stimulate muscle sense organs and act as cues for lassitude. The reason for this is that the behavior of lassitude, originally dependent on the chemical products of fatigue in muscle tissue, may be conditioned to other cues. The individual now acts as though he were tired because he is in a situation associated with such action on some former occasion. A college student who had never engaged in hard labor but who was an enthusiastic tennis player and who played a hard game undertook to work during his vacation with a crew building a skid-road in the forest. With a mattock in his hands for the first time he attacked the mountain side in much the same fashion that he played tennis, with all his might. But his smashing attack left the mountain practically undamaged and within three hours the student had reached a state of extreme exhaustion. He had not the strength to return to camp until he had rested for several hours. He returned and rested for the night. On the next morning he had, since he was in excellent physical condition, made a good recovery from his physical fatigue. But when he took up his mattock again it could be observed that his fighting spirit had entirely disappeared and he began the day with the air of a man hopelessly tired. This behavior was the result of associative learning. This was the way he had last used his tool. The hod carrier, the lumber piler, the ditch digger, in fact every man who spends his time at hard labor very soon learns to adjust his speed from the beginning of the day to a rate that will not fatigue him beyond the point of overnight recovery.

Tasks which involve routine habit only are notoriously easier than those which require frequent decisions or the exercise of judgment. One reason for this is that the routine habit has from long practice been often reduced to a minimum of exertion. Excess movements have been eliminated because they involved the annoyance of fatigue, which broke up the habit and allowed a new routine to be formed. Many a housewife with slender arms can vigorously beat the ingredients for a cake for a period that would leave her brawny husband exhausted. Coordinated movements use less energy than uncoordinated movements in which muscles are working at cross purposes. Fatigue depends not so much on the results accomplished as on the manner in which the work is done. In selecting the optimum gear ratio for a bicycle it might be argued that it is only necessary to arrange to have the push required an easy one. But this would demand many more thrusts of the leg in covering a given distance. And fatigue depends on the number of movements as well as on the work done by each movement. In each thrust some of the energy of the muscle is required to overcome the viscosity of the muscle itself. Before skill is developed, muscles have not only to lift the weight and overcome their own viscosity but to work against other muscles.

Fatigue may be cumulative. When rest is interfered with or disease interferes with recovery, the effects of one period of work last over into the next. A state of lasting exhaustion may be reached. The fact that severe fatigue acts as a disturber of sleep aggravates many states of fatigue and prevents recovery from them. It is into such a condition that the person suffering from neurasthenia is driven.

It has been mentioned that habitual routines are comparatively free from fatigue. The situations that prove exhausting include states of conflict in which muscular tensions are chronic and which interfere with sleep and prevent rest. They also include situations which require close attention, because these also involve the continuous tonic contraction of many muscles. Any new situation offers cues for conflicting action, and general tension and fatigue are the normal effect of new experiences. Some persons are more fatiguing to us than others because they exact our continuous notice and stir us to confused response. We find some persons "restful" in that their behavior is adjusted to our habits and allows us to be at ease in their presence. It is not at all unusual to discover that a nervous breakdown from exhaustion has as its inciting cause some member of the family other than the patient, someone who is "difficult," hard to "get along with," irritable, exacting.

The physical symptoms of fatigue, in addition to the diminished capacity for work, often include a rapid and weak heart, rapid and shallow breathing, poor circulation and cold extremities. The fatigued muscles do not respond normally and movement becomes incoordinated. There is a close association between accidents and fatigue. Muscular tremors may be present and the individual is subject to sudden "starts," in which many muscles are involved. Insomnia and nightmares may be included. The muscles lose their tonus. In a state of extreme fatigue the body loses some of its power of resisting infection and the individual may succumb to colds or other disease.

Fatigue is, of course, only one of the causes of inadequate emotional reinforcement of action. Disease and many forms of constitutional defect may also be responsible for inadequacy. To the psychologist fatigue is of the most concern because it can result from purely psychological causes in conflict and tension and is often avoidable through a proper reeducation of habit.

THE NERVOUS BREAKDOWN

IN 1911 G. V. Hamilton published an account of some animal experiments in which his animals were set a very difficult problem. This problem consisted in being confined in an enclosure from which there were four exits. Three of the exits were always closed, but not the same three in any consecutive trials. On the first trial it might be exit number 2 that remained open; on the second trial, number 3, and so on.

If it were the same door that always led to freedom the problem would be simple. Rats quickly learn their way through the walls of old houses and can return to food that they have once located. A local warehouse has contended with this facility in rats for many years. In a supposedly rat-proof storage building the ice cream cones are regularly found by rats and many cases will be empty when time for their delivery comes. But in Hamilton's problem no ordinary repetitive habit is a solution. A habit of attacking one particular door results in a baffled action three times out of four and so tendencies to avoid all doors are established. But the avoidance of all doors leaves the animal driven by hunger and confinement. The only routine habit that would solve the problem consists in establishing a fixed order in which the doors are tried. If such a habit is established, the situation does not prove upsetting. The animal moves from one door to the next, and when it finds one that yields to pressure, the animal makes its exit.

In this problem situation rats would grow increasingly ex-

cited and rush from one door to another and back to the first
again, or persist in violent efforts to get out by one of the locked
doors. When college students were placed in a like situation
sixty per cent of them promptly formed a habit of regular exploration. Only one made several tries at the same door, one try
after another. But students who were put through the problem
in a state of excitement caused by a continuous shower bath in
the enclosure, or by electric shocks from a wire grid placed on
the floor, or by the continuous sound of an automobile horn
behaved very differently. Only sixteen per cent of them formed
the habit of a routine exploration of the doors in order. Fifty-
seven per cent made useless repeated efforts to get out at a
locked door.

We are reminded of Anrep's experimental nervous breakdowns in dogs when confronted with a discrimination that was
beyond their ability to make. When the circle and the ellipse
which led to food or shock were made almost alike, the dogs
broke down, lost their tempers, trembled, and lost the ability to
make the original discrimination which they had thoroughly
learned a short time before. Horton and I observed something
very similar in our cats in the puzzle box. The cat which escaped
in an early trial by backing into the post which opened the door
unfortunately learned in the next few trials to avoid the post.
Its solution was now useless, but it was persisted in until eventually the cat backed some forty times without escape, sometimes
circling the box three times as it backed. This cat showed evident excitement and upset. It panted, mewed, clawed frantically
at the edges of the box and occasionally flung itself down on the
floor.

Hamilton finds the results of his experiment analogous to
many human experiences. A woman who is confronted with an
insoluble problem, a recurring situation that does not result in
a routine habit solution, may develop neurotic symptoms, or a

nervous breakdown. Two of Hamilton's illustrations from his extremely enlightening book, *An Introduction to Objective Psychopathology*, may be described here. One of these concerns a housewife (p. 262) who had an incorrigibly adulterous husband. In her reaction to this source of distress she was driven from one device to another. Weeping, pleading, threats against his life, moves toward obtaining a divorce, refusals to have anything to do with the husband, attempts to be more pleasing than the husband's mistress, attempts to make the husband jealous by paying attention to other men were all tried, one after the other. Eventually she entered on a neurotic invalidism. Trial and error has failed to establish an escape from her distressing situation. To the maintained annoyance furnished by the husband's behavior there has been added the effect of her own exhaustion, and the situation is beyond her own capacities of solution. Invalidism is the only recourse by which she can be saved from more serious damage.

Hamilton contrasts this with the behavior of another housewife whose problem lay not in a difficult husband but in a difficult kitchen. The small size and inconvenient arrangement of this room demanded much effort and many choices. In order to cut bread a space must first be cleared, and before a space can be cleared another space must be found where the utensils to be removed for the bread board can be set down. This housewife thought out her troubles and adopted a system which included the disposal elsewhere of utensils not in immediate use, and efficient stereotyped habits soon relieved the burden of household work.

Hamilton emphasizes the difference between blind trial and error which characterizes the behavior of his rats in their enclosure and the behavior of the woman with the amorous husband, and the rational behavior of the housewife who reorganized her kitchen. The first housewife was not rational in that she did not choose one course and stay with it consistently. She failed to distinguish the possible lines of action which might lead to solution. These might include consistent efforts to reform the husband, or an agreement in which their common life was established as a business arrangement for the benefit of the children, or a legal separation, or a divorce. But vacillating between these courses makes the success of any one of them improbable or impossible.

The ability to make such deliberate and considered choice between possible lines of action depends on many things. In states of excitement, as illustrated by Luria's murderers or suspected students, or Hamilton's excited human subjects who were compelled to find their way out of the room while receiving continuous electric shocks through the floor, the capacity for planning is impaired. Emotional reinforcement drives the person into immediate and confused action, whereas the essential of deliberate choice is a period of hesitation in which articulate beginnings of action may compete for control. Failure to discover a solution may be caused by emotional stress which interferes with the ability to think the problem over. But failure to discover a solution may also be caused by inadequate emotional stress. The person in trouble may not have the capacity for a degree of excitement which will break up his old and inadequate habits and drive him to new adjustments. Hamilton blames the neurotic invalidism of the wife with the incurably amorous husband on her failure to make a rational elaboration of her problem. It is quite possible that equal blame for her condition lies in an emotional inadequacy. Her husband caused her distress, but he did not evoke, as he would have in some other women, a degree of rage which would have produced some kind of settlement. He made her angry, but not angry enough.

The essential for nervous breakdown is a persistent failure to establish a habit which removes a maintaining stimulus responsible for excitement. If we are confronted with a consistently hopeless and inevitable misfortune, adjustment is normally fairly certain, strange as that may seem. The death of a husband is seldom followed by a nervous breakdown. We learn to accept death as irrevocable. There is nothing to do about it. No matter how disturbing, it remains as a fact when the disturbance has exhausted itself, and associative inhibition occurs. The ceremonies that surround death have, as Janet points out, a great social utility because they emphasize the fact of death and make the whole community aware of it, just as the ceremonies of marriage serve to emphasize the irrevocable nature of the union and to notify rival suitors that they must look elsewhere. They remove lingering doubts and indecisions in the married pair themselves.

But when the husband is not dead but only occasionally extremely annoying, nervous breakdown may result. If he continues as a stimulus to conflicting responses, to incompatible lines of action the cumulative effect of the tensions maintained by conflicting action systems is to produce exhaustion and an impairment of the ability to make decisions. Once the vicious circle is entered on, the final effect may be a neurotic episode, a breakdown, which is itself a variety of solution. Like the tea guest in a Gulf Island home recently who was stung on his tongue by a yellow jacket and who found that the whisky bottle which his elderly spinster hostesses had urged upon him had been filled with furniture polish, the cure may be worse than the disease. Just as he forgot about the sting, so the victim of the breakdown may no longer be disturbed by her erring husband. Her neurotic invalidism has reduced him to less importance as a problem.

Both Hamilton's animals and Anrep's dogs were subjected to nervous breakdown by being placed in situations which prolonged tension and conflict. The sight of any door had become a cue for avoidance but at the same time a cue for approach.

The animal being tense with these opposed action systems in conflict, and with the excitement incident to the interference of the two systems, exhaustion follows and diminishes the chance of a solution. The normal result of conflict is excited activity and a new variability in behavior, an eventual escape from the troublesome situation, and the fixation of the method of escape as a habit response to the distress. On future occasions the excitement will be less in evidence. In the animals a solution was beyond their capacity.

Behind every nervous breakdown and its eventual neurasthenic or psychasthenic symptoms and states of anxiety lie conflicting attitudes and a major indecision. Strong motives impel to divergent courses of action. Behind most nervous breakdowns lies also a defective system for emotional reinforcement of action which may have its effect through endocrine disorder, disturbance in sugar or calcium metabolism, or an indefinitely long list of other physiological conditions. Fatigue or exhaustion may in some cases be a primary cause. But physical inadequacy alone is not a sufficient cause. Many persons in extreme poor health remain mentally well adjusted. Severe invalidism which makes energetic action quite impossible may be met with a serene mind and no signs of distress. There are actually many cases in which such a physical illness causes recovery from neurasthenic symptoms because the illness has reduced the strength of the drive or of the desires involved in the conflict. The patient has become too weak to care. Old age may also have this effect and be the final cure for hysteria and anxiety.

Even in its most severe forms the nervous breakdown preserves its adaptive character. Perhaps it would be more correct to say that even in nervous breakdown people remain adaptive organisms. That is, the breakdown represents a solution of a distressing situation, even when the solution appears distressing. When the original difficulty is concerned with the failure to keep "face" or to hold to an adopted rôle about which social ambitions and social habits have been organized, the breakdown manages to save something from the wreck. The young man who has for years thought of himself as a budding pianist and now faces failure because of paralysis, can, by the aid of his paralysis, think of himself as an unfortunate pianist but still a good one. Except for his physical infirmity he could even now be playing to enthusiastic audiences. The wife who has thought of herself as the object of her husband's love and now finds him devoted to another can explain to herself that she has, because of her hysterical illness, withdrawn from competition, not been worsted in it. And she can at least regain his attention, if not his love, by her baffling symptoms. The man who is used to acting the promising young business man and who now cannot by any other means hide the fact that he has failed may enter an invalidism that excuses his dependence on his wife's earnings.

The symptoms of the breakdown are as if chosen for the purpose of escaping an intolerable situation. They are not actually so chosen. They are more likely to have been hit upon just as the cat hit upon its manner of escape from the puzzle box. The fact that they served for escape from distress leaves them associated with distress. In order to forget the symptoms or to retrain them it would be necessary to repeat the distress and manage some other way out.

It is usual for the victim of a breakdown to insist that his symptoms are peculiarly his own. No other person's suffering was ever just like his. He is different from other people. Physicians do not understand him, he is convinced. If he acknowledged the justice of the physician's diagnosis his symptoms would be threatened with cure, and a cure is often the last thing that he wishes. The neurotic resists help for his symptoms because they are not his real trouble. His pains and aches, his deafness or his paralysis, his daily rise in temperature are his defense against the fundamental conflict that originated his breakdown. If he loses his symptoms he will have to return to the front. Or if the girl recovers from her illness she will have to confront the obnoxious marriage. If the mother gets well, her daughter will leave her to return to teaching.

The breakdown is a habit adjustment. Like all habit adjustments it tends strongly to be self-maintaining. If the adopted symptoms fail, others will take their place, unless there has been a fundamental reorganization of the interests that were in conflict. The very multitude of symptoms often exhibited betrays their necessity. The patient is playing safe, and if some are discredited, others remain.

The unreasonableness of symptoms is natural enough because they are not chosen by reflection and argument, but are seized on as they occur. Pains and aches which have transient but real causes will be responded to as intense because the response is facilitated by the total situation. Because of the exaggerated response the pain becomes subjectively intense. In this sense the pains are real enough. The pain has the subject's whole and devoted attention.

The self-maintaining nature of a nervous crisis is the chief obstacle to a cure. Any threat to the continuance of the neurotic behavior meets a defense like the defense of a child in a tantrum. He closes his eyes against distractions, raises his voice to drown out parental arguments, or runs to his room and locks the door against persuasion. The neurotic may use these same measures. More often the adult modifies his childish tantrum. He drowns argument not by screams but by visible expressions of pain or weakness. He avoids like poison persons who have proved unsympathetic.

In an excellent popular account of the nervous breakdown by the late Beran Wolfe there are listed what he believes are the essential characteristics of such crises. The patient does not realize the meaning of his symptoms. This means that they were not first named and then acted upon, but that they were hit upon by accident. In the second place, the symptoms are all egocentric. They are like no other symptoms and thus cannot come under the physician's rules. In the third place, the onset of symptoms is always just before or just after a crisis such as a marriage, a separation, a disclosure, a test of skill or knowledge. The crisis threatens the patient's character rôle. He is apt to prove unequal to a normal sex life in marriage or unequal to the standard set by the college examination or for the concert pianist. The symptoms must make him feel secure in his rôle. His pains or his weakness must act as a scapegoat and take the blame for his failure to meet the crisis. By his symptoms the patient is excused from competition with others. The symptoms are not under voluntary control. Their selection has been inarticulate and not planned. This means that the symptoms are not directly subject to verbal cues and not open to argument.

All this only goes to show that the nervous breakdown is not a nervous breakdown. The central nervous system is still operating normally and effectively. Behavior is being adapted to situation by the same processes of learning that are illustrated in any habit formation. The breakdown is primarily a social breakdown. The game being beyond his strength or beyond his preparation and skill, the player stops playing. This describes the behavior of Anrep's dogs or of Liddell's pig which, after being tricked systematically as it stood before a box into which it had learned to expect an apple to fall at a signal, eventually stood rigid and refused to investigate the box.

The additional features of the breakdown, that is, the features which are added to the refusal to make a choice or to withdraw from a dilemma, consist in learned acts which justify this retreat and refusal to other persons. The retreat is often right and proper, but this is not realized by the victim. The contemplated marriage would be a mistake, but the fiancée does not know how to retreat except by becoming ill. The soldier is not equal to front-line fighting, but neither he nor the army authorities can afford to recognize that fact directly. The responsible business executive whose affairs are going rapidly to disaster should resign and call on others to settle them, but this course would demand that he explicitly acknowledge his incapacity and substitute a rôle of incompetence for that of competence. He resigns in effect by going to bed or by developing a terror of street traffic which keeps him from the office. He can do this and still think of himself as a good business man.

The bizarre, distressing, unreasonable and often disastrous means by which the nervous breakdown achieves escape from trouble and conflict is a simple consequence of the fact that it is a solution under extreme stress. Rational judgment, the normal period of hesitation and verbal trial and error, is replaced by excited flounderings which escape voluntary control. Luria's description of the difference in the behavior of children and that of adults when they are confronted with a decision will be remembered. The child goes into immediate confused action. In the adult the conflict blocks action until those tentative movements which constitute thinking have with the aid of verbal associations resolved the conflict and allowed one system to exclude the other. But if the adult is in a state of excitement and stress this period of reflection is disturbed. Murderers just arrested by the Moscow police and brought to Luria's laboratory were like small children rather than calm adults. Offered a simple choice, they showed a childish confusion. This was also true of the students suspected of wrong political opinions who were waiting in line to be interviewed by the board which had power to remove them from the university and to ruin their careers. It is interesting to note that in those cases in which a murderer later confessed, he recovered his voluntary control and behaved like an adult. Students also, when a decision had been rendered in their case, made such a recovery whether the decision had been favorable or unfavorable. Murderers and students now were free of conflict. They had nothing to conceal.

One major indecision or a state of apprehension, which is much the same thing, will make impossible normal reflective choice and cause a severe disturbance of judgment. The victim of a nervous breakdown is in the condition of the accused murderer or of the suspected student. The origin of his difficulty is, however, not a transient external threat but a conflict of well-intrenched habits and desires. He can look forward to no simple measure of relief like confession or the decision of his case. Until he reorganizes his life and makes peace among his conflicting desires he will continue to be in difficulties.

We have for some pages lost sight of the possible physical basis for breakdown. There are writers who believe that illness or physical defect is the primary cause of all such disasters. We may call them organicists since they hold that defect in the function of some organ or organs is to blame. There are other writers who explain such breakdowns in terms of conflict. These we may call functionalists. Both organicists and functionalists are right, and both are wrong. Most breakdowns would not have occurred without an initial physiological inadequacy, and all breakdowns depend on the effects of physical exhaustion after the breakdown has commenced. But no breakdown occurs without conflict. Physical weakness alone is consistent with a calm and serene mind.

XIX

THE PSYCHONEUROSES: HYSTERIA

INJURY to the optic nerve or to the area of the cerebral cortex to which its fibers are relayed can render a man incapable of sight. He will no longer respond to visual stimuli like a normal man. The destruction of a brain area through the effects of disease may interrupt brain paths essential to certain types of response. The destructive changes in the walls of blood vessels which are called arteriosclerosis may result in the entrance of a bit of detached artery wall into the blood stream, and when this has reached the finer branchings of the arteries of the brain the circulation is locally blocked and a portion of the brain may cease to perform its function of transmitting neural impulses. The result is popularly called a "stroke" and may result in an impaired ability to speak, or an impaired ability to use the muscles served by the affected brain region.

The disorder of behavior resulting from such injuries to nervous tissue is clearly blamable on the physical injury. There are other types of interference with the mechanisms of mind. Cannon and Rosenblueth in their monograph, *Autonomic Neuro-Effector Systems,* have reviewed the evidence that responses to nervous impulses depend on the production, either in the nerve or in the effector, of a hormone-like substance. Acetylcholine, the chemical mediator for the nerves which serve to contract the skeletal muscles and to produce specific movements, is highly unstable and its effects are confined to very limited areas. Sympathin, the chemical mediator for the sympathetic system, is more stable, and can through the blood stream give rise to contraction of muscles or the secretion of glands at some distance from the tissue served by the excited nerve. It is highly probable that these chemical mediators will be found involved in behavior disturbances. It is also recognized that many diseases, including pulmonary tuberculosis, syphilis, and various gastro-intestinal disorders, have characteristic effects on behavior and change the style of our conduct.

Disorders of behavior, usually termed organic, which have their origin in injuries to the central nervous system or which interfere with its operation in the conduction of nervous impulse or its activation of muscle and gland, lie in the field of medicine and not in the field of psychology. There is another group of disorders of behavior in which there are no signs of injury to nervous tissue and no conspicuous defect in the manner in which the central nervous system performs its tasks. These disorders are called *functional*. Medical men are in the habit of describing them as of mental or psychic origin. This does not mean that there is no physical basis for the disturbed behavior. All behavior has its physical basis. Calling them mental in origin is only a recognition of the fact that they originate through associative learning, for mind is synonymous with learning. Similarly, when medicine speaks of a mental cure or of a mental treatment, this also means a cure or a treatment undertaken by directing learning and establishing habits, not by the administration of drugs or a diet or by surgical interference.

Psychic origins of mental disorders have been illustrated in the chapter on the nervous breakdown. Conflicts are established through learning, not through lesions in the nervous system caused by disease. Habits of dependence upon parents are the effect of training. New interests which interfere with these habits are also brought about by training and the exposure to new situations. The resulting conflict may therefore be described as having a psychic origin. The theoretical distinction between functional and organic disorders appears to be clear and unambiguous. But it is not so in actuality. The reason why it is so difficult to make the distinction in practice is that conflict may have physical effects in exhaustion and endocrine disturbance which provide an organic basis for troubles whose origin was primarily mental. Similarly, a physical inadequacy which interferes with the emotional reinforcement of action may make difficult or impossible the solution of a conflict, and the physical inadequacy is now complicated by mental factors. In the case of the nervous breakdown it may safely be declared that both conflict and physical inadequacy are always involved. When we speak, therefore, of functional disorders of behavior, it will be understood that the conspicuous occasion for the disorder lies in a learned adjustment to a difficult situation. This will not deny the probability that physical inadequacy contributes its share and may have been the original reason for the difficulty of the situation. The psychoneurotic is likely to find many situations difficult, situations which a person in normal physical health would have readily met.

One large group of distressing symptoms of functional origin is conventionally included under the name *hysteria*. *Hystera* was the Greek name for the womb, and the use of that name for the symptoms in which we are interested derives from an early belief that displacements of the womb accounted for the behavior of the hysteric.

Very few terms in medicine are so vaguely defined as hysteria. It is not a disease entity with a definite group of symptoms associated with a recognizable cause. The name is applied to almost any persistently annoying and distressing behavior that is patently the result of learning and is at the same time not under the control of the patient. Fits, blindness, deafness, loss of the sense of touch in definite areas of the body surface, or other forms of anesthesia, anorexia or loss of appetite, amnesia or the loss of memory for specific events, paralyses, trances, somnambulisms, compulsive movements not under the patient's control, and remarkable simulation of the symptoms of physical disease may all be included.

All of these symptoms—the seizures, anesthesias, paralyses, compulsions, amnesias, the mimicry of organic disease—have a number of characters in common. They are beyond the control of the patient and do not respond to ordinary command or entreaty from others. They are not voluntary acts which will respond to verbal cues. The hysteric's inability to move his arm is a real inability. He cannot, by taking thought, bring his arm to move. Conscious voluntary acts are under control because we can, by controlling their verbal beginnings, start the train of action or, by using another cue, side-track it. This is not true of the hysteric paralysis. If it were true, the failure to use the arm would be classified as malingering and not as hysteria.

Added to this lack of voluntary control over the hysteric symptom is another characteristic. Nearly all the symptoms of hysteria differ from organic nervous disorders in that they give evidence of organization into desires and purposes. The paralysis may not be "chosen" by the patient, but it is the sort of thing that might well have been chosen under the circumstances. It serves to relieve a situation. It is a solution of a problem. By being paralyzed, the patient avoids some difficulty, gets his way, escapes an intolerable pressure of circumstance. A young woman on three occasions has succumbed to a paralysis of both legs which makes walking impossible. A neurological examination discovers nothing wrong with her nervous system or her muscles. But the paralysis has on all three occasions appeared on what was to have been the final day of a visit to the home of pleasant and sympathetic friends. Her own home is a place of discord and intense quarrels. When she is confronted with a return to her family she finds herself paralyzed. The visit is prolonged for several days until she recovers, and this recovery is associated with the obvious impossibility of extending the visit further.

A soldier in an American military hospital in France during the war lay in bed paralyzed. His legs would not support him. If the attending doctor had been able to find an injury to the nervous system which would have accounted for the paralysis it would be accounted as organic, not functional. But there would have been other symptoms associated with the paralysis. The art of diagnosis of injuries to the nervous system is remarkably developed. Furthermore, if the paralysis had been caused by a physical break in conduction pathways, the soldier would not have been observed on certain rare occasions, when his attention was absorbed elsewhere, to move his legs under the bedclothes. A paralysis or a deafness which comes and goes is presumably not the effect of a lesion in the central system.

Above all, it is to be noticed that the paralysis was the sort of thing that a man might well learn to do to avoid return to the battle front. It was a successful answer to a difficult situation. At the front are danger and discomfort. The contemplation of a return is acutely disturbing. In the hospital are warm food, comfortable quarters, pleasant nurses and safety. Any man might choose these in preference to the first-line trenches, even if this involves a less glorious war record.

The staff judged that the man was not malingering. He was not, in their opinion, sustaining his legs in their revolt by conscious control. Such a diagnosis is not always certain and there are usually medical officers who disagree with it and judge that threats of punishment may be effective. But in such cases threat of punishment is often not effective. That is our reason for pronouncing the behavior involuntary. Verbal associations with threats do not affect it.

The cure in this particular case was somewhat drastic. A visiting French physician was making rounds with a member of the hospital staff and, on reaching the soldier patient, volunteered to cure him if the resident physician did not object. He was invited to try what he could. What he did was suddenly to turn and spit in the soldier's face. It required the help of several able-bodied men to hold the paralyzed soldier away from his "benefactor."

The probable history of such a case of hysterical paralysis is this. For the soldier the slight wound that brought him to the hospital was an escape from very disturbing and annoying conditions. The announcement that he is recovering and can return to the front in a few weeks calls up the distress of the trenches. This distress is renewed by reminders of his recovery. He is like the cat in the puzzle box which likewise discovered an unconscious solution. Lying in bed, the soldier thinks over the situation. He learns of some other soldier who could not be sent back because his legs were paralyzed. What is it like to be paralyzed? Why, like this—and he experiments with his legs. What would it be like to try to walk and have one's legs fail to respond? He finds what it would be like and tries this out several times.

The next morning he starts to rise from his bed with his attention on something else and discovers to his surprise and joy that his legs will not work. The explanation is simple enough. He had practiced starting to move out of bed without using his legs and, with his attention elsewhere on this occasion, the habit has gone through as practiced. It was without intention or choice. He was not thinking about his legs or their movements. The soldier realizes that he did not deliberately refrain from using his legs and that he is not to blame for their behavior. And any later feeble efforts which' he may make to walk involve intentions which include a return to the front. This proves as difficult to "will" as it would be to "will" to strike oneself a smart blow in the face, or for a child to pick up and drink the castor oil. There is now a real sense in which the man cannot voluntarily walk. Threats and punishment might turn the scales and enable him to walk, or they might not. French practice is reported to have cured many such paralyses and hysterical disabilities by the use of severe electric shocks which made the hospital as disturbing as the front.

Flinching at a threatened blow is a habit, not an instinct. But there are few persons who can by inner resolves control the action. Habits are not under voluntary control unless they have among their starting component movements cue words which can serve to begin the action or which can be displaced by other words and the action thus be side-tracked. Furthermore, part of the conditions of any action lie in the posture of the moment. Magnus has described a reflex behavior of the decerebrate cat. If its head is turned to the right, the right leg will be extended and the left leg will be somewhat relaxed and flexed. This serves to maintain the cat on its feet if it is standing, but the reflex is entirely automatic. If a mouse runs across the room in front of the cat from left to right, this adjustment takes place as the head turns and the cat is kept in a position from which it could jump toward the mouse. This is a restriction of the cat's possible movements. Under these circumstances the cat may jump toward the mouse or it may refrain from jumping, but it could not possibly jump away from the mouse, or scratch, or perform any movement incompatible with its postural set for jumping in the direction in which its head is turned. In order to scratch or to jump to the left there would have to take place a thorough readjustment of posture.

The voluntary actions of men are also limited by such postural backgrounds at any moment. At any given instant there is a very limited number of actions that can be performed. The hysteric soldier might attempt to control his legs and walk, but the attempt would be futile because the attitude practiced while he was dallying with the idea of paralysis does not allow walking.

The paralysis in such functional cases does not amount to a total inability to use the paralyzed member; it may consist only in an inability to use it for a particular action. A student of the piano had prepared himself for a concert career by very hard work. Shortly before his first important recital he sat down to his instrument one morning and found that his hands refused to play. This condition made necessary not only canceling the engagement but entering another career. He had no difficulty in using his hands for any other purpose. He could perform other tasks. He could serve himself at the table, use his typewriter, throw and catch a ball, but over the keyboard of any piano his hands became cramped and stiff.

Some of the background of his disability was clear. In spite of tremendous industry he had reached only a fair degree of skill and musicianship. Some of his friends were much concerned over his determination to be a concert pianist because they recognized that his talent was only second-rate. These doubts the young man undoubtedly shared, but they were usually in the background when he practiced. Signs of conflict were not lacking. To his friends his insistence on his first important recital had about it an air of desperate resolve. The desperation was evidence of an ambivalent attitude, a division in his own actions. We do not know just what accident caused his dilemma to be settled by the device of paralysis. He could, of course, have become ill, or found that he needed more practice, or discovered any one of a thousand other ways out, such as enlisting in the navy. But his state of distress was such that he was incapable of calm planning. It is very probable that overexercise, or the use of his hands in carrying a heavy suit-case, had actually brought on a slight tendency to cramp. This cramp appears unexpectedly as he sits down to practice for the recital. It has not been foreseen and was not chosen. Its beginnings were inarticulate. But it suddenly appears as an excuse which will solve his troubles and save him from a demonstra- tion of his inferiority. He is tremendously interested in it and tells his friends the bad news. Left to itself, his fatigue and tendency to cramp would have disappeared with rest. But it has now been verbalized. He cannot sit down to the piano without wondering in advance whether or not his hands will perform, and this means that he sits down to the piano set for the new habit. He cannot play.

Two of the three occasions on which I myself have suffered from a loss of voice and have been compelled to speak in a whisper were during the day preceding speeches which I had engaged myself to make without realizing that they were on subjects quite outside my own interests and range of information. This could not have been mere coincidence. In my anxious state a slight huskiness calls attention to the voice. The voice is tried out in various ways. Sure enough, it is impossible to produce anything but a whisper. Excuses are made and relief follows. But the voice does not return until the speech has been made by my obliging substitute.

A six-year-old schoolgirl was nauseated each morning as she started to school. When a change of teachers was arranged the nausea disappeared. Her case is like that of the pianist. Both confront an event with dread. Both have in their distressed condition hit upon a line of behavior that saves the day. The pianist is excused from his concert and the schoolgirl from her appearance at school. Just as it was with the cats in the puzzle box, the action that saves the day and changes the situation is preserved as a habit. The mode of escape is associated with the distress from which escape is made. So long as the mode is successful and leads to escape, no retraining is possible because this would require that the particular form of distress be associated with some other action. But the distress is gone when the escape has been made, and there can be no new associations attached to distress in its absence.

A mother who has brought up a large family, put them through school and has done much entertaining for them has had frequent experience with the guest who was subject to the common hysterical attack which consists of uncontrollable laughter and tears. The victim at the party was always a girl, and always a wallflower. She sits about without attention, in a state of maintained hope. Another might have escaped from the intolerable evening by developing a headache and going home. But that somehow does not occur to her. The strain increases and eventually some incident starts her to laughing, which becomes uncontrollable. The hostess discovered a treatment which was always promptly effective. She led the girl to a third-story room out of hearing of the party and there, without any expression of sympathy, left her. Recovery was always prompt.

It is regularly true of hysteric seizures that they require an audience. The excitement which reinforces them derives usually from social difficulties. Such episodes are closely related to embarrassment and stage-fright. They precipitate a situation which has become intolerable. They may actually be the solution for the trouble. Instead of remaining unnoticed, the wallflower is now the center of sympathetic attention. In a previous generation fainting was the mode of escape from many social predicaments. Since the predicament is essentially social, it is natural that fashion should to some extent control the mode of escape. One male student of the present generation has on three occasions slipped to the floor unconscious during an interview with an instructor in which the student was urging a change of his grade. This was the only way he knew to end a difficult interview in which he had not had his own way. Girls have during the last generation tended to abandon this device.

Hysterical anesthesia or loss of sensitivity is of particular interest because it practically always serves a present purpose. It eliminates trouble and annoyance or the reminders of trouble. Janet described such an anesthesia in a girl who was caring for her sick father. On one occasion, she was helping him to rise from his bed when he had a convulsion and died, falling on the girl who lay under the corpse for an hour and a half or two hours. She later declared that her left arm, side, and leg were not her own and developed occasional paralysis or occasional anesthesias in these regions. Stimuli to the left arm were undoubtedly reminders of an intolerably painful incident, and she has succeeded in substituting for the normal responses to a touch on these areas other responses which do not call up the painful experience. An hysterical anesthesia is merely a habit of responding to a stimulus as if it had not occurred. The person who is hysterically blind has merely established certain habits of responding as if he did not see. That he actually does respond to visual stimuli is usually easy to establish.

The hysteric anesthesia is not a true anesthesia. The patient responds to stimuli in the affected area but his response is the response which he believes would be given if the area were not sensitive. With a so-called "glove" anesthesia in which the insensitive area covers the hand, but not in the pattern or with the limits which would accord with the distribution of any sensory nerve, the patient may be blindfolded and, if sufficiently naïve, he may be induced to say "No, I don't feel that" on each occasion that the hand is touched.

Railroads, steamship companies and bus lines have to deal

with many suits for damages in which injuries bear the marks of hysterical origin. These *traumatic neuroses* originate usually in some incident which might well have caused severe physical injury and which has caused some slight injury to the plaintiff. A woman is riding in a railway coach and happens to be just rising from her seat when the engineer brings the train to a rather abrupt stop. She is thrown heavily on the back of the next seat. In this instance she leaves the train without being particularly aware of being hurt. That evening in telling her relatives whom she is visiting all the details of the trip the incident is remembered in due course and described with the emphasis necessary for holding an audience. This recalls experiences which the others have had with sudden stops. They grow indignant over the lax ways of railroads and engineers and the callous disregard of the comfort of passengers. Someone mentions that the railroads would mend their ways if they had to pay for accidents like that. It is agreed that this would have been a perfect case if there had been any injury. How does she feel now? The woman makes a few exploratory movements. Yes, there it is. Her back hurts. She was, after all, somewhat shaken by her experience. But her back hurts quite badly. With her sensations there may be mixed the effects of the fatigue resulting from spending a day on the seat of a train. The others become very sympathetic. She is put to bed. The next morning she recalls the conversation before rising and makes a tentative, very tentative, test of her back. The pain is there. She feels it whenever she tries to move. If she had important and absorbing affairs to attend to, the pain would have gone unnoticed, but she is at leisure to attend to it. She finds that it is impossible to rise from bed. The rest, including a sympathetic lawyer, is plain sailing.

When the case has been settled (the one described, for a considerable sum) interest in spending the damage money may help to break the habit of staying in bed and nursing her hurt. Recovery is likely to be delayed only by the necessity of making it seem reasonable to the public. The line between conscious or articulate malingering in which plans for making the company pay and for simulating injury are well formulated, and unconscious or inarticulate self-deception is often impossible to draw. There is often a mixture of the two. Conscious acting is added to unconscious acting.

The habit of a limp may long survive the pain which led to the formation of the habit and be quite unconscious in that limping occurs without verbal deliberation or guidance. If the case had gone against the passenger, recovery would have depended on the extent to which she was committed to her rôle by the attitudes of her friends in her presence. Such an injury responds quickly to any suggestion of a cure which will save "face." A new liniment or massage will have miraculous results.

Many physicians have learned to be extremely cautious about suggesting symptoms to hysteric patients. It is now recognized that the remarkable likeness between some purely hysterical illnesses and the standard symptoms of the disease usually depends on the detailed questions of the physician who is in search of symptoms of some disorder which he has in mind. Even the best of us must occasionally take himself in hand to keep from cataloguing troubles which would have been unnoticed save for an unusually sympathetic inquiry about our health.

It should be noted that what has been said about hysteria gives no reason for believing that "nerves" are behaving badly. The operation of the nervous system may be faultless. Hysteric habits are formed just as useful habits are formed, through association of stimulus and response. The fault lies not in the neural mechanism of learning, but in what is learned. At the same time, the evidence points strongly toward an organic fault in numerous cases. The fault is found in the physiological structures which operate to furnish the energy of movement. Almost any defect in this energizing system may give rise to hysteric behavior. A heart which causes distress on slight exertion will direct habit into an extreme conservation of energy and distress may come to be avoided by unusual and annoying devices. The physical defect may be the underlying basis for the development of hysteric conduct. Or the physical inadequacy may follow on "mental" stress in the sense of conflict and exhaustion. Two university girls illustrate the origin of hysteric behavior in the stress of a difficult situation. Both entered college with vague anticipations of social triumphs, anticipations formed in part by reading stories of college life or by visions of that variety of college life which flourishes only in Hollywood. Both girls failed to get on with their associates or to be popular with men. One of them was brought to the attention of a college adviser because she had deceived her sorority sisters with a romantic account of a wealthy and talented suitor. Occasional rich gifts were exhibited. These she had herself purchased and charged to the account of her parents. She wore an engagement ring which the others assumed to have a value proportionate to the size of its "diamond." When the supposititious nature of the fiancé was discovered by the other members of the college sorority the affair was taken with a seriousness that could be explained only by the disappointment of the others on finding that the report of such big game in the neighborhood was false. But when the whole situation was explained, sympathetic fellow members undertook to relieve the isolation and social failure of the romancer, and there has been no recurrence of the hysterical lying. In this case there was no original physical defect, but only a defect in social habits and ambitions which put too great demands on the physical system. Sleepless nights and hours of tension had their effect in allowing an irrational solution and a solution ultimately unworkable.

The hysteric lying of the other disappointed girl took another form. She began to relate scandals to her associates which served two distinct ends. By her slanderous statements about certain other members of her sorority she vented her resentment of their success and popularity and at the same time the nature of her stories insured her at least an occasional interested auditor. This case did not meet with the sympathetic treatment given the first, and hysterical lying continued throughout a college career and for some time afterward. She had been always fat, homely and unattractive. Early in her school career she had hit upon the device of securing transient attention and quasi-companionship through gossip and slander about persons envied by herself and her listener. This device had been established in much the same fashion that another girl would have learned to smile or to flatter or to offer cheerful assistance or to dress pleasingly.

The Freudian theory of hysteria is that it represents a conflict between the ego and an unconscious wish which is out of harmony with the ego. The wish has been repressed but has an energy of its own derived from the libido. To this the chief objection is that to personify ego and wish, to treat these as agents with purposes of their own, is to desert the forms of scientific description for a sort of primitive demonology. The only agents known to us are complete persons, and the division of the person into a list of *dramatis personae* reads into the nature of the subordinate characters in the drama characters which they do not possess. Furthermore, the introduction of the libido as a source of energy is quite unnecessary. The energy of any wish lies in the muscles and nerves, and the occasion for the liberation of that energy is the stimulation of sense organs. When a man sits on a tack it is not necessary to suppose that the energy with which he moves is supplied by a libido. There is fairly direct transmission of nerve impulses from the sense organs at the seat of trouble to the muscles involved. Nor is it necessary to explain his behavior in terms of a pleasure principle or a reality principle.

Janet has pointed out another fault of the psychoanalytic account of hysteria, an account which represents the repressed and unconscious wish as always sexual in nature and its triumph as due to the imperious nature of sexual drive. The fault which Janet points out is that many hysterics do not have an imperious sex drive. They are far more often persons in whom this source of excitement is at a distinctly low ebb. They do, it is true, often complain of not being loved, but this is no evidence of sexual desire. It rather indicates in them the desire for security and protection common to inadequate and depressed persons. They have no energy for loving others, but want the attention of others without any expenditure of energy on their part. They become specialists in getting something for nothing. The hysteric is almost always strongly egocentric and has the other symptoms of inadequacy. The reason that the hysterical behavior has been developed as a solution for a conflict is that there is not adequate energy for a true solution. The hysteric seizure, or anesthesia, or paralysis, can be regarded as a success only in the control of the immediate situation, and it disregards the public outside the family, or disregards all remote effects for the sake of immediate relief. The person with available energy can reach an emotional reinforcement adequate to a thorough reorganization of habit and a solution that is more than temporary relief. The hysteric is deficient in drive. He does not, as the Freudians assert, suffer from an excess of drive.

In this connection it should be noticed that the majority of the forms of misbehavior which we classify as hysteria *restrict* the world to which the patient responds. His blindness, his deafness, his paralyses, his convulsive attack which disregards much of the social situation in which he is placed, all serve to simplify his world. By failing to see, he is no longer responsible for what he would have seen. His deafness is an excuse for disregarding unpleasant advice or the reminders of duty.

I have observed on two occasions very similar behavior in puppies. On being for the first time placed before a large mirror on the floor, both barked at the sight of the image and approached the glass. Both eventually went behind the glass, to find nothing there. Both of them, when they were on later occasions placed before a mirror, elaborately disregarded it and would look in any direction but toward their reflection. By refusing to look in the glass they solved a disturbing and annoying situation, a situation which included another dog which would mysteriously vanish. Both solutions were unconscious in the sense that the dogs did not plan them but merely hit upon them.

Hysteric episodes occur in the life of every person. But we are forced to the conclusion that there are some persons who are properly described as having an hysteric personality. The evidence for this is that there are people of whom we can predict that they will tend consistently to hit upon time after time the kind of adaptation which we call hysteric. They do not, of course, make up a distinct type. We should, if we could agree upon standards of classification, find something resembling a normal distribution of hysteric episodes. In some persons there would be comparatively few; in others there would occur many, and the great majority of people would fall between these extremes. And the position of individuals would tend to be rather stable from year to year. The majority of those whom we call hysterics remain hysterics in spite of treatment. Through psychoanalysis or other means the specific forms, the specific habits by which they express their inadequacy may be changed, but new forms of hysteric adjustment are likely to appear.

One reason for this is that hysteric behavior is often based on underlying physical inadequacy. The unusual and distressing ways in which the hysteric adjusts to his problems derive from abnormalities in physical drive or the physical sources of energy. There are frequent instances in which a proper diagnosis of organic disorder followed by restoration to physical health has had the further result of a sharp decline in hysteric forms of adjustment. There are many other instances in which physical disturbances such as the menopause are followed by the development of hysteric adjustments in women who were previously in good mental health.

Another reason for the stability of hysteric traits is the conservative nature of habit in general. The small girl who has learned to control her family by bleeding at the nose on critical occasions may be deprived of this instrument of control by having the nasal membranes involved cauterized. But if she has for two years dominated her household by this means, she is probably by this time so used to that domination that she will discover new means of achieving it. Failure to get her way will prove so distressing that new habit adjustments may be expected. The cats with which Horton and I worked in our laboratory were much less active in their attempts at escape if they had been habituated to life in a cage.

A third ground for hysteric behavior which would probably operate to insure that new hysteric adjustments would take the place of those for which a cure had been found, is the inarticulate nature of many desires. A desire for which we have no name, a desire which is not recognized by its verbal description, is less amenable to self-control or to the control of other persons. The fear for which we have no name cannot be dealt with. An enjoyment of a sadistic experience in which erotic excitement accompanied a struggle with another child during which the other child was made to weep may have been forgotten. It is forgotten in the sense that we could not now name the original circumstances or assign them a date. But there may remain of the experience a strong but unacknowledged interest in physical coercion or an interest in inflicting pain, of which the possessor is unaware. He has no words for it. He cannot control it by accepting or rejecting its verbal cues. There is good reason for asserting that hysterics in general are marked by a lack of insight into their own motives. They are torn by impulses for which they have no words.

An hysterical seizure is, for instance, in some cases a reenactment of an exciting event. A girl disturbs her friends by becoming distraught on several occasions and then falling to the floor and struggling for a time. Questions finally elicit the fact that this is a repetition of her defense against the erotic aggression of a young man with whom she had gone canoeing. She had not recognized the reenactment and the action was not under her control because it began before she had any warning of what she was about to do. When the recognition was established and the initial movements of the seizure were associated with this verbal recognition, voluntary control was possible.

The actual associative history of this voluntary control was probably this: at first the scene is reenacted as a matter of motor habit. Some erotic cue or reminder is sufficient to begin the scene, and the intense excitement of the first occasion was responsible for a thorough redintegration. When she has been led to describe the original experience in words, the beginnings of the action are associated with verbal recognition. The final associative step is to use the words now aroused as cues for inhibitory action which will "side-track" the involuntary movements of the seizure. This is what the psychoanalysts achieve when they report that bringing a suppressed wish into full consciousness relieves it of its charge of energy.

The chronic hysteric lacks insight into his own motives. If this is the result of years spent in a family environment in which strong tabus prevent the discussion and verbalization of inevitable and natural desires, it will not be overcome by "bringing into full consciousness" any one childhood incident or any small group of repressed wishes. It is, however, quite conceivable that a prolonged psychoanalysis might supply much of the insight needed for voluntary control. The extent to which this is actually achieved in practice would be very hard to determine.

XX

PHOBIAS

THE lives of many people are affected by irrational fears of an astonishing variety of things. There are cat-fears, dog-fears, mouse-fears, fears of stairs, of darkness, of thunder, of riding on trains, of bright lights, of certain foods, of snakes, of bats, of infection. There are persons who cannot bring themselves to remain alone in a small closed room, or to cross an open space. There are fears that attach to particular persons, and the fearful individual cannot bring himself to confront the object of his fear. There are people who cannot spend an evening alone in the house, and people who avoid high places. Medical usage has attached to the more common of these fears formidable names compounded of the Greek term for the thing feared, together with the Greek word for fear itself. *Phobos* in the Homeric poems means *flight*. The fear of enclosed places is called claustrophobia; fear of open places is called agoraphobia. By a long list of such terms medical men have concealed their ignorance of the nature of these common fears from the public and from themselves. The patient who cannot bring himself to make a voyage by train may be told by his physician that he is suffering from siderodromophobia. The patient is not enlightened by the term, though he may be caused to realize that the time spent by his physician in acquiring it must be recompensed. The conventional list of phobias has also served well the lazy college instructor, for the list furnishes a wealth of examination material. We shall here be content to describe a fear of high places as a fear of high places, rather than as a case of acrophobia.

All such fears have one paradoxical feature. They are very seldom experienced. The person who suffers from an extreme fear of cats cannot bear to remain in the same room with a cat. She has learned to avoid cats. The man who fears the elevator is never found in elevators. The person who is desperately afraid of being alone in an open space is almost never desperately afraid because he never allows himself to be caught in that predicament. Phobias are fears that are almost never experienced.

There is another characteristic which most phobias share. This lies in the fact that either the phobia as a whole or some essential feature of it is not discussed by its owner. Either the original experience was inarticulate, as would be the case in terror aroused in a young child who had not yet acquired enough vocabulary, or the original experience had elements of shame which forbade its description to other persons.

These two characteristics of the phobia are well illustrated in a recent account by G. Milton Smith of a phobia originating before the age of three. This is the case of an intelligent youth of nineteen who had an intense fear of darkness which made him incapable of remaining alone in his room at night unless in bed. Under hypnosis he recalled being alone with his father who had, when the boy was three years old, been taken to a sanitarium and died there without being seen again by the child. On the occasion of the remembered incident the father had suddenly thrown down his paper, risen from his chair and with his face contorted in emotion stamped about the room shouting. The boy ran down the dark hall and, looking back, saw his father coming behind him. When the boy reached his mother's room she met the pair and quieted the father who sat down and wept. The mother very solemnly warned the boy that he must never tell his experience. After several sessions under hypnosis in which other details were recalled, the young man did some experimenting with staying in the dark and found that the fear of darkness had disappeared.

Here is an extreme terror brought on by an incident which is apparently the basis for a lasting fear of the dark. But it is to be noted that this fear of darkness is seldom experienced because the first occasions on which it appears have led to the formation of habits which avoid being alone in the dark. The actual terror is thus give no chance to appear. If the child had been often terrified in the dark, terror would have led to such a reinforcement of action that a new habit adjustment would have been made. In order to get rid of a fear of darkness, *darkness must be experienced* and attached through association to some response other than terror. In order to get rid of a fear of elevators the first essential is an experience with elevators. But the elevator-phobe will not ride in elevators. His one terrifying experience has led him to the habitual avoidance of them. One hasty cure of such an elevator-fear which had persisted for many years and become a serious handicap to the business man who suffered it was achieved by enticing the possessor into a tall office building on the excuse that he must at least look at an elevator. He was assured that he need not ride in it. When he and his impatient counselor had arrived before the elevators the phobic was seized by the arm and literally pushed into the car. He was frightened but made no scene, perhaps because of the presence of the elevator girl. He was told that the ride was to continue and that an attempt to get out would lead to his being taken for an insane man in custody.

The terror whose effects had operated for over ten years did not fully materialize. The man was annoyed and somewhat frightened, but such a state is usually not maintained for long, and after a number of rides up and down he was willing to go to other office buildings and try their elevators.

The second common feature of phobias, the fact that they or some of their essential features are not discussed, is illustrated in both the case of the elevator fear and the fear of darkness. The man who feared darkness had been warned by his mother to keep silent about his experience and so far as he remembered he had never mentioned it before. The elevator-phobe was ashamed of his fear and had made many elaborate excuses for refusing to enter an elevator. He had arranged his business routine with great care so as to avoid a need for elevators. In each case it is probable that discussion would have favorably disposed to a cure. This is not always the case. Some fears survive a very complete recall of the original incident and frequent discussion. Their elimination depends on conditioned inhibition through actual exposure to the frightening stimulus.

We can be rid of some fears through talk alone, particularly if the fear centers about talk. A young woman, a student in a hygiene course, was sent to consult a psychologist because she felt as though she would faint whenever blood was mentioned. She had stopped going to her hygiene lectures. In this case also the actual fear was not often experienced because she had learned to avoid courses in which there would be mention of blood. The hygiene course, unfortunately, was required of all students and this led to the discovery of the phobia.

The psychologist undertook a very simple course. He established a certain amount of confidence and good-feeling, managed to provoke the girl to laughter by an amusing anecdote or two, and, while her pleasant and relaxed attitude still held, brought up some mention of her difficulty. What was being done was explained to her. She was told something of the nature of inhibitory conditioning. By degrees the conversation became more sanguinary without bad effects. Eventually the young woman who could formerly not hear talk of blood without growing faint became something of a conversational menace to others because blood was her favorite topic.

Instances of another common fear, the fear of blushing—or, as the psychiatrist takes pride in describing it, erythrophobia—are numerous among young people. A girl who suffered from this fear had learned to protect herself by always sitting in the rear of the classroom. If she was called on to recite in any class she did not answer. Occasionally she withdrew from a course in which continued refusal promised to be difficult. In her case a method like Dunlap's negative practice was used. She was persuaded to try the next time she was among friends to bring up the subject of blushing and to boast that she could when she chose blush more readily and more furiously than anyone present. She followed these instructions on a number of occasions and eventually lost her ability to blush so readily and ceased to be troubled by it in public. In her case the blush was a part of a general embarrassed state brought on by social confusion. After several experiences in which blushing had been noticed by others and her awareness of this notice had interfered with her attention to what she was saying, she had learned to avoid such storms of confused emotion by remaining silent and keeping out of notice. When blushing became a social asset and the topic of conversation among friends, there was no longer any state of confusion and blushing failed to appear. Free discussion had added its effects to her cure. Before consulting a psychologist she had not been willing to talk about her phobia and had no opportunity to establish the control that articulate discussion would provide.

Many phobias depend for their very existence on not being discussed. The resulting dissociation from speech (which renders them unconscious in the Freudian sense) makes it impossible for the subject to direct his own actions toward the feared situation. It is not necessary to recover the actual memories of the original incident, as Freudian theory would hold. The memory may be fictitious and still be effective in making the situation articulate. New verbal associations with the beginning of the undesirable response may be established, associations which had nothing to do with the original learning. These new verbal cues may then be made the cues for inhibitory conditioning, the substitution of harmless responses for the undesired ones. This is the "mechanism" behind the psychoanalytic theory that the recovery of a repressed memory into full consciousness brings a cure.

That Freud uses the word "unconscious" in the sense of "inarticulate" is evident not only by an examination of his use of the word but also by his own direct statement. In his *New Introductory Lectures* he says: ". . . we can infer it [an unconscious intention which produced a slip of speech] with certainty from the occurrence of the speech disturbance, but it was not able to obtain expression; it was, that is to say, unconscious. If we subsequently bring the intention to the speaker's notice, he may recognize it as a familiar one, in which case it was only temporarily unconscious." In this statement "expression" can mean only verbal expression, and recognition must mean the application of the right word.

It is quite accurate, therefore, to say that most phobias have an unconscious or inarticulate motivation and that when this becomes articulate the cure may often take place. It is, however, quite possible to be badly frightened and to recall the frightening incident without having the recall effect associative inhibition of the fear. A workman on a bridge may have a fall and be able to describe the accident in great detail, but he may nevertheless be afraid to venture back on the bridge or even to go on with his calling.

A woman who was possessed by a mouse-fear had gone to

great lengths in her avoidance of the terrifying beasts. A skilled man had been engaged to mouse-proof her house. All possible entrances were covered with wire netting or blocked off. Even the tops of the two chimneys were protected. As a result of the phobia it had been years since she had seen a mouse, but the mere mention of one was enough to cause her to leave the company. She was inured first to conversation about mice, then to the presence in her room of a small and very innocuous china mouse, next to a more realistic mouse of rubber, and, following that, to a stuffed white mouse prepared by a taxidermist. The final step, a live mouse in a cage, was eventually tolerated and by that time the phobia had lost its force. This elaborate series of graduated cues for retraining was, possibly, not necessary, but its results were successful. The "cure" had obviously been attended by considerable talk about mice and this must have contributed to the negative adaptation of terror.

The term "phobia" is used to describe fearful attitudes toward distinct and namable things. But the same attitudes of frightened avoidance may be connected with more generalized features of situations. There are many forms of social timidity in which the disturbing feature of the situation is not easily named after some prominent constant feature such as a cat, darkness, running water, or the smell of ether. Social timidity may depend on very complex relationships toward other persons. A young man may find himself incapable of more than short and embarrassed replies when he is talking to his employer, though he has no difficulties with his fellow employees. His timidity and the exciting nature of an interview with the employer derive from the fact that there is conflict in his attitude. He may be strongly impelled to boast of his work, or to point out that he deserves an increase in pay, or to call attention to faults in a rival, but these actions have been rehearsed with the employer absent. When the two are actually face to face the situation is changed and the employer's manner may discourage the planned speech, or habits of deference conflict with the firm demands that were practiced while the clerk was alone.

The history of a case of social timidity is often like the history of a typical phobia, and the two essential causes of its prolonged existence are the same. There has been an unfortunate incident. We have made a rude remark or a blunder and find ourselves laughed at or eyed strangely; we discover that we are not dressed as the others are dressed and this competes with our conversation for our attention. Tension and excitement result from the confusion in behavior and the competition of action systems. In confusion we retreat to a corner or flee from the party. When we are next invited to a similar affair we feel an anticipatory embarrassment which is merely an associative response to some advance reminder of the party. We may now retreat before the catastrophe. We may become incapable of forcing ourselves to attend such gatherings.

A young man left college for a berth on a ship bound for a northern cruise for eight months. There were no women aboard the vessel. On the evening of his return he attended a dance with several of his fellow students. He was missed soon after arriving at the dance and was eventually discovered hiding in a service entrance in a state of "nervous chil[1]." Daydreams and reading during the voyage had not prepared him for any feasible approach to the partners with whom he earnestly desired to dance. He had become incapable of speech with a girl in a party dress surrounded by other students.

Social timidity perseveres because in order to overcome it we should have to face the company, and the shy person ends by protecting himself from occasions at which his shyness would be in evidence. Just as the victim of a phobia seldom experiences his fear, so the shy person seldom exhibits his social confusion.

His shyness is evident only in the set of habits which protect
him from terrifying contacts. Also like the phobia, shyness
maintains itself in part by the lack of discussion of humiliating
incidents. Refusals of invitations are made by some conventional formula. One is too busy, or not interested in such affairs. The humiliation that provoked the avoidance is not mentioned. As in the case of the phobia, mere discussion may lead
to cure. Through an account of the humiliating experience to
a friend it is associated with words. But the friend's reception
of the account may be very different from the agonized spirit
in which the confession is made. The friend did not suffer the
humiliation and may be provoked to laughter. His laughter and
his attitude may prove "catching." We have so often shared
the experiences of others on occasions when both are provoked
to laughter or other emotion by the same situation that the
expression of the emotion in another tends strongly to evoke it
in us. If we first confess and then share the laughter of our
companion, we are eventually led to substitute amusement for
shame in recalling the humiliating experience.

This would, of course, work both ways. We may tell some
experience which we have found highly amusing and have it
received in stony silence or with averted looks. This reception
has its effect on our attitude and we now recall the amusing experience only with a blush or with a "gone" feeling of depression. Queen Victoria's "We are not amused" would change the
affective value of any narrative.

Both a tendency to phobias and a tendency to social timidity
may result from inadequate emotional reinforcement of action. The individual who is put in a state of excitement but
lacks the reserve energy which would compel action and reorganize habit to meet the difficulty tends strongly to escape
by flight and to fix habits which avoid the disturbing situation
instead of attacking it. Phobias and social timidity are there-

fore often found in the same individual. They may be almost never in evidence. Men have succeeded in keeping from being alone for a period of fifteen years, without friends or family becoming aware that a most elaborate routine has been worked out to avoid that catastrophe. We may discover that a person whom we judged to have much social poise and to be equal to any social occasion gives that impression because she takes extreme care to avoid meeting persons outside the small group to which she is adapted. With her friends she is at ease. She has learned their ways and found how to respond to them. But she will not confront a strange company.

XXI

NEURASTHENIA, PSYCHASTHENIA AND
ANXIETY STATES

DURING the World War every army had its cases of functional nervous disorder which incapacitated soldiers for duty. Hollingworth has published an account of a large number of American cases hospitalized at Plattsburg, N. Y., in his *Psychology of Functional Neuroses*. One of his most interesting observations was that there were significant differences in the types of nervous breakdown suffered by enlisted men and by officers. The men inclined strongly to the ailments which we have described as hysteria. They showed much more tendency than officers to develop paralyses and anesthesias, or to simulate disease symptoms or epileptic attacks. Their officers more often exhibited "nervous indigestion," states of anxiety accompanied by nightmares and loss of appetite, an inability to make decisions, periods of quickened pulse and heightened blood pressure.

All of these symptoms manifested in greater degree by the commissioned officers are the normal results of inadequacy in the physical apparatus for the emotional reinforcement of action and may be brought on by exhaustion, by the results of intense and prolonged conflict, or by physical defects which antedated military service. If, among the symptoms, states of exhaustion are conspicuous it has been common practice to describe the condition as *neurasthenia*. If we are more impressed with the patient's inability to make decisions or to control thought, his condition is called *psychasthenia*. If the chronic tensions and associated disturbances of pulse and digestion are conspicuous, the trouble may be called *anxiety neurosis*. But these names are neither universally accepted nor can they be made to fit the cases unambiguously. The majority of cases show in some measure all the symptoms named.

Why is it that more officers fell into such states than enlisted men? Hollingworth's answer is undoubtedly the correct one. He gives two reasons. The first is that the officers carry a much heavier responsibility than the common soldiers. The second is that officers were as a group more intelligent and better educated than the men.

An enlisted man in the army has comparatively few important decisions to make. These are made by officers. The private does not have to choose what he will wear, what he will have for breakfast, the hour at which he will rise, or how he will spend his time on duty. He lives under orders which prescribe not only what he shall do but the manner in which he shall do it. Such decisions as he must make are the decisions of immediate action—where to try to place his bayonet, whether to take cover in this shell hole or that. Most of the elaborate organization and discipline of an army is aimed at the prevention of any need for decision by the enlisted man. The officer, on the other hand, must look to the provisioning and quartering of his command. He must decide how the orders of his superior are to be carried out and how objectives are to be reached. Failure of attack or of defense is blamed not on men but on officers. In addition, the officer must deal with the varied personalities of his command. All responsibility requires deliberation and choice. Decision, when high stakes are involved, takes much energy.

There is also some evidence that differences in intelligence and training affect the type of neurotic response to intolerable situations. The hysterical tricks by which the enlisted man escapes duty are not open to the more intelligent person who can himself see through them. In order that a paralysis that keeps a man from duty shall be classed as hysterical and not as a case of malingering, the device must be inarticulate and unplanned like the cat's escape from the puzzle box. Education and intelligence reduce the possibility of inarticulate and uncontrollable tricks of escape. The more intelligent man not only realizes how others will react to a paralysis that has no basis in physical injury; he must also face himself. The tricks of the hysteric are recognized as not consistent with the stage directions for his rôle.

The hysteric has the better part. When he has without conscious plan or intention developed his escape and his functional blindness or deafness or his epileptoid seizure and this has been accepted by the examining physician as a valid reason for being invalided home or sent to a base hospital, his troubles are over. His illness satisfies the authorities, the public and himself. He, being a naïve person, finds nothing in his functional disability to contradict his rôle of soldier or to impeach his faith in his own bravery.

The French are reported to have reduced somewhat the number of hysterical evasions of service by making the base hospital less pleasant than the front-line trenches. This was accomplished by obligatory "treatments" which included enemas and acutely uncomfortable and long-continued sessions with an induction coil. At the point where these became severe annoyances a cure of the hysterical symptom was often achieved. This is more or less in line with the tradition of military discipline which assigns punishment without much regard for the nature of the excuse and thereby reduces the number of breaches of discipline to a minimum. The English and American practice was more sympathetic and admitted the hysterical paralysis or hysterical seizure as an excuse from service. There were naturally more cases under this policy.

With the naïve (or cynical) solution of the hysteric not open to him, the officer does not find a way out. His distress, which is the result of prolonged conflict, is unrelieved and at this stage his symptoms are those which we have described as anxiety. Tensions keep him from sleep or trouble his sleep with fearful nightmares. He has periods of rapid pulse. The well-known effects of excitement on digestion are in evidence. One-third of the physicians in a well-known clinic are reported to be themselves under medical care for stomach ulcers or conditions associated with ulcer. Cases are extremely rare among Negroes. The army officer has no prospect of relief. His responsibilities continue while his command sleeps. An added source of anxiety is the necessity of keeping his state from the notice of his men and his brother officers. Psychasthenic symptoms are then added. Prolonged and unrelieved tension makes him incapable of decision. He begins to extend his worries into the past and the future. He worries over yesterday's troubles as well as today's. Control over his thoughts is gone, and day-terrors are added to his nightmares. Obsessions interfere with his attempts at deliberation. He cannot bring his attention to his problems. If alcohol is available and he has an experience of its relaxation, this may add to the confusion. Eventually movement and action, because of his exhaustion, become painful and he complains of a chronic fatigue which rest will not cure. All exertion demands tremendous effort. To what actual physical exhaustion he may have as a result of his prolonged state of tension, is added a changed habitual attitude toward work and duty. The behavior first caused by actual fatigue may become attached to the sight of the task and a man may feel tired on viewing his work for the first time in the morning though he has had a night's rest.

The terms neurasthenia (nerve-weakness) and psychasthenia (mind-weakness) were originally used in the belief that the first condition derived from physical exhaustion of nervous tissue and that the other was purely an affection of the mind. The terms are no longer apt save for the reference in each to deficient strength. Both sets of symptoms probably involve one or more of the physiological mechanisms that provide for muscular action, respiration, heartbeat, vasomotor tone, muscular tonus, blood sugar and the rest. Habit is also obviously involved, and the symptoms represent a habit adjustment to the physiological deficiency. One failure or one reprimand may break up the attitude of confidence that is essential in commanding men or in making plans and carrying them out.

G. V. Hamilton's *Objective Psychopathology* describes with much insight many instances of functional breakdowns in civilian life. A woman marries and lives on a farm. During the early years of marriage a number of children are born. At the age of fifty or fifty-five she finds herself performing all the household tasks that she did in her youth, with some additions because of the added members. Habits usually require an emergency for their disruption, and though the children are now grown the mother has been relieved of none of her routine. By this time decreasing physical strength has made the load too heavy. She is in a state of chronic fatigue, but gradual habituation has inured her to this and no sudden crisis has appeared to upset the routine. Then the mother has an illness, a slight attack of influenza, and goes to bed. Her task must be performed by others. There is a physical recovery. But when she attempts to get up and resume her work she finds this impossible. There are aches and pains which are hard to account for. The mere sight of her familiar tasks brings on fatigue. The physician is again consulted and finds nothing wrong. He inquires carefully about her symptoms. She finds that she has a considerable number of those he mentions. These are now verbalized and become a part of her response to the threatened resumption of duties. She is in the position of the soldier about to be returned to the front trenches after a month in the hospital.

She may develop a new set of habits and interests which center about her own sensations and health. Pains which she had disregarded for years in her zealous performance of duty are now cues for calling the doctor, staying in bed, and particularly for conversation. The stroke of six is no longer a signal for rising but for relaxing on her pillow. A disturbed and either sympathetic or indignant family gets up and starts the work of the day.

Hamilton found that effective measures in such a case included going over the whole situation with the family to make clear that the patient was not capable of the heavy tasks which she had up to the time of her illness performed. If a definite redistribution of duties that recognized the partial disability of the patient was made, the individual could be encouraged to take up the lighter load and an adjustment might result. The danger was that the new assignment of duties would give way to old habits and that this would be followed by a new crisis.

In so far as the patient's adjustment lies in the adoption of an assortment of symptoms and a state of hypochondria or morbid attention to her health, we might refer to the adjustment as hysterical. She would have reacted to difficulty with the type of solution more characteristic of the common soldier in war time. The development of neurasthenic or psychasthenic symptoms would usually require more than heavy duties. The hysteric solution may be superficial and temporary, but it represents an actual solution that does not lead to impairment of the ability to adjust. Neurasthenia and psychasthenia follow not on dis-agreeable tasks or excessive labor but on fundamental conflicts within the personality, on divided loyalties, on unresolved rivalries of desire. Hysteric solutions resemble other solutions of problems except that they are annoying to associates, out of the control of the patient, not rational, and usually limited to "getting by" a temporary situation. Being without plan, they do not take the larger situation into account. A child may learn to rule the family by temper tantrums or by making scenes and yet be in excellent health, physical and mental. The soldier whose paralysis is accepted by the medical officers as a disability is temporarily out of his troubles. He is enjoying the lesser of two evils. The mother who compels her daughter to give up teaching for service at home by the device of illness when the daughter leaves for her job has merely used a cruel and un-usual method of getting her way. When the device succeeds, she is in a normal state of health.

In neurasthenia and psychasthenia we are dealing with very different conditions. Prolonged conflict has so exhausted the resources for action that the process of adjustment itself is altered. We are confronted with an impaired mind. The victim becomes unable to make adaptations that would have been quickly achieved in his normal state. All decisions are difficult for him. Choosing what he will have for breakfast becomes a heavy task. The cure of an hysteric habit may be achieved through training in insight or through so simple a measure as provision for its failure. When the hysteric symptom does not achieve success and relief it is supplanted by other habit ad-justments. But the cure of neurasthenia and psychasthenia nearly always requires rest and always requires a thorough re-organization of interests and desires.

In neurasthenic depression there are many physical symptoms

which are natural accompaniments. Chronic fatigue, its out-standing symptom, has been mentioned. This is in large part actual muscular fatigue produced by long-continued states of tension. Though nothing has been accomplished, the muscular activity necessary in conflict results in physical fatigue. The victim is fighting himself. Fatigue symptoms are exaggerated because conflict interferes with rest and sleep. Many neurasthenic symptoms can be reproduced by compelling an individual to remain awake for two nights.

Added to the actual fatigue which would be apparent in a chemical analysis of the victim's muscles, there is a fatigue of mental origin. This means only that during actual physical exhaustion new habits and new attitudes have been established. When physical exertion becomes painful, as it does in fatigue, we learn to conserve effort and avoid the pain. To the neurasthenic the very thought of his duties or the thought of meeting people, of conversing, is a cue for avoidance. Rest will not relieve this state. It can sometimes be relieved by a radical change in surroundings, a change to an environment which does not offer reminders of physical exhaustion. Removal from the family presence and from the household is in many cases a spur to recovery.

Besides fatigue, there may be vasomotor disturbances, cold hands and feet, "nervous chill," and odd illusions of heaviness or of great size in body and limbs. The vasomotor system serves the muscles used in action and for the maintenance of body temperature. It is part of the emotional reinforcement of action which is, in the neurasthenic, no longer adequate to its function.

The neurasthenic always develops an egocentric attitude. He is interested in nothing which does not affect his immediate comfort. Every remark made tends to be interpreted as bearing on his situation, or tends to be completely disregarded. How

could this be otherwise when any effort is so painful and exhausting? There is no energy to spare for remote interests, or
interests in the welfare of other persons. Before his breakdown
he may have been an enthusiastic follower of sport or a collector
of stamps. He may have taken an interest in the education of his
children and in their play. He may have been devoted to his
business and fond of his business associates. But none of these
interests will aid him to a relief of his present state, and all of
them demand still more of the effort that he has learned to
avoid. Instead of serving others he learns to exact from others a
maximum of service and protection.

This need for service and protection leads the depressed person into many strange forms of conduct. Janet describes tendencies in the patient to torment the immediate members of his
household on whom he is dependent. He seems to enjoy tortur-
ing just those members of the family who are most sympathetic
and loving. Janet believes that this conduct serves two purposes.
It reaffirms the neurasthenic's power over the persons on whom
he depends. And a quarrel, hurling abuse at devoted friends or
family, serves to stimulate a short-lived excitement during which
the patient becomes almost normal. The spur of a family quarrel
has only a brief effect and must be often repeated.

Sulking and pouting serve to call out protestations of devotion and affection from other members of the family. The depressed patient reiterates statements of his own worthlessness,
of the futility of his life, and these will continue so long as they
bring reassurance from those about him. (Janet, *Les médications
psychologiques*, vol. ii, pp. 197 ff.) The patient tends to make
scenes for the same reason. These will be followed by a reconciliation. They resemble those quarrels of lovers which tend to
occur as mutual interest wanes. The making up after a quarrel
is a more thorough relief. The neurasthenic's jealousy of anyone

else who is also served by a devoted friend is easily understood. This jealousy does not spring from affection, because the patient has no energy for affection. Its source is the threat to security which the friend's division of favors represents. Anyone who has any influence over the protector is bitterly resented.

A neurasthenic mother has become dependent on her daughter. When the daughter graduates from college and becomes interested in a young man, there is a campaign of opposition at home. The young man's character and appearance are criticized. On evenings which the daughter had planned to spend in his company the mother develops a terrific headache and her anguished groans move the daughter to break her engagement with the suitor. One candidate after another is driven away. After several years the daughter begins to realize the situation and to understand her mother's tactics. She eventually suffers a nervous breakdown herself, torn between interest in marriage and loyalty to her mother.

In another similar case the mother was unsuccessful in her jealous defense of her daughter and there was an elopement and marriage. But the situation was not accepted by the mother, who developed a severe illness which had so genuine an appearance that the daughter left her husband to devote herself to her mother's care. This same mother took many opportunities to humiliate her daughter in public and at the same time professed for her a great love. It is true that she felt it necessary to have the object of her cruelty always near her, but this nearness was essential in order that the mother could be served by the daughter who at the same time was an object for the abuse which stimulated the mother to a condition almost normal.

Throughout this chapter the terms "neurasthenic" and "psychasthenic" have been used without much distinction. The underlying difficulty and the general symptoms are much the same in both. The only distinction that can be made is that indecision is more conspicuous in one case, and exhaustion in the other. There is great need of a new term to indicate a state in which the emotional reinforcement of action is inadequate. Such a term would embrace chronic anxiety states, neurasthenia an psychasthenia.

XXII

DREAMS AND FANTASY

THE physiological basis of sleep is not known. Various suggestions that it is the result of fatigue products in the blood stream and their effects on nerve conduction, or a special sleep hormone, of an increase in the distance between the surfaces where one nerve cell has its functional connection with the next, or that there is a "sleep center" in the mid-brain all remain purely speculative explanations. It is much more profitable to consider the circumstances under which sleep occurs and the conditions that interfere with it. H. M. Johnson, who has carried out elaborate and careful observations on sleep with many laboratory subjects, describes it in terms of progressive relaxation of the body muscles. Just as general tension is cumulative, each new addition to the tension of muscles furnishing stimuli that bring further tension, so relaxation is, in Johnson's view, a cumulative affair. As one group of skeletal muscles relaxes, the loss of sensory impulses from the relaxed set diminishes the total of neural disturbance entering the central system and causes further relaxation. The connection between sleep and fatigue probably lies in the effects of fatigue in producing relaxation of muscles. In fatigued muscles action is painful and is therefore avoided.

The precautions that we take in order to sleep indicate that relaxation is one of its important conditions. We draw the blinds and turn out the light to shut off stimuli to our eyes; we take what steps we can to insure quiet and prevent the muscular tensions that would result from auditory stimuli; we lie down and thereby relax the elaborate system of anti-gravity reflexes that is in continuous operation while we are sitting or standing.

Sleep is not, however, identical with relaxation or perfectly in accord with the degree of relaxation. Jacobson's *Progressive Relaxation* reports that extensive general relaxation can be achieved without sleep, and it is well known that men can walk or maintain a sitting posture during sleep. G. W. Crile reported in his *A Mechanistic View of War and Peace* that he had seen companies of British infantry on the retreat from Mons with many soldiers asleep on the march as a result of having been in almost continuous retreat for several days. Men shuffled along; at an irregularity in the road they would stumble and be aroused for a moment after their recovery and then fall quickly asleep again. The first-aid station for their wounded did not resound with the usual cries and groans of the wounded but with snores and heavy breathing only. After eight hours of sleep the wounded had recovered sufficiently to make their usual outcries in response to pain. Motorists often drive for some time asleep and may wake only as the car leaves the road. Sleep is not entirely dependent on darkness or quiet or freedom from activity. These are only conditions favorable to sleep, and if sleep is long deferred it will prevail over light, noise and movement.

In the higher animals sleep is necessary to life. It is doubtful whether a man may go five days without it and live. But men do not often die of insomnia. After two days or more without sleep it becomes an imperious tendency and will take precedence over severe pain.

Johnson has exploded a number of popular beliefs concerning sleep. The general public is now familiar with his findings that the sleep of normal healthy young men is disturbed by occasional shifts of posture at intervals of from five to fifteen minutes during the whole night. Only the aged or those weakened by illness sleep "like a log."

It is also known that the soundest sleeper makes some response to stimuli. Passing cars or a voice in the room will produce a faint stir of activity and slight changes of pulse and respiration in the soundest sleeper. The sleeper is not cut off from the world about him but only tends to make minimal responses to its events. These slight responses are probably faint stirrings of the action that would be associated with such stimuli in the waking state. To a spoken question the sleeper tends slightly to make an answer. If he goes so far as to respond audibly, his answer will probably be bizarre or absurd. He does not respond to the noise of the passing car just as he would if he were awake because any response depends fully as much on what the person is doing at the time of the stimulus as it does on the nature of the stimulus. In the absence of waking movements and waking postures the response of the sleeper is out of touch with the situation and appears meaningless. Such responses are probably slight movements of the last act associated with the noise, but there are complications introduced by the sleeper's posture and his sleeping activities.

Sleep is often occupied with strange fragments and strange combinations of action because the sleeping posture and sleeping activities offer a background very different from the background furnished by waking activity. These fragments of action have their own serial associations established usually in the activities of the previous day. If we have just purchased a new car and driven it for the first time, that night our dreams are likely to have traces of our driving activities. We may dream that we are driving on a country road but that the vehicle is a strange one and that we are lying in it on our back unable to see the road ahead of us. This perception is the combined result of the actual posture which we have in bed together with the associations established during our driving day. The last association of the noise of an automobile horn, for instance, may have been some movement of driving. The noise of a horn during sleep tends to revive this movement as the associated response, but this, despite sleep, is combined with some perception of our actual posture in bed. Dreams of being unclothed in public have a like origin. Some noise or some reminder stirs in us the actions performed recently in some public place, but this is combined with the perception of our actual unclothed state. Or we may have been working on some problem and attitudes connected with this are revived by transient reminders during sleep. We may go on with the problem to a solution. A large proportion of dreams can be interpreted as attempts to find a way out of a difficulty that has recently occupied our waking attention. The dream solution is sometimes good. But the chances are that, because we are detached from waking posture and surrounding conditions, it will fail to take everything into account.

These movement fragments that constitute dreams may arise from inner stimuli as well as external stimuli. A slight spasm of the pyloric sphincter or other unusual activity in the stomach, a cramped position in bed, being too cold or too hot may account for impulses which are in the central system routed into motor pathways of recent action. Most dream material comes from the activities of the preceding day because these were the last associations with many cues. If we dream of Italy we can usually recall, if we set about it, that during the previous day someone had in our presence mentioned Italy or that we had noticed an item of Italian news. Childhood events are also represented occasionally in dreams, but not the events of intervening years unless these were associated with unusual emotional excitement. Very often, when material from childhood or intervening years does appear, it will be discovered to have had some recall during the last twenty-four hours.

Probably most dreams are not recalled. Every person has had the experience of waking and realizing that he has been dreaming but being unable to remember and recount his dream. This is especially true if we shift our position and open our eyes before making verbal notes on the dream or before practicing its verbal description. The dream is now lost. The regular practice of recounting dreams to other interested persons may establish a habit of reviewing the dream for report. I have known two persons who claimed that they never dreamed, who both, after they had been for some months in the company of others who recounted dreams at the breakfast table, began to relate as many dreams as the others of the company. Memory is dependent on verbal associations established at the time of the experience. We can report accurately only those events which we were observing, and observation must have consisted in practicing the description as we watched the event.

The use of dreams by the psychoanalysts for the uncovering of the inarticulate desires and aversions which are responsible for conflict and neurotic symptoms depends on several features of the dream experience. In the first place, dreams are motivated in the same ways in which waking behavior is motivated. Action tendencies are aroused by stimuli, and the dream fantasies are associations with maintaining stimuli responsible for the aroused tendency. In an infantry company whose commissary failed to provide food at the end of a long hike many of the man reported dreams of being in the presence of groaning Thanksgiving tables or of searching for food or of anxiety over food. If stomachs had been filled such dreams would have been impossible. A satiated man does not dream of food because the responses associated with satiation are incompatible with eating. When the stomach is full, the attitude toward food is more likely to be that of slight aversion. Dreams of walking are possible when the dreamer is relaxed in bed because this relaxation is compatible with slight movements of walking. But no soldier asleep on the march could dream that he was lying down at rest. None of the drivers who have described to me dreams that took place while actually driving has reported dreaming of any other action than driving. Sitting erect, clutching the wheel, holding the foot on the throttle all eliminate any trace of the adjustments we might make to lying down or fishing a stream. The erotic dream is essentially dependent on maintaining stimuli from tensions in the genitals which have in their turn been aroused by contact stimuli or through association with other stimuli actually received during sleep. The general physiological state, of course, is another determiner of such tensions.

If the previous day has been occupied with a major worry or conflict, this will have established so many associations not yet reconditioned that nearly any activity aroused in us will call up our unachieved desire. Dreams are therefore diagnostic of our desires, and the Freudian contention that censorship of social control is less evident in sleep than in waking is well justified. This control depends partly on the stimuli which accompanied the social situation, on such things as the presence of other persons or our own postures and attitudes. The absence of such inhibiting stimuli makes the dream a freer expression of desire than waking thoughts, and a much freer expression than our waking actions. We are, for that matter, more free in our waking fantasies when we are alone than when we are in company. When others are about, not only the seeing and hearing of these others but also those social tensions, particularly facial, which we maintain in the presence of others keep us to the mark. Our "company face" regulates our behavior. Social control is not, of course, completely absent from dreams because we have many habits of conformity which depend on our own postural stimuli or which are modifications of the desire itself.

Freud contends that the dream can be viewed as a protective

device to enable the dreamer to continue sleep. This contention is essentially correct. The impulse to sleep, whatever its physiological origin, is undoubtedly part of the stimulus situation affecting us; and any desires for activity which are present must be compromised with this impulse.

In the nightmare, whether the cause of the dream is an intense digestive discomfort or erotic tension or a conflict of tensions left from some problem unsettled during the day, this impulse to sleep is defeated. Excitement reaches a point at which overt action prevails and we jump out of bed or cry out and so waken ourselves. In psychasthenic depression the tensions of the day remain or are easily revived during sleep and one of the most common complaints is of insomnia or of successions of terrible dreams. In the somnambulist an action system that often includes something of plan and foresight reaches the point of actual movement. We recognize the condition as sleep because he is responding to very limited features of his environment. He may notice enough to avoid obstacles and make his way to the point that he has in mind or climb ladders and perform skilled feats of balance on cornices, but there is much that he disregards. He may walk past us without taking any notice. He may answer when spoken to, but his answer does not take in the complete situation and may fail to make sense.

Havelock Ellis has asserted that when the sleepwalker is wakened, he never remembers what he was about or the nature of the dream fancies which accompanied the action. This seems to be rather generally true though I have had two accounts of dreams that accompanied walking for some distance. Just why it is true is not clear. I suspect that giving an account of a dream requires that it not only be dreamed but also noticed at the time. Memory, as Janet contends, is based on narrative, and a dream which is not narrated as it occurs is as difficult to report as a waking experience which is not narrated to oneself.

Daydreams are of the same stuff as dreams that accompany sleep. They are naturally somewhat altered by the fact that we are sitting or standing or working at a task. If we are asleep in bed with muscles relaxed except as activated by the dream we may dream that we are flying or floating in the air. But flying daydreams would be more rare. Daydreams are often as hard to recall as dreams during sleep. The old-fashioned phrase, "A penny for your thoughts," often found its hearer unable to state what he had been fancying. I have with a companion spent several hours painting a boat, one on each side and not within each other's range of vision. Suddenly my companion asked me what I had been thinking about and neither of us could recall the substance or any part of our afternoon's reverie though we were convinced that we had filled the time with daydreams. A sudden alertness wipes out the pattern of the dream.

Jung has well described the differences between two types of thinking. There are times when thought is occupied with inarticulate fancies which we cannot recount to another person because they were inarticulate. He calls this *autistic* thinking and contrasts it with the self-communion that takes linguistic form. Many of our thoughts are inner conversations which vary from incoherent stray phrases to finished sentences. James Joyce in *Ulysses* has made an effort to record such inner thinking as it occurs. His character who does the thinking in the book is probably much more a word thinker than most men because he is conceived by an author who is tremendously interested in words for their own sakes.

There is no sharp line between autistic or private thinking made up of stray bits of action, lookings, listenings, and rational thinking in which words predominate (sayings). The private thinking can be only very roughly communicated to another person. We are suddenly asked what we are thinking about. "Italy," we say, or "the Bay of Naples." The vague and

private detail which was something like a view of the bay we had
once seen from a small boat may not be conveyed at all to our
questioner. If twenty persons are asked what they think of when
the word "Italy" is pronounced, there will be twenty different
replies and all they have in common is that they have something
to do with Italy. One person sees a map in which Italy is colored
green with a blue sea about it; one sees the Coliseum in the late
afternoon light; one reacts as he did to hearing "O sole mio"
sung by a strenuous tenor in a Neapolitan hotel; another has
faint stirrings of eating gnocchi or relives his reaction to the
presence of goat's milk in his morning coffee. None of these
private associations can be fully reported or communicated. In
so far as actual words formed part of the association, however,
these can be reported and accurately reproduced by the hearer.

The psychoanalysts have undertaken to examine and interpret the autistic thinking that goes on in dreams. In such an
examination the dream must first be put into words by the
dreamer, and in this it undergoes thorough changes. As it occurred it was incommunicable, and only partly remembered.
The process of giving it a verbal description is an opportunity
for many changes and alterations because the speech takes the
listener into account. After the dream has been described the
dreamer may be asked to continue to name the associations
which occur to him after the telling, or to state what some
element in the dream makes him think of. We may be able
to judge the nature of the motivation behind the dream from
these replies. The dream is pronounced evidence of an unconscious wish for escape from parental domination or evidence of
an unconscious hostility toward the analyst or evidence of a
perverse erotic interest which has never been acknowledged by
the dreamer in so many words. If the dream imagery pictures
the outcome of an escape from the parent, or the outcome of

a hostile attitude toward the analyst, or the outcome of a perverse desire, this interpretation is justified.

A young business man reported a dream. He was in an inner
office. There entered a beautiful girl dressed in black. He approached her and was about to embrace her when he noticed
that two older women were standing in the doorway which led
to the outer room and that they were looking very severe. He
walked boldly to the door, closed it, and returned to the visitor.
The dreamer when he told the dream had not realized that the
description of the two rooms applied to his own office as well as
to the dream office, that he had a secretary and a filing clerk
who worked in the outer office and that his fiancée had called
on him during the previous afternoon. The two clerks had not
actually stood in the doorway on this occasion, but he had possibly anticipated such a move. This dream was obviously a repetition in large part of the afternoon's episode. No far-fetched
associative symbols were involved. The addition of the door-
closing to the actual events was a natural afterthought. The
only element of unconscious desire that was evident lay in the
fact that the dream was recounted to an acquaintance without
any recognition of the locale or of the participants.

But there are dreams in which such symbolism does play a
part. A man who was a few weeks later discovered in an embezzlement and arrested, recounted the following dream: He had
ascended to the top of a long hill. At the top he found a precipice on the other side and at the foot of the precipice was a
dark pool of water. Looking over the edge he slipped and clung
for an agonizing moment. After some time he grew more exhausted and realized that he would fall. He did fall, but the fall
proved very gentle and he floated on the surface of the pool
with a great sense of relief. It is quite possible that this was an
account of his desperate situation with his firm and that the
dream represented a possible solution—to let go and take the

consequences with an anticipation that a term in jail with everything settled would be a great relief. It is possible that this was the reference in the dream, but this would be very difficult to establish. The reference of symbols depends on the individual experience of the dreamer and is subject to few rules. Freud has shown a tendency to list certain stock symbols. The serpent, an obelisk or any straight object means the male organ. Doorways, circles or enclosed figures represent the female. The return to the womb of the mother would be represented by an entrance into a darkened room. Whether dream symbols are as conventional as these lists of meanings would indicate, it is impossible to say. There is great danger that their acceptance by the analyst causes him to read such references into dreams where they do not fit. It is quite true that many dreams seem to the friends and close acquaintances of the dreamer to have obvious references which have escaped the dreamer himself. Symbol and metaphor play a large part in all thinking and are the basis for the extension of words to new meanings. The best treatise on psychology that has yet been written, Janet remarks, is the dictionary.

That the impulse to sleep, however, symbolizes the desire for a return to the mother we may well doubt. Sleep is a part of our physiological make-up and needs no such far-fetched explanation. Freud is correct in finding signs in most dreams of the impulse to return to sound sleep because this impulse, whatever its physiological cause, is unquestionably present.

Dreams protect sleep. Fantasy and daydreams protect idleness. Fantasy tends to appear when men fear and avoid action. In the flight from reality which has been described by Freud this disinclination for action is evident. This is a partial explanation for the exotic and romantic nature of fantasy. If we daydream about our familiar surroundings and our job this tends to lead us into activity. Daydreaming about Tahiti or

Samarkand carries no such threat. No forgotten task will be brought to our minds so long as they are occupied with adventure in strange lands. The inadequate person learns to occupy his mind with the distant and the romantic and so to protect himself from current annoyances.

If the early sounds of household activity tend to call us to the day's duties or if yesterday's anxiety begins to threaten sleep, a pleasant dream may erase the tension of muscles which threatens to arouse us and the dream allows us another half hour of rest. This tendency to dreams and fantasies is acquired as all forms of escape are acquired. It is the identical process by which the infant learns to quiet himself by sucking his thumb. The thoughts that have on some occasion proved sufficient to distract us from our restlessness tend afterward to be suggested by this restlessness. The timid person who is worried over some problem of inadequacy or some impending and dreaded meeting has discovered that daydreams of Tahiti or novel-reading or the cinema erase his anxiety from his muscles and bring relief. Distraction is habit-forming for just the same reason that food or opium is habit-forming. Essentially bridge and thumb-sucking are alike in that they are forms of escape from discontent.

XXIII

MEMORY AND FUGUES

D URING the World War a young American of twenty-two
was drafted and sent to a training camp. He had finished
college with a fine record and was something of an esthete with
interests in art and literature and music. At camp he was placed
among an illiterate and "tough" crowd from a big city. He
found camp life and military discipline intolerable. He had
never before come in contact with the obscenity and rough
horseplay that interest so many youths. His previous life had
been effectively sheltered.

After a short period in camp he disappeared. He was discovered several months later in a distant part of the country and
identified as a deserter from the army. He had assumed another
name and was earning his own living as a clerk. He professed to
be quite ignorant of his name and family and of the fact that
he was in the draft army. He had no memories beyond being on
a train several months before and was completely vague about
his early life. On being returned to his camp and visited by his
parents and the family physician he did not at first recognize
them. After several days of very sympathetic treatment in the
military hospital his memory returned. He now faced court-
martial as a deserter. But the court did not hear the case because
he killed himself before the date set for his hearing.

It is easily understood that for some youths who had been
brought up in circumstances like his the close association with
rough companions that is a part of barracks life would prove

intolerable. There were a number of severe breakdowns from this cause. When a man is resented bitterly by his non-commissioned officers for his habits of precise diction, his better education, his attempts at personal comfort, life can be made very miserable for him. The motive for leaving camp was clear.

But that he should proceed to forget his name and antecedents seems hardly credible. It is, however, quite possible, and there are a great many records of such *fugues* or lapses of memory. It should first be noticed that this is not at all a loss of habits or of the general effects of previous learning. He is not in the least like a visitor from a strange culture or a man without a culture. He retains his ability to speak English, his habits and his skills. He is equipped to get a job and earn a living. He has not forgotten his geography, but only where he himself had lived. He has not forgotten the common American names, but only which name is his own. He knows what soldiers are but has forgotten that he is a soldier. In fact, his forgetting seems to be a carefully planned move to avoid military service. Remembering would involve him in calamity.

Such forgetting has all the marks of a voluntary and planned line of action. But we are compelled to admit that such fugues may be involuntary. Janet quotes the case of a wife who, in such a fugue, left Paris for Marseille and there spent eight days. Her husband sued her for divorce and charged that this had been a romantic interlude. She was quite unable to recall at the trial where she had gone or with whom she had been. The decision went against her. Later with the aid of hypnosis the whole episode was recalled and proved to be quite innocent, but the recall was too late. Her memories of the period were not open to voluntary recall, although they were still intact.

To return to the soldier. He was on his return treated with great consideration by the military authorities and the probable sentence of the court-martial would not have been extreme.

Nevertheless, he found it impossible to face the future as a deserter from his country's army. His training had made him conscientious and he fully realized what he had done and how this would be received by persons of his own class. His loss of memory was a change of rôle. But the change of rôle, however he may have come to begin it, carried such a relief from his troubles that reminders of his former status only served as cues for the action of escape, which is the affirmation of the new rôle. Hearing his former name is a signal to think of his new name.

In a recent case an elderly man was brought in by the police to a public hospital unable to give any account of himself. Under hypnosis he told a variety of astonishing yarns which it later developed he had heard as a small boy from an adventurous uncle. He told them so convincingly in the first person that the physician interested in him was persuaded that he had discovered a remarkable case and had the séances recorded. Memories recovered under hypnosis are not necessarily truthful and are motivated as well as ordinary memories. The old man's identity was discovered by publishing his picture and it was found that he had a wife and family in another city. He was again put under hypnosis, but whenever his real name or his family or his place of residence was mentioned he was overcome by excitement and refused to continue his hypnotic state. His motive was obviously escape from his family and we are led to some suspicion of pretense in the continued refusal to acknowledge his identity. Mr. X is obviously the one person that he refuses to be, the one rôle that he will not play.

A man was taken from a train at the request of the conductor, who notified the police because his passenger first asked him what destination had been marked on his ticket and some time later followed this by asking where he himself had boarded the train. The puzzled traveler proved to be a barber who had been missing from his shop for three weeks. He could recall nothing of the interval. It was quite blank until he found himself on the train, and his curiosity over his own movements and intended destination was very natural. When arrested he had in his pockets several hundred dollars in cash. This was more cash than he had ever had before in his life, and it is very probable that the *amnesia* or loss of memory was an escape from troubling thoughts over the source of the money. Here again we cannot be absolutely certain about the involuntary nature of the forgetting, but it appeared genuine.

No other writer has equaled Janet's analysis of the nature of memory, and his description throws much light on these temporary disturbances. Janet calls attention to the fact that when we say, "Do you remember . . ." we do not at all mean, "Do you have visual images or auditory images of the experience?" We judge the ability to remember by the ability to give an account *in words*. Animals do not have memory in this sense. The dog rushes up to his owner after an absence but he does not remember *that this is his master*. "This is my master" is a verbal statement. The dog has no language and is totally unable to make verbal statements. He merely reacts to the master with obvious joy. But this is not remembering. It is merely reacting with joy. The dog cannot say to himself that this is the same man or that this is Dr. Brown. Small children likewise, when they have not yet acquired much language, cannot be said to remember. They have habits and likes and dislikes that show evidence of past associations, but memory waits on their ability to witness and describe verbally an event and then to report it to another person. Janet's own illustration is of a young woman who lived through a very distressing death scene. Her father was lying drunk in the apartment and her dying mother struggled and fell from the bed. The girl with great effort got her back and wiped her lips. The mother died. After this the girl would often, if she were in a room with a bed, reenact the

whole death scene with evident distress. But she did not remember that her mother had died or that there had been such
a scene. She reenacted but did not remember. She was sure that
if her mother had died she would have been told. Her mother
was therefore only absent. The girl could give no verbal account,
but her reliving of the experience was vivid.

This throws much light on the fugues that have been described. The loss of memory is the loss of an ability to describe
or narrate a past event or a past situation. The person suffering
from such an amnesia is not at a loss in finding his way about a
house which has been familiar, but he cannot tell in words his
own relations to that house. His actions betray his familiarity
but the house is not recognized.

The inability to give an account of a period of one's life is not
always regarded as abnormal. Social workers concerned with the
administration of relief may encounter it daily. A large part of
the public is sufficiently untrained in describing and narrating
to be quite incapable of giving any connected idea of their own
biography. The relief worker may get from them by patient
questions a few high points or outstanding events, but to reduce
these to an ordered narrative the relief worker must take charge
and arrange the events in his own fashion. Simple people have
no biography. They have never attempted a connected account
of their lives. They remember that John was born the spring of
the big snow and that Martha was born during harvest. But
they do not use our highly intricate and conventional calendar
and cannot name the date. John is obviously older than Martha,
but if both children had died in infancy the parents may now
be undecided as to which was first. Several years ago a Viennese
journalist had many interviews with an illiterate Austrian peas-
ant who had worked his way, at first with a horse and cart and
then on foot, from Austria through Siberia and across Bering
Strait to Alaska. The book which resulted, *Thirty Years in the*

Golden North, is a remarkable tale of adventure, but the journalist was not able to put events in either their geographical or their temporal order. The illiterate adventurer was often too close to the border of starvation to bother with place names. He had no system of dating and was unable to tell the year in which most of the events had happened. What order was given the account was done with the aid of a map.

In the *fugues* which have been described the victims were educated persons, and their inability to account for the period covered by the fugue is surprising because they have the skill and the language necessary and can account for other periods in their lives. Functional losses of memory like these strongly resemble voluntary changes of rôle. The only things forgotten in many instances are the items that would compel the recognition of the deserted character part. It is as if the small boy who has been playing all morning that he is a fireman should change after lunch and be a soldier. He now disregards his fire truck and if he imitates its gong occasionally it will be inadvertent. He is now a soldier and his actions are ruled and integrated by that rôle. He carries a gun and marches, instead of dashing to fires.

For those occasional short periods of loss of memory which follow head injuries and occur frequently in football we have no adequate explanation. Many players have, following such an injury, gone about their affairs for the next few hours and, in two cases recounted to me by the victims, for a day or more, but have later been unable to give any account of the period following the injury. In some instances the player has continued in the game, but later remembers nothing.

Some amnesias are accompanied by radical differences in behavior, and the writings of Morton Prince have treated these as changes in personality. For over a generation the public was much stirred over the notion that two personalities could occupy the same body alternately with characters and interests as different as those attaching to Dr. Jekyll and Mr. Hyde. A girl leaves college where life has been rather too much for her and is discovered a few weeks later a waitress in a cheap restaurant with no memory of her college status or her former life. She has taken on a different manner to suit her surroundings and gives a very different general impression. Or a lawyer with a large income leaves a tangle of professional and domestic affairs including a mounting debt and is discovered in a small shop selling candy and toys to the children of a nearby village school. Here he has fitted into his new rôle and his manners of the big-city prosperous lawyer have become rustic. Prince reports another type of case, a case in which there are two or more "personalities" and some of these are perfectly aware of the others and enjoy teasing and annoying them. I confess to complete scepticism over these descriptions. I suspect that the women involved were playing up to what the physician obviously hoped for.

We are all aware that our behavior and our thoughts alter with changing mood. When we are depressed we tend to think of depressing things and our actions are those of a depressed person. The associative cues for all thought and action include not only what we see and hear but our own attitude; and the influence of attitude is apt to be greater than the influence of external cues. When we are elated we think of assets and when we are depressed we think of our debts. A too heavy meal makes us dwell on memories of sea voyages that were rough and on motor roads that had too many curves. Most habitual drunkards have a drunken line of action and speech to which they always revert when drunk. Janet explains in such terms the alterations of personality that seem to take place. Usually a period of depression marks the beginning of a fugue. The individual finds life too burdensome and escapes to a simpler environment. The return of physical energy brings a return of more active be-

havior and the return of the memories of a more active life. I
was once asked by a friend about to undergo an appendectomy
what it was like. My own memories were of a pleasant hospital,
bright summer weather, a room with many flowers, cheerful
nurses and a chatty surgeon. This was told the friend. The next
morning I visited him after the operation. He opened his eyes
when I spoke and then closed them and murmured something.
I leaned closer and asked him what he had said. It was, to paraphrase his brief and profane statement, to the effect that I had
grossly misstated the facts. But I had already on entering the
sick room and smelling the ether recalled many of the painful
details which did not occur to me the afternoon before.

Many fugues are the result of a state of lowered vitality and a
lowered capacity for facing life. The change of emotional state
plus the change of scene and neighbors operates to exclude
thoughts of home and of the character part that was being
played. This does not constitute a fugue, but is a fertile ground
for its development.

It should be mentioned that an association test will betray
the presence of the verbal associations that are denied by the
amnesia patient. When the stimulus word is uttered and the
subject has been told to respond with the first word that comes
to him and in the shortest possible time, either the response
word will be appropriate to his deserted personality or he will
show the signs of evasion, the lengthened reaction time, repetition of the stimulus word instead of responding, or an emotional
reaction.

Freud claims that all unpleasant memories tend to be repressed and pleasant memories to be retained subject to recall.
This is doubtful, and a number of experimental studies have
given very ambiguous results. If recall is attempted when we
are having a similar unpleasant experience, the advantage will

be with the unpleasant rather than the pleasant. With slight hunger or slight erotic emotion the cues for relevant desires are present. The cues for nausea are not likely to be present in a laboratory test. But probably memories of nausea are as efficiently or more efficiently evoked by a slight qualm than are memories of pleasant food evoked by slight hunger.

Both memory and its occasional functional loss are characteristically adaptive, as is behavior in general. The registration of an experience which establishes the associations through which it can be later recalled is an adaptive result of training. We learn only gradually the art of putting experiences into words. The acquisition of this art comes through years of practice which is governed by trial and error. We discover that certain expressions produce in others the form of cooperation or the response for which we are set. We learn to modify our descriptions to fit the audience, for any narrative is determined by present conditions as well as by past events. We speak always with a present motive. Speech is a form of escape from something disturbing in our situation. Our early conversation is aimed at direct relief. The baby learns to indicate his wants because the sounds that he makes have on past occasions brought relief from these wants. The motives that operate in adult speech become extremely complicated and hard to trace. What is it that drives our friend to unburden himself at length on the subject of his recent stay in the hospital or his admirable handling of a recent business deal or to hold forth at such length on the state of the country? We can often understand the motive if we give it our attention. The condition of our own health can obviously be a source of unrest, and our preoccupation with it in conversation when we can find an interested listener derives from anxieties over threatened illness and the fact that we are adjusted to receiving sympathy from others. That need for sympathy when we are in trouble depends, of course, on past training. There are families in which children are not given sympathetic attention during their minor ills. Such children would find less need for sympathy and less occasion to elicit it through conversation when they are older.

We learn to notice those features of an event that will interest our friends. I believe it was Watson who mentioned that the most important part of golf is played in the locker room. We learn eventually to do those things and to notice those things which will be readily listened to by others. We select our vacation place according to its talking points as well as its physical comforts or its promise of relaxation or diversion. We also fit our account of what we have done to our listener. Our vacation is remembered differently for Aunt Martha and for our boon companions. We tell each of them different features of the trip and our manner of speech is fitted to their reception of it. All memories are essentially narrative and are adjustments to a present situation. Memories change with present needs and present interests.

The fugue represents the extreme of such a change. It is now highly undesirable to be the person we have been or to have the responsibilities that we have been carrying. The same unwillingness to be Mr. John Doe that leads one man to give an assumed name when he is questioned may, in extreme cases, lead another to think the assumed name in his own inner reflection. The fugitive from justice denies his identity and that part of his history that would lead to the discovery of who he is. The depressed individual learns not only to deny his name to others but to avoid thinking it himself. It is highly significant that nearly all fugues are accompanied by a radical change in scene and that restoration to the family and the home or the appearance of family friends usually leads to an acknowledgment within a short time. In the home environment there are too many cues for the real name. It cannot be avoided. While on the excursion to strange places that accompanied the fugue, these reminders were absent. The functional amnesias thus appear to be, like the symptoms of hysteria, adaptive reactions to disturbing conflicts within the personality.

XXIV

THE FAMILY AS A SOURCE OF CONFLICT

THE principle of gravitation, though we assume that every particle of matter including our own bodies continuously behaves in accordance with it, does not enable us to understand the physical geography of the earth's surface, its hills and valleys, rivers and snow caps, or the movements of the living creatures who occupy that surface. But the principle of gravitation, though not one person in a hundred or perhaps a thousand can state it as a physicist would state it, is illustrated in all the changes in the earth's crust and in all the movements of animals. And in its terms we can predict many events in our world.

There is a certain likeness between the principle of gravitation and the principle of associative learning. In terms of association only, we cannot predict what will happen to any person or what habits he will form. We know only that his actions in the future will derive from his behavior in the past and that his responses can become attached to new features of his situation and that new patterns of response rise from combinations of the old. The principle alone will not tell us that this child will grow up to be a banker or a baker or a drug addict or a wise and humane physician. We only know that whatever he is caused to do is likely to be repeated when he meets again some of the circumstances in which he did it. But we do not know what he will be caused to do because we do not know what stimuli will be brought to bear on him, what his environment will be or what the manners of his neighbors.

We can tell something of him in advance from our knowledge of constant states. We know that all men, whatever their culture and whatever their history of individual accident, will tend to learn some type of behavior which will be consistent with a maintained blood temperature. They will have learned some artifices by which to warm themselves when cold and to cool themselves when warm. They will learn to find salt that will maintain the definite proportion of salts normal in the blood stream. They will learn to rest and lessen effort when the ratio of carbon dioxide to oxygen in the blood is above its normal. We know that they will acquire some habits that will keep blood sugar within definite limits. We cannot predict just what these habits will be, whether the blood sugar will be provided from the meat of seals which the hunter has learned to harpoon or from the bowl in the Child's restaurant to which money earned by selling insurance gives access. We know that after maturity some manner of relief from sexual tension physiologically produced will be discovered, whether through the approved ways of marriage, by clandestine arrangement, by perverse means, or by sublimation in exercise and work.

In order to know the particular methods that a man will use to restore his constant states we must have two other kinds of information about him, as well as know that he is capable of learning by association. How the creatures without mind, the grass and the trees and the lower forms of animal life, will meet such disturbances we know in advance by observation of other members of their species. But creatures with minds, that is, creatures that can alter their forms of defense, are less predictable. In man we must know something of the *culture*, which will give us some information of other constant states which are not physiological. His neighbors will enforce upon him their manners and speech. Departures from the folkways on his part will upset and annoy his fellow tribesmen because such departures will threaten their own habits. Their annoyance will last until they have in turn disturbed the man himself and brought about a trial and error conformity in his behavior. The customs with which we are surrounded thus become like the constant states which guide our learning. The breach of a custom has effects like a departure from normal temperature or from normal water content; it can be equally disturbing and by being disturbing it coerces learning and brings conformity.

If, then, we attempt to examine the situations which lead to conflict and neurosis in the individual we must know something of his cultural surroundings. Even the problems of getting food, keeping warm, satisfying thirst, or relieving the system of waste are tremendously complicated by social demands on conduct. If a lack of food has distressed us it is not enough that we find food and eat it. We must get it by approved ways and eat it with certain manners, else we may suffer annoyances which are far greater than the annoyance of hunger. Many persons have starved with food about them but with social conventions barring the way. When it is a question of finding a mate, this becomes still more complicated because two independent learning systems are concerned. There must be cooperation between two separate individuals. Food does not have thus to be courted.

There is another source of information about a man that is as necessary for predicting his behavior as is a knowledge of associative learning and a knowledge of his cultural surroundings. That other source is his own past. He is at any moment a creature of habits which resulted from previous learning. If we know his culture we know that he will earn his living in one of the prevailing ways. Knowing his past, we can know also which one of these ways he will use.

This is intended as something of a warning. If we believe that from family relationships arise many failures of adaptation and many distressing conflicts and so undertake an examination of the family to discover how it produces these failures and these conflicts, we must bear in mind that the particular culture is the general background of all action and that our results will apply only to the types of families that we have examined. In other cultures our findings would be very different, because in other cultures families would be very different.

It is quite possible to apply our knowledge of the nature of learning to many common situations in family life and to add to our understanding of their results. We can in terms of associative learning anticipate the effects of many situations, or we can learn to avoid certain undesirable effects by interfering and altering the circumstances which produce them.

The most ambitious psychology of the family so far is that offered by Freud and other psychoanalysts. They have outlined the drama of the individual in terms of his early experiences in the family. The experience of birth, the early attachment to the mother centering around the breasts as a source of pleasure, the early encounters with regulation of eliminations, together with hostile attitudes originating in the failure to get enough milk, weaning, jealousy of the next child, the frustration of erotic wishes, combined with intense and prolonged fixation of desire upon the father, are held by Freud (*New Introductory Lectures*, p. 164) to determine the main outlines of the personality and to furnish the basis of future conflicts and neuroses.

The Freudian account has gone astray in two respects. It has read into the drama of the infant a great deal that belongs only to the psychology of the adult because it is not based on the observation of infants. And it has attempted to write the dramas of all infants as one drama in spite of the tremendous differences in circumstances encountered by infants in different families. We are attempting to understand why one person becomes neurotic and another does not. To attribute this fact to a very limited number of features of early environment is bound to fail. But it must be recognized that the Freudians have brought to light a great many facts whose existence had not been suspected, and that many of their explanations of individual traits, particularly those having to do with erotic interest, will probably stand the test of time and observation.

Among the common familial situations that lead to serious conflict when the children in the family reach maturity, one of the most important concerns the dependence of the child on its parents, particularly the mother. In early months this dependence is almost complete. The infant lives by what Overstreet has called in adults the nuisance technique. Disturbances of the infant's constant states which produce restlessness and crying are eventually relieved through gaining the mother's attention. Cold, hunger, pins, cramped position, colic, all serve as motives which guide the child to keep the mother distraught until she in her turn escapes by performing the necessary service for the child. The manner of her care has been determined in advance by the traditions of her culture. There are things that mothers do and things that they do not do. Departure from these brings its own punishment from the adults about her.

But the care of the child, particularly the twenty-four-hour care of a very small infant, becomes in the mother first a habit and then a permanent interest. Other interests have yielded place to it and eventually the mother is in her turn dependent upon the child. Her life becomes identified with the welfare of the baby and her motherhood an essential part of her personality. With the loss of the child she would find herself adrift and purposeless.

Whether or not there is a strictly erotic component in the child's attitude toward its parents depends on the extent to which it receives from them erogenous stimulation which creates erotic tensions. To call the child's interest in the mother incestuous as Freud does is absurd save in those cases in which the mother has specifically incited it. Actual fondness for the mother derives from the fact that appeal to her is associated with practically all the annoying situations of infancy. For her the infant has interests motivated by hunger, cold, pain, ennui, and by a mass of habits which are all drives in that their interruption is disturbing.

The time arrives when the child begins to develop interests of its own. When school is begun new habits must be learned and increasing self-dependence established. By the age of sixteen not only have most children advanced far toward forming interests outside the family, but approximately one-half of all children have developed an intelligence superior to that of their parents. Settled habits have been established toward mother and father. Parents are no longer thrilling or exciting as are new acquaintances from without the household. In a static culture the habits of obedience to parents are likely to remain. The parents have the advantage of greater wisdom and information. But in a rapidly changing culture the younger generation may be actually in better touch with the times than the older, which has the handicap of adjustment to a world which has now become old-fashioned. The present American father and mother of fifty first adapted themselves to a world without electricity, without telephones, automobiles, trailers, oil burners, airplanes, cinemas, the radio. Their world in many ways resembled more closely the world of Shakespeare's day than it did the present. The boy or girl of sixteen is often more skilled and better informed in details of the modern environment than the parent. Ideas and morals change less rapidly than the physical environment, but they do change; and the older man may find himself one of a Tory minority that looks in fear at social changes which do not in the least daunt his children.

The development of outside interests and new ideas and new skills by the younger generation threatens the family pecking order. The ascendance of the father, in so far as it is based on superior strength and superior intelligence, is challenged. One of the main interests of numerous college students becomes freedom from interference by the parents. Parental care and supervision, necessary for survival in the early years, become harsh annoyances. By the time that a child who is increasing in size and strength and intelligence has reached adolescence the parental habits of care and supervision are often left several years behind. By the time that parents have learned the degree of responsibility that may be allowed a child of five, the child has become seven. Parents' habits tend to be static. They do not, like the child's strength and intelligence, have a natural biological rate of change. During the war at least two colonels of draft regiments and probably many others had requests from mothers that they see to it that sons wore their heavy underwear beginning October first.

In the adolescent himself growing interests plus static parental rule mean a confusion of habit. Proneness to submit to care has become habitual, but this conflicts with the new interests established outside the family circle. The volumes written by the last generation of psychologists and educators blamed this state of "storm and stress" on the physiological changes of adolescence. This was a mistaken notion. There is no special psychology of adolescence. In primitive cultures in which there is less difference between the interests of adults and children such "storm and stress" periods fail to appear. In our own culture in those special cases where children are protected from outside contacts until seventeen or eighteen, the emotional crisis is postponed until there is this exposure to new interests.

In many instances parents, usually mothers, react to this increasing independence of children with extreme annoyance. The most conspicuous instances are in those cases where the mother has lost her husband by death or divorce or has ceased to feel affection for the stout, bald and stodgy person who has replaced her bridegroom, and centers her interest in her son. Especially when he is an only son the mother often fights bitterly his increasing independence and eventually finds ways to overcome it. She may contribute to and welcome failure on his part, or illness, because these serve to keep him with her. Especially when she is threatened with displacement by a bride will she become jealous and exert herself. Jealousy of a daughter-in-law often breaks up a marriage, with disastrous results to the son.

If the widow is left with a daughter instead of a son the transfer of erotic interest is less likely to form part of the situation. In addition to lifelong habits of care and supervision there are, instead of erotic interest, habits of dependence on the daughter's services. By one means or another the mother manages to prolong the daughter's dependence. The rôle of mother and the authority that goes with that rôle are difficult to lay aside, particularly if there is no other part at hand to play.

If son or daughter has no physical inadequacy the development of outside interests leads to a revolt against continued dependence on the mother, and eventually to freedom. The strength of the revolt and its emotional reinforcement may be measured by the strength of the habits of dependence which have been cultivated in the child. Toward the mother an ambivalent attitude is formed, a mixture of obedient affection and of hostile irritation, or, in the extreme, of love and hate. Of these two, the dislike or hate is the attitude which tends to be unconscious and unmentioned because social conventions and the mother's own verbalization give fluent expression to the attachment, but leave the hostility without words.

Where children have been allowed to take their own initiative or have been put upon their own responsibility as rapidly as they developed the capacity for that responsibility, this conflict is avoided. There are a great many families where the parents have had either sufficient insight or sufficient indifference to bring up their children as free individuals, capable of making their own decisions. There are other families in which this has been made impossible and sons and daughters of thirty-five are not trusted to make their own plans. In many such instances a year away from home at the critical age, from sixteen to eighteen, would have been sufficient to achieve independence and the capacity for life as a separate personality.

In our local clinic Stevenson Smith once noticed that a small boy from an orphanage who was seated at a table about to take a test allowed the pencil which was placed before him to roll slowly to the edge of the table and fall to the floor. The boy watched the pencil as it rolled but made no move to pick it up. Becoming curious, Smith tried out the same situation with some fifteen orphanage children. Nine of them behaved like the first and made no move to save the pencil from falling. The next fifteen children who visited the clinic, none of them from institutions but children living with their own family, were exposed to the same situation. Without exception they reached promptly for the pencil when they saw it in danger of rolling off and either placed it in a safe position or held in their hands. In a large institution it is far easier to discourage children from taking the initiative in such tasks as opening windows or moving furniture, and to have these done only by an adult or at the command of an adult. To allow the children to make decisions on their own initiative would lead to a certain amount of confusion and trouble. The result is to make the institution child less likely to attack problems on his own responsibility. Undoubtedly many homes approximate this training. Other homes encourage initiative to develop. In some families the mother insists on the selection of all playmates and the child acquires no capacity for making approaches to others. A boy from a well-to-do and carefully protected home may grow up with no ability to make friends and as an adult be limited to those who make advances toward him because of his wealth. There are many cases of children too carefully reared who fall into low company by virtue of the very care of their upbringing. The dependent child does not suffer the effects of his overprotection until he is thrown on his own resources.

Enforced obedience and discipline have effects which depend on the manner of the enforcement. The difference between a slave and a free man lies not in the amount of labor that they perform or in the physical comfort in which they live. Woodward's *Life of Washington* describes Washington's puzzled surprise when he found that the free workmen in Philadelphia regularly laid up six times as many brick in a day's work as his slaves did on the plantation. And many slaves lived in better quarters with more food than the free worker could provide himself. The objection to being slaves is an objection to acting in accord with the plans of others. Slavery must therefore be enforced at the start with severe punishment. If its discipline is constant and consistent the slave becomes adjusted to that state and often incapable of making his own plans or acting on his own responsibility. Many stories of southern slaves after their liberation illustrate this fact. Return to the owner and to his service was often voluntary.

The condition of a child in the family is somewhat the condition of the slave. If the parental enforcement of obedience is consistent and regular, the child becomes accustomed to falling in with parental commands. Prussian family discipline has for generations been of this absolute character and is undoubtedly at the foundation of the obedience to the state and the ready transfer of this authority to whatever régime is in power. Modern German nursery schools, according to Lewin, emphasize this discipline. Children are to be accustomed to prompt obedience and are not to be given reasons for orders.

In many families there can be no consistent enforcement of discipline because family authority is divided, or because there is conflict of interests between parents, or because one parent commands in erratic and inconsistent fashion. When a father sometimes becomes enraged because a child disturbs the household with noise, but on other occasions tolerates or encourages such noise, the child can form no regular habit and is provoked to anger and revolt. Goodenough has collected information that the number of temper tantrums per month indulged in by a child is closely associated with the number of adults in the household. The more grown-ups, the more tantrums. The explanation is obvious. The more grown-ups, the more interference and the less consistency in that interference. Not only children break down under such circumstances. I am told of a carpenter who recently withdrew from a contract to build a house after a week's experience with the three women for whom it was to be built.

The overdisciplined child is in the condition of the slave adjusted to slavery. He may prosper so long as he does not encounter responsibility. But he is socially inadequate and may also be socially timid. Irregular and capricious discipline has a different effect. Emotional excitement and revolt are its results. The final results depend somewhat on the physical constitution of the child, on his capacity for emotional reinforcement, on his "spirit." If "spirited," the child tends to develop a resistance to capricious discipline. This may eventually lead to running away from home to find independence as soon as possible. In many cases such a boy is left not only with a hatred of the father but with an angry resentment of all authority. The active revolutionary often has this background.

Similar relationships often hold between mother and daughter. A mother who is domineering and intelligent, who tends always to lead the conversation and who always dictates the plans may have a daughter who, being spirited, is stirred to revolt and competition. She learns to compete with the mother at getting attention and in having her own way. But if the daughter has less physical energy and spirit she will learn not to compete with the mother, to be silent in the mother's presence and to keep her thoughts strictly to herself, if revolt has been thoroughly inhibited.

College advisers are sometimes visited by mothers with large and able-bodied sons in tow. The son is not doing well in his courses. If the adviser directs questions at the boy in an attempt to find his interests, the mother answers for him. The boy sits passively, giving the interview rather little attention. He is not going to be called on to speak, because he is never called on to speak in his mother's presence. The mother explains how devoted she is to his success and how zealously she superintends his study. In spite of this he fails to master his subjects. She has herself sat with him every evening while he prepared his mathematics assignment for the next day. The adviser is in an embarrassing position. He may hesitate to urge that the boy be left quite to himself, probably to fail in mathematics which has undoubtedly become highly distasteful to him. His real interests are not mentioned in his mother's presence, because this leads to argument and his mother wins all arguments. He should, of course, be turned out "on his own" and allowed to work under his own power.

Illness and physical defect in a child are likely to bring about corresponding overcare from parents. The blind child who receives sympathy and from whom nothing is required learns to use his infirmity to excuse him from effort. Among blind college students there are great differences. Some insist on performing much the same tasks that other students are called on to perform. Others demand special consideration whenever they can. The record of one successful girl who later earned an independent living by her music was a record of Spartan treatment in the family, deliberately undertaken by wise parents. When she stumbled over a piece of furniture she was calmly admonished to look where she was going. She had her own share of household duties which equaled the share of the others. Excuses for her were not made in her presence. On the treatment of the handicapped child by the family will depend in large measure the nature of the rôle that he adopts, the way in which he describes to himself his part in life.

There are countless other specific family situations which lead to trouble. One child may have set a school standard which is beyond the ability of another to reach, and failure brings acute distress and a conviction of guilt and inferiority. In the youngest of the family either too much assistance and affection from the others may be a poor training for facing the world by himself, or the experience of living among persons who are all his mental and physical superiors during his growing years may deprive him of initiative. A father's attempts to drive his son to carry out his own unachieved ambitions may place the son in a profession that he hates and insure his failure. We cannot create interests in children by forcing them to tasks. Even an infant's interest in his bottle can be made negative when an anxious and tense mother notes that the prescribed amount has not yet been taken and forces the nipple into the infant's mouth. The bottle becomes a cue for shutting the mouth and turning the head away.

In the development of the erotic interests of children many parents are so concerned over premature sex activity that their sole contribution to the training of the child is in the observation and enforcement of strict tabus on speech and behavior. In a past generation this attitude extended into the school system and it was the practice to submit high school and college youths to lectures on sex morality which aimed to associate erotic interests with such fear and disgust that their expression would be controlled until marriage. When these lectures, which were given by a curious group of ignorant and emotional speakers, were successful the result was undoubtedly serious trouble in many later marriages. Attitudes were established which made impossible the normal enjoyment of marital relations. A too successful repression of erotic interest prepares good soil for the development of perversions.

In the place of such lectures as used to be aimed at making sex disgusting, there followed a movement to give instruction in sex hygiene to children. This included efforts to induce parents to desert the tabus which grow up about the subject of love in the family and to encourage free discussion. This practice is undoubtedly an improvement, but it also has its questionable side. It is quite certain that romantic love depends for much of its interest and much of its emotion on these tabus. And if we conclude that the romantic attachment is an important aid in bringing about the violent readjustment of habits which must be achieved when a bride and groom from different households set up a home of their own, the freedom from tabu cannot be pronounced an unmixed good. Freedom from tabu amounts to a freedom from glamour. This is, however, probably not a serious danger. Instruction in the physiology of digestion which makes clear what the beefsteak will be like an hour after it is eaten robs few people of appetite.

In many families there develop preferences of the parents for one child or the other. This tends to be a preference of the father for a girl and of the mother for a boy. If the parents are given to quarreling or uttering other expressions of hostility or distrust, attitudes are built up in the children which endure to alter the children's own adult relationships in marriage. Hamilton's *Research in Marriage* and its popular résumé in *What Is Wrong with Marriage* by Hamilton and MacGowan offer some slight evidence that girls who were led by the mother's hostility to dislike the father keep the patterns of this dislike and tend to express it later toward their own husbands. They fall readily into recriminations and suspicions that they have heard expressed in their own childhood. The extent to which mutual hostility between parents is reflected in marriage difficulties in offspring is not yet accurately known, but it undoubtedly represents a strong tendency. The same remarks apply to the boy in the household. Hamilton reports that boys who admired their mothers and sisters and believed them beautiful and attractive were more often happily married than those who did not.

It would be absurd to attempt an exhaustive account of the familial sources of conflict and maladjustment because their variety is infinite. We have done no more than to consider a few illustrative situations and their effects. Familial problems will change rapidly with the extensive movement of the American population to cities and to apartment life which is now in progress. Youth organizations, organized play and sports, the movies, radio, the motor car are all encroaching on the influence of the family on the development of interests and personality traits. There are modern families in which the chief conflict centers about the use of the family car. With a new generation the psychology of the family may offer a new set of problems.

XXV

MARITAL SOURCES OF CONFLICT
AND NEUROSIS

A BULLETIN of the United States Department of Agriculture on the subject of pigeon-raising states that pigeons may be led into a comparatively lasting mating by placing them for a number of weeks in adjoining cages so that each is the most prominent object in the other's field of vision. Although the federal government has not yet covered that item in its advices to citizens, there are canny mothers of marriageable daughters who realize that adjoining deck chairs on an ocean cruise or their equivalent may do for human attachments what propinquity accomplishes for the pigeon. In the United States the conventional history of a marriage has been supposed to begin with an interest aroused in the young man. A glance through the women's magazines or through the last edition of the Sears-Roebuck catalogue would lead to the conviction that the Trobriand Island native's belief that the eye is the seat and source of love is shared in our own country. Advertisements that would recognize the old Russian admonition to use the ears also in the choice of a mate are non-existent.

The eventual fortunes of most marriages depend on the organization of desires which has taken place long before the marriage itself. Each party to the union enters it with hopes and ambitions, some of them articulate and some of them nameless. Obviously no census of these antecedent desires could be taken. Their existence can only be inferred from the varieties of disappointments that can be observed in later behavior. In many cases what the young man or woman wanted out of marriage is not known to him or her. The longing is inarticulate. The outcome may be deep-seated and lasting gratification or a recurring sense of frustration and anxiety, and in neither case may the person himself be able to put into words the source of his gratification or of his frustration.

It is a common error to assume that erotic drive is the one outstanding motivation of marriage. If this were the case, frustration would attach to marriage only in those cases in which there are actual barriers to erotic relief. We find, however, that disappointment and frustration are not limited to the unmarried and to that small proportion of the married in whom there are such barriers. Disappointment is fully as prevalent among married persons as among spinsters and bachelors. The reason for this is that the motives which lead to marriage are often more concerned with social status and prestige, with security and protection and service, with income, with a need for a companion to whom one can speak without fear and restraint. The intimacies of love can introduce a relationship that is free from the elaborate and difficult guard that must be placed upon public utterances or general conversation. Many marriages are responses to the pressure of friends and relatives, to the assumption that marriage is the proper state for everyone. Social pressure may lead into marriage persons in whom the sexual drive itself is absent. The choice of a beautiful wife may have little or no connection with erotic interests. The man may find his daydreams concerned with triumphant appearances with her in public, expressions of envy among his male friends, a stir in the dining room of the grand hotel as he and she make their entrance. Her beauty serves to reassure him of his own power. A girl may find intense gratification in marrying a man with the prestige of intellect or income. The public respect with which he is received is flattering to the woman who can hold the affection of such a public character. None of these are erotic motives.

There are marriages in which children are part of the plan. The rôle of mother and father has been adopted before the event of the birth of the child. There are other marriages in which only one of the pair has looked forward to that event and the birth of the child arrives as a kind of natural catastrophe to the other. In most instances the tremendous reorganization of habits and interests that a baby forces upon the young married pair is made without difficulty. The excitement of the new experience serves to reorganize desire and ambition to meet the new duties. But the change of rôle is a violent one. The girl who has been devoted to her own immediate interests and has been living in a whole-hearted pursuit of pleasure in which the important decisions concern the style of the next dress or the choice of a hairdresser or a shade of nail enamel is compelled to devote herself for twenty-four hours a day to the care of a baby. If, instead of leisure, she has been absorbed in ambitions of a career, the arrival of a child may be even more upsetting. Unless her physique and spirit are equal to the demand for a reorganization of habits and personality, she may be left with persistent conflict. Her resentment of the child is usually unconscious or inarticulate because such resentment is not acceptable to the public. She does not put her hostility to the child into words because there is no occasion for rehearsing even inner speech on that item. The argument with friends and relatives would be lost before it was begun. But the child may be made to feel the inarticulate hostility. No one has made a census of the number of American mothers who believe that in them the world lost a brilliant writer or a brilliant interior decorator. Health and spirit and intelligence serve, of course, to reconcile the child with a career if ambition has been deep-seated.

Very little has been written concerning the disturbance of rôle that is imposed on the father by his fatherhood, but this too leads to inarticulate resentments that in inadequate males often result eventually in the desertion of the family, with or without the excuse of a functional amnesia. One of the motives when men marry is the escape from boarding house and hotel quarters, food and associations. The girl he marries may have been impelled by desires for the comfort and prestige of an attendant male, and be quite without any interest in the provision of a home. Her daydreams have concerned appearances at the theater, at social gatherings, at public eating places with an attentive squire. His daydreams may have dealt with the type of evening and the type of home life made familiar to the public through the advertisements of the American Radiator Company.

Between two persons who approach marriage with such different hopes there is bound to be misunderstanding. If the social tabus surrounding love and its expression have built up in the bride and groom a strongly reinforced romantic attachment, this will during the honeymoon period facilitate the break-up of old habits and interests and lead to the discovery of compatibilities. During this period quarrels may be frequent because of the clash of habits, but the excitement of the quarrel may provide the variation in behavior that discovers new ways around the difficulty. Disagreement and temper may be followed by reconciliation and concessions on the part of one or both.

After the readjustment of habits, the prolonged state of romantic excitement disappears because it depended on obstacles and conflict. Romantic emotion is replaced by routine habits. Husband and wife learn what to expect of each other and to adjust to each other's behavior. The excitement may be revived by threats to the new régime. The loss by death of a husband or wife usually causes more intense and lasting grief than the loss of a lover. The loss of a marriage partner involves much more serious disturbance of habit and interest and character rôle. Since marriage, once entered into, becomes an economic arrangement, a recognized social status, a partnership for mutual aid, a means to free conversation and intimacy, and eventually a complex and conservative habit system in itself as well as a means to the relief of erotic drive, threats to the continuation of the marriage may place a severe strain on the individual and will often lead to breakdown. An established marriage may maintain itself against misunderstanding and marital conflict because its interruption would threaten to disrupt all those habits which are formed about the household routine and those habits which lie behind the social rôle or character which the partners are maintaining. The higher divorce rate which prevails among apartment and hotel dwellers than among people living in their own homes indicates the conservative influence of household habits. Changing from one hotel to another or from one apartment to another may require very little change in habit.

Even in cultures where marriages are the results not of previous attachment and romantic love but of arrangements by parents, affection and tolerance normally develop and husband and wife adjust to common living. This adjustment is like any habit adaptation. A mutual "addiction" develops that is like the addiction to a long-continued diet or the addiction of a child to its mother and a mother to her child.

It was stated at the beginning of the chapter that propinquity has the same effect of establishing erotic interest in human beings that it has in pigeons. There are certain obvious exceptions to this. Brothers and sisters do not normally develop such interest in each other. Incest, or the mating of individuals with members of their immediate family, is an extreme exception and not a rule. It would be very rare even if no social tabus enforced it with punishment and social disapproval. The reason for the rare occurrence of incest is that in human beings attitudes toward other members of the household are established before sexual maturity and before erotic drive attains its full effectiveness. Immature members of the same household fix their attitudes toward each other without the reinforcement of sexual tensions and these attitudes forestall the possible development of erotic interests. A close analogy is found in the unwillingness of a child to share in the eating of the rabbit which has been raised as a pet. Love and courtship involve attitudes so unlike those which are built up by daily contact in a household that they are excluded toward housemates. It is quite significant that this natural avoidance of incest applies only to housemates and that a brother and sister reared apart may fall in love, while a brother and foster sister reared in the same household do not. Associative inhibition of erotic interest has been prepared by the non-erotic attitudes, rivalries, jealousies, cooperations in play and household duties that are associated with the housemate during childhood.

The reason for devoting so much attention to the absence of erotic interest in those who are members of the same household during infancy and childhood is that the same determining factors may lead to the development of a like indifference between husband and wife and may lead to the associative inhibition of marital love. The presence of husband or wife during periods when affectionate behavior is inhibited by fatigue or by anxiety over finances or by the demands of caring for children or by illness may make that presence a cue for the new attitude and this may supplant the other. Depending on the circumstances, affection may undergo what has been called positive adaptation and the pair become increasingly attached, or negative adaptation and affection be gradually supplanted by other attitudes.

At its best marriage includes some of the deepest gratifications known to man. Establishing a lasting partnership in love with mutual confidence and mutual enjoyment serves as an anchor which enables many persons to ride out storms of adverse circumstance. Such a partnership enables both parties to face the world. When not at its best, marriage is responsible for many breakdowns of morale and mental health. What the outcome of any marriage will be depends to an important extent upon the desires, conscious and unconscious, which lead up to it. No two persons want the same things out of marriage, and what is wanted depends on previous experience. A certain amount of daydreaming and novel-reading or play-going may have directed a girl's desire toward a prince charming who is not adequately represented by the insurance agent with a taste for following the races whom she eventually marries. There may be no living girl who would fit the romantic dreams of a boy who has depended on reading and fantasy for the details of his love object. The girl whose early experience has established an interest in mothering and managing may find a husband who was not looking for care and direction but for someone to dominate. The man who had established a strong dependence on his mother and is incapable of making responsible decisions for himself may find that his wife has equal tendencies to rely on others and that together they are helpless. Appearance and dress play an important part in first attraction but in these days of standardized and much publicized fashions they have little to do with traits of personality.

Ordinarily this discrepancy between desire and reality is not serious. Unless there are deep-seated conflicts of habits and interests between the two, each learns to desire the other and the earlier desires are forgotten for new interests. Wives adapt to golfing husbands or to business addicts. Husbands, somewhat less readily, learn to tolerate formal dining or a household planned for bridge parties. It is only where the conflict of interests involves the deeper and more conservative traits of personality that adjustment is certain to fail.

Hamilton's *Research in Marriage* places the blame for most marital difficulties on the training and environment of the individual during his childhood. This conclusion is drawn from the results of a study in which one hundred married men and one hundred married women were persuaded to answer some four hundred questions bearing on their marriage and their previous history. They list as first of the impediments to adjustment in marriage the mother who, having no normal sex life with her husband, turns her affection upon her son and takes measures to render him completely dependent on her. If the son is brought to rebel eventually, this rebellion will be against all women and his marriage cannot be successful. If he does not rebel, his attachment to his mother will prevail over his attachment to his wife. They mention also the rarer case of the son who has been led by his father to despise his mother. It appears essential that a boy have developed favorable attitudes toward mother and sister in order that he may have ready such an attitude for his wife. Hamilton reports very few cases of girls who developed overdependence on the father. The father is usually too little concerned with the girl's upbringing. But he has many instances in which the mother's hostility toward the father or her expressions of contempt and disdain organize in the girl an attitude that is readily attached to the husband. To the attitudes established by prudish training in the early home environment Hamilton attributes many forms of inability to reach full relief of erotic tension and this, in either partner, tends strongly to render a marriage unhappy. The attachment of disgust and shame to what is related to love often results in the destruction of a marriage. The partner is despised.

It should be noted, however, that neither male impotence nor female frigidity is the direct occasion of neurosis. It is quite possible to live an active and long life without erotic experience. It is only in so far as these misdirectings of interest lead the individual into conflict and into intolerable situations that they threaten mental health. Impotence, for instance, which has been the result of the inhibition of erotic tension by a terrifying experience or by prudish training, leads to nervous breakdown only through its secondary effects. In the rôle or character which the majority of all males adopt through social direction there is included the part of the male. This involves notions of physical strength and size, of the ability to command respect and attention, and particularly to command the respect and attention of the opposite sex. A knowledge or a suspicion that he is not capable of taking the proper part of a male in love-making interferes seriously with this rôle and may lead to tremendous efforts to compensate for the lack. Delusions may develop and the man find that he is a reincarnation of the Messiah because this would explain his lack of interest in Eros and at the same time endow him with gratifying prestige. Or, where the deficiency is not absolute but only enough to cause misgiving, the man may find it reassuring to devote himself to the courtship of many women. Don Juan's life is a desperate attempt to prove to himself and others against his own inner suspicions that he is a male. Such demonstration the normal individual does not require. Boasting of conquests with the opposite sex has the same origin. In many cases the boasting has no foundation, but serves to preserve the rôle of masculinity.

In some instances these forms of behavior appear in late middle age and are the signs of a diminished physiological drive. After forty many men become more susceptible to transient love-making because they are aware that they are becoming inadequate to the masculine rôle.

Preoccupation with sex has obscured the fact that most marriages which encounter difficulties are threatened by non-erotic factors. The number of failures blamable on extremely divergent habits and interests is undoubtedly very large. When one of the pair has married out of his class, adjustment may depend on the social environment in which the marriage is placed. The "squaw man" may be well married so long as he himself goes native and and lives among his wife's people, but an attempt to introduce her into his own cultural environment may be disastrous. The habits of the more complex civilization can be fitted into the less complex more easily than can the ways of primitives be reconciled with a more sophisticated culture.

The failure of the husband to earn enough to sustain the rôle of the wife may lead to a loss of her respect. Two very similar instances in which women married men of lower economic status have recently had very different results. In one, the married pair withdrew from all touch with the girl's well-to-do relations and quickly adjusted themselves with the aid of romantic emotion to a life far different from the former life of the girl. In the other case, the maintained contact with family and relatives forbade the acceptance of the new rôle of poor man's wife and the necessary unpretentious status. The wife developed, with the assistance of her family, a tendency to hysterical illnesses that required expensive medical attention and eventually a separation from the husband and a return to the family.

In American middle-class families the husband is normally the bread-winner. His occupation demands a considerable share of his interest and energy. He meets more people during the day than his wife. The slight demands on time and energy made by a modern apartment leave the wife with more leisure. The husband's free time may be occupied with plans and daydreams that concern his business. The wife's freedom from responsibility is a source of unrest and dissatisfaction not always compensated for by bridge, clubs, music, shopping and the movies. So many more women than men develop hysterical illness that until the war hysteria was by many authorities regarded as a women's disorder. The combination of leisure with the lack of a satisfactory rôle favors the development of morbid forms of adjustment. An astonishing number of widows follow their release from marriage by the death of a husband with the development of new interests and a new life. Many women forced by marriage to take a subordinate place in the family find this a chronic source of discontent in an age in which the formal educations of the husband and wife are equal. The modern American use of life insurance frees these women for lives much more in accord with the rôles for which their training and the current social opinions of women's position have established them in their thinking. Widowhood brings freedom to express these notions in action in public life, charities, travel, business, and in new friendships.

XXVI

SOCIAL STATUS AND CONFLICT

THERE exist biological sources of unhappiness and maladjustment. Pain, disease, physical injury, famine, flood, storms, cold and heat all are capable of producing human distress. But the distress they produce is not distress at its worst. They result in death or in adaptation. We can grow used to an arduous life. Exposure to the weather, if it does not kill, loses its terrors. Hard labor is met with increasing strength of muscle and a greater capacity for exertion. Men become used to a diet that leaves hunger always gnawing. For acute distress and prolonged distress man himself is the most effective cause. The one thing that he cannot adapt to is himself.

In adapting to the world man alters his own nature and his habits. These alterations become part of him. He now not only defends those physiological constant states that are essential for life itself; he must also defend his new habits and ways. *It is in the conservation of his acquired nature that most of the sources of unhappiness arise.* A civilized man must not only have food; he must have the kinds of food to which he is used. He must not only keep warm; he must wear clothes that meet his taste. He may even starve to death rather than break the tabu against asking help, or he may risk death to maintain the good opinion of his fellows. His adaptations to his fellow man are the origin of his more serious troubles. Starvation carries with it none of the agonies that may be suffered by human beings who are in a position to gratify their physical wants.

The reason why men are the worst enemies of men is that learning can cope with trouble if trouble will only remain the same. Happiness in the sense of an adjustment that avoids breakdown is possible to Eskimos who live in constant danger of starvation or to slaves or to a hopeless cripple. It is to unpredictable change that adjustment is impossible, and man himself is the most variable thing in nature. Adaptation to his fellow man is the most difficult of all the adaptations that man is called on to make.

Among the adjustments that men make to their human surroundings, none is more important in giving unity and meaning to a man's life, in making him a consistent and understandable personality, than those habits which make up a man's notion of himself. He learns to guide his conduct in terms of verbal formulas. We have called these formulas his rôle. The rôle is made up of the acknowledged attributes of "I" or "Me." It may be present in thinking only on occasion. There are many times when a man *forgets himself*. When the rôle is present in some form, when a man "remembers himself" or remembers "who he is," the bits of speech or the fleeting words or gesture in terms of which he remembers serve to call up or to inhibit action and to make action consistent with the rôle. Knowing or acknowledging in so many words that he is industrious or lazy serves to guide action to ways that are deemed industrious or lazy. Knowing that he is a failure serves to make behavior appropriate to failure. Knowing who is "boss" serves to maintain the pecking order. A man may act as if he were well until he knows (remarks to himself) that he is sick, whereupon his conduct changes. A twelve-year-old may play contentedly with nine-year-olds until he recalls that he is older. He must then take the part of his years and cease to play as an equal. When we speak of realizing one's age we mean using the name of that age as a cue for appropriate action. The captain may talk with an enlisted man on equal terms until he remembers that he is a captain. The enlisted man may so far forget himself as to address his officer as man to man. When he "remembers himself" his attitude will change.

All this amounts to what we call *self-control,* which is the control of action in terms of the accepted description of the self. "Am I a man or a mouse?" If the answer is "man," we steel ourselves for manly action. But the inner answer may be "mouse." In that case we behave differently. The late Beran Wolfe in his extremely shrewd account of the nervous breakdown (now published with the title, *Calm Your Nerves*) borrows an expression supposedly translated from the Chinese for the description of this character part and its effect on action. He calls it "saving face." This description applies to an enormous number of human actions and attitudes.

We derive our notion of our rôle or "face" largely from others. This is partly because it is expressed and remembered in words and the words are learned from our fellows. It is also because the approval of others manifestly attaches to certain rôles and not to others. When small boys play war games, only threats and punishment compel the smaller and weaker boys to act the enemy. This part is often left to the dog or to the small brother without being really accepted.

A large proportion of all conflicts and nervous breakdowns concern failures to live up to an adopted rôle. The reason for this is that the success of a rôle depends on the acceptance of that rôle by other persons and this acceptance is often difficult to obtain. If the rôle is not well conceived and threatens the rôles of others, it meets resistance. It may conquer this resistance and all other obstacles, and we may retreat to an asylum where bizarre rôles are tolerated so long as they are not too intimately associated with action. There we lead the life of a king, modified by adherence to the hospital rules. We may wear our decorations and make an occasional royal speech if we do not object to eating at the table with commoners and taking our duty at the dishes afterward.

In feudal society the adoption of a rôle was regulated and forced. The son of the cobbler was assumed by his neighbors to be destined for the cobbler's bench. He might have childish deviations from this and fancy himself occasionally a knight or baron, but this kind of nonsense was not tolerated by his fellows as he grew older. It met ridicule and hostility and eventually corporal punishment. He dressed as the cobbler's son, ate the food of cobblers, pulled his forelock before the gentry as artisans did, and in general deported himself in a way that was taken for granted by himself and all others.

In a modern democracy there is, at least in public utterances and in the formulas of the public schools, no such forced assignment of rôles. In the United States children are sent to schools which presume to fit them for any save criminal parts in the community life. Ambition in the cobbler's son to be President is fostered and praised. It becomes a duty to improve oneself, that is, to adopt a rôle higher in social value than that of one's parents.

A large number of nervous breakdowns occur as individuals are confronted with a test of their adopted rôles—as the young pianist approaches his first concert, the officer his first command, the teacher her first classes, the freshman girl her entrance to college life, the young man or woman the event of marriage. In all these the rôle has been more or less accepted and has dominated and unified behavior. It is now threatened with failure. The young man has studied music and practiced the piano. In answer to the question, What are you going to do? he has replied, "Be a concert pianist." The public tolerates and encourages such an ambition; but it takes more than this tolerance to make an artistic success. The public must eventually be faced and won.

In these anticipatory breakdowns the conflict is between ambition or intention and a defense against hints of failure. The performer who anticipates offending his audience, the officer who fears that he lacks "power of command," the lover who fears that he may meet ridicule or scorn from his bride, the teacher who dreads not being able to interest her class and maintain discipline all face the test with confusion and conflict in their tendencies to action. The great majority of breakdowns just precede or follow such tests of rôle.

When there is a breakdown it will have certain interesting characteristics. The most outstanding feature of it, whether it takes the direction of an hysterical amnesia or paralysis or anesthesia or takes the form of a neurasthenic depression and leaves the victim prostrate, will be that "face" will be saved. In some fashion the rôle will be preserved. The pianist will not be shown up as not a pianist at all. His piano-player's paralysis makes it possible still to think of himself as a great pianist who would, if it were not for his disability, be playing to enthusiastic crowds. The young man who wanders off on the eve of his marriage is enabled to keep from thinking at all about his marriage. His amnesia, in fact, consists of a refusal to think about what will remind him of his marriage. The officer who cannot confront an actual engagement develops shell shock and is invalided home, still an officer. The reason that he is not winning medals at the front is his functional deafness. Nearly all those who now talk enthusiastically of the glories of the past war are men who managed somehow to avoid participation and at the same time continue to think of themselves as gallant soldiers. The men who took part in actual fighting had the romantic interest in war quite drained away. Romantic enthusiasm did not survive actual front-line experiences.

Each college year sees a number of student breakdowns which are excused by relatives and friends as due to overwork. Actually the normal response to overwork is fatigue and exhaustion which lead to rest. The student breakdown even when it follows hard work is seldom the result of the work. Usually work has ceased for a long period before the crisis. The actual difficulty is some conflict between rôle and actuality. Here is, for instance, a docile girl who has received good marks throughout grade and high school. Modern schools grade their pupils according to effort and docility and not according to actual achievement. Splendid marks are attainable by very slow pupils. When she reaches the university there is keener competition and more objective grading. As a result she manages to receive only average grades in spite of increased effort. She cannot reconcile herself to average grades or face her family where her record has always been a matter for pride and comment. She begins to lose sleep, to become despondent, to find herself unable to study. A crisis may result in hysterical illness, or chronic anxiety and exhaustion make it necessary to withdraw from school.

In many such cases the only thing necessary for a profitable college career would have been an accurate notion of her own capacity and an acceptance of her limitations. If she had been in the habit of thinking of herself as an average student instead of as an outstanding student, all would have gone well because that rôle would have been practicable.

Confusion may be introduced into a rôle by the failure of others to accept it. The part is not well played and fails to be supported by the rest of the cast. Or confusion may derive from conflicting interests within the individual. The good citizen and father may develop a taste for drink that carries him away periodically and leaves him with a damaged opinion of himself as well as with a damaged reputation. An ambitious student may become involved in a love affair that leaves him no longer singleminded in his devotion to work. Every evening represents a conflict between courtship and study.

A boy has been encouraged by his family to think of himself as a great inventor. From childhood he has made sketches of new devices for accomplishing this or that result. Friends of the family are proudly told of his inventive genius. No one expects an immature boy to carry ambitious designs through to completion. He fails to get the training in engineering that might make possible actual accomplishments. He is already an inventor to himself. But eventual public recognition depends on actual accomplishment, and of this he is incapable. He may, as a result, withdraw from reality and develop the delusion that he is working on plans to revolutionize the airplane or the automobile. These plans are never finished. They now serve only to excuse him from other efforts at a career and to bolster up his rôle. Many books are forever being written but are never finished. They are pretenses which really deceive few persons but they allow the author to avoid losing face.

The Freudians call the activities which tend to restore a threatened rôle *defense mechanisms*. They are not proper mechanisms because their action is not predictable in advance. But their results are predictable. We can predict that the rôle will be maintained somehow in the great majority of cases. The rôle, which is our adopted social status, is a conservative habit system which will respond to any interference by producing excitement and the variation of behavior which will normally lead to escape from interference. The man whose rôle is threatened is in the position of the cat in the puzzle box. By one device or another he will escape with minimal change in his personality and in his conception of himself.

When the best of us is criticized his natural reaction is defense. We do not immediately change our self-estimate. We discover ways to preserve our self-esteem and to disregard the criticism or reinterpret it. When a college teacher overhears a student speak disparagingly of his teaching it is fairly certain that his reflections will be occupied for some time with self-defense. Who is this student, after all? He is probably one of those college drifters who have no interest in intellectual matters. Pearls have been cast before swine. The student is stupid and unable to appreciate the merits of good teaching. The quality of students is growing worse each year. The teacher had not noticed it before. Or the student probably resents the amount of real work that he must do in this man's class. We do not expect the teacher to accept the judgment and congratulate himself on having heard it in time to mend his ways. That would require sustained broadsides of inescapable criticism. Conceit has more lives than a cat.

Much of our ordinary conversation turns out to be made up of such defense of rôle and status. Each person tells in turn of some bit of clever work for which he was responsible. The business man happens to recall a number of very astute deals in which he has recently proved his merit. The athlete explains how the breaks went against him at the last track meet. The resident of the small town senses the attitude of the visitor and points out that it has the largest cheese factory in the world or that a noted Hollywood hero was born there. Distinguished ex-citizens by a kind of sympathetic magic enhance the value of their fellow townsmen because they share a feature of his rôle. "We are both Eagles," the barber remarks when the governor is mentioned.

The original motives behind desire for social value and high status are obvious. High status carries with it authority, credit, attention and deference. These we have learned to value because they have resulted in many forms of gratification and relief. They have now become interests in themselves. We first learned to get favorable attention because that was the means of ridding ourselves of hunger or cold or sticking pins. Attention eventually becomes an interest for its own sake.

In like fashion social position becomes an interest which is intense in youth and into middle age. The old may learn to disregard it. They become used to their status and adapted to its limitations. But youth in choosing a rôle chooses it in terms of its social prestige. In that rôle parents may be only an impediment. They may dress less well than it demands or they may be less dashing or less brilliant. They usually carry associations of deference or obedience which are intensely annoying in the new rôle. It requires strong public opinion to force many youths to filial behavior once they have gained independence. The parents are reminders of a status that has become highly distasteful.

Sudden wealth often permits rôles, hitherto possible only in fantasy, to be expressed in action. Stories of the Florida real estate boom in which many paper fortunes were made in a few weeks describe many disruptions of families and many desertions of wives who had shared humbler days. The sudden realization that he is a man of wealth may lead the *nouveau riche* to behave like a man of wealth, to behave, that is, like his own notion of such a man. This notion may be fantastic, but it will develop into action. When circumstances move the other way and the man used to wealth loses most of his income, he may find life intolerable on the pittance of ten thousand a year which is left him.

Dominant rôles begin their appeal in early childhood. Whether or not they are adopted depends on experience. The small boy who plays regularly with larger boys may adjust himself to following rather than leading. The boy who has played with other boys slightly younger or smaller or less intelligent than himself becomes accustomed to the exercise of power and domination becomes a settled interest. The boy who plays chiefly with girls of his own age or younger may become accustomed to power but finds himself not prepared to exercise it over males of his own age. He may adapt himself by withdrawing from competition with males and be directed into esthetic or other interests in which he may continue to exercise authority over the other sex.

Failure and disgrace consist in the destruction of rôles. *Social status* might be defined as "what others treat one as," or the classification applied to the individual by his associates. In failure and disgrace social status has been reduced to a social value lower than the adopted rôle. The frequency with which this event leads to flight from the community, to mental breakdown, or to suicide proves that it is the situation which above all others makes adaptation difficult.

XXVII

THE PSYCHOLOGY OF INSANITY

W E HAVE so far paid scant attention to the forms of mental disorder which presumably have their chief cause in injuries or physiological disturbances in the central nervous system. In the functional nervous disorders which have been previously described, the brain and spinal cord are working normally. It is true that neurasthenia and psychasthenia involve physiological inadequacies in the mechanisms for the reinforcement of action, but in them brain pathways are intact and normal learning is in evidence. The brain mechanisms for progressive adaptation are not refusing to operate. What gets learned may be distressing enough, but the learning itself takes place according to rule. We may even regard the nervous breakdown as a manifestation of the adaptive defenses of the individual, and the hysterical symptom as a form of adjustment to unusual circumstances. The embarrassing and awkward results are not the fault of the central nervous system.

There is another class of mental disorders in which the distressing behavior is primarily caused by actual destruction of brain cells or by physiological conditions which affect the ability of the central organs to perform their normal tasks of conduction. These disorders are of only incidental interest in psychology and their treatment lies not in psychological devices but in medicine. The treatment of nervous breakdown is also primarily in the hands of the medical profession and should remain there because an essential condition of cure may be the restoration of physical health and resources. But the functional nervous disorders which involve breakdown have contributing causes which lie quite outside the field of traditional medicine, and the cure of such disorders will require that physicians have recourse to a knowledge of learning and habit which is not now a part of medical training.

Our interest in the mental disorders of organic origin will be limited to certain of their mental symptoms and will not include their physiological bases or their methods of treatment. But there are some interesting and characteristic ways in which men react to disease of the central nervous system. It is not only the outer world that we adapt to. We adjust ourselves to our own traits, to our own strength or weakness, to our own degree of intelligence or to its lack, to our own failing memory in senescence, a failure undoubtedly based on the changes in an aging brain. Reaction to our own reactions makes up the bulk of our behavior. If our balance is suddenly upset while we are standing, an adjustive movement takes place. But the movement itself is a change in our situation and is responded to by further change. In the more inclusive sense of the words, consciousness and awareness are made up by our own secondary responses to our own movements. We may absently brush aside a tickling hair on our forehead or ease our cramped position on a chair without being aware of it. Awareness of our own movement requires that the movement itself be responded to, be noticed. Noticing our own primary responses to an external situation is itself a secondary response. In this book we have used the word "consciousness" to indicate secondary responses only when these were articulate. But this is a restriction of the term made for our own purposes.

The psychologists of a generation ago drilled themselves to what might be called tertiary responses, responses to secondary responses, awareness of their own consciousnesses. Their chief difficulty was that they had to invent and practice their own specialized language in order to deal with such tertiary responses. Common speech is developed in connection with primary response. We name objects and events in connection with our primary adjustment to these objects and events. Our secondary responses to these primary responses have not the public importance that develops language.

When degenerative brain changes or abnormal physiological conditions (of blood pressure, drugs and poisons, endocrine secretions, bacterial invasions) alter primary behavior, the secondary adjustments to that behavior are of necessity also changed.

Disorders of the mind proper, that is, disorders of the capacity for progressive adjustment, are called *psychoses*. Among the psychoses with definitely known causes are paresis, caused by syphilitic invasion of the central nervous system, and the psychoses originating in alcohol and drugs. The result of syphilitic invasion of the brain may be far-reaching destructive changes which include the destruction of nerve cells and consequent interference with the conduction of impulses through the central nervous system. This has immediate results in the loss of certain reflexes and the impairment of coordinated movement. Speech may be difficult as well as skilled movements of the hands.

The patient's mental symptoms, which usually first call attention to the disease, are undoubtedly his own adjustments to the primary disturbance in behavior, his attempts to compensate for or to conceal his inadequate response. The deterioration of memory is probably caused by actual interruption of associative pathways. The patient cannot remember engagements or the details of his business when he receives the usually efficient cues for such remembering. This interferes with his judgments and causes errors which are obvious to the patient as well as to his friends. He gives up his more exacting interests and becomes careless in dress and deportment and reckless in his business. His reaction to the inevitable criticism and social difficulties into which he is led is the very natural one of annoyance and defense. His failures to achieve what he has easily done in the past lead to suspicion directed at others.

This initial development of suspicion directed at friends and family is an extremely common early symptom of central nervous system disorder. We are all habituated from infancy to having our intentions and plans blocked by the interference of other persons. We are all ready on the basis of these experiences to explain our failures by the hostile intentions of others. The paretic may attribute his digestive disturbances to poison secreted in his food. It is the same food that he has always eaten. And, so far as he knows, he is the same eater. The difference must obviously be in the food, but concealed. His suspicions are naturally directed toward those with whom he has the most dealings, his immediate family and associates.

If depression results from the condition of the central nervous system the delusions associated with depression will be present. If he is not depressed, delusions of persecution may evolve into expanded ideas of his rôle, ideas that he is wealthy, powerful, strong, immortal; but these delusions will have little effect on action save to render it careless and neglectful of his former interests. His behavior is still for the most part adaptive, but adaptation to the deficiencies of his own nervous system and his own primary behavior leads to the social failure which we call insanity.

Two forms of alcoholism may be distinguished, the chronic and the episodic; the latter drinker may go without alcohol for a period of months between sprees. In the chronic heavy drinker there occur degenerative changes in nerve tissue and elsewhere that lead to maladjustment in behavior. Memory and consequently judgment are affected. Failure is rationalized by ideas of persecution. The loss of ambitions and the failure of emotional reinforcement lead to the belief that nothing is worth while except alcohol.

In the episodic drinker permanent degenerative changes are less in evidence. He characteristically goes entirely without alcohol for a prolonged time after a spree and then has another period of heavy drinking and almost complete abstinence from food. After several days of this, delirium tremens may set in, with hallucinations of vision and of things crawling on the skin. Food produces nausea.

One prominent psychoanalyst is convinced that all the alcoholics that he has treated are homosexuals. This is probably not a fair sampling of them, but it points out what is probably the case, that alcoholism is generally a symptom of underlying maladjustment. Of two men who both have the experience of getting drunk on a number of occasions, the one with a source of chronic conflict and distress is much more likely to develop the habit. The depressant effect of alcohol relaxes tensions. If this source is, for example, a homosexual interest in which sex tensions are aroused but direct relief is prevented by social obstacles, the relief from excitement and the relief from the original tension itself may be achieved by alcohol. Drugs which produce relaxation operate as a consummation of the motive in the sense that they rid the organism of its restless activity. The fact that being drunk is followed by extremely unpleasant nausea and weakness does not teach any lesson because by the time these unpleasant results have appeared the tension is gone and cannot be associated with the effects. But when through a gradual recovery and a new accumulation of erotic tension the individual again reaches a state of "jitters," the last association with that state is the act of drinking and this tends now to occur. The habit at first tends to be episodic. It is only by the accidental discovery that a drink during the inevitable "low" period relieves this quite different form of distress that the habit of drinking during this state is formed. The drinker who requires a "pick up" in the morning has acquired two separate alcohol habits, one associated with stress and excitement, the other with the distress of the morning after.

It is fairly certain that any other form of recurring or chronic distress or chronic conflict may lead to alcoholism. Men drink from many causes other than frustrated homosexual interests. Marital and business difficulties, disappointed ambition, or the disturbance of a rôle may also lead to alcohol.

Drug addiction, particularly morphine addiction, has been discussed in another chapter. Of it also we may say that the average person in good mental health can be exposed to morphine without forming the habit. From the work of Spragg with chimpanzees which was mentioned before we must acknowledge that regular doses of morphine eventually have an effect which makes abstinence distressing, and a habit is thus acquired. But, as in the case of alcohol, only an individual who is unstable and subject to chronic distress from other sources is likely to form the habit on a limited number of doses of morphine. The great majority of addicts are neurotic individuals, failures, misfits, individuals with inadequate reinforcement who have discovered morphine as a relief from tensions.

When addiction has been established, the original drive for which the morphine was a relief and the new drive based on abstinence from the drug make together an imperious motivation which will lead to getting the drug at almost any sacrifice. Habits of polite or moral behavior which stand in the way of relief are promptly broken. The abstinence symptoms include great restlessness, an inability to sleep, tremors, fears and hallucinations. Complete withdrawal of the drug with careful medical supervision and with provisions for diet and exercise will eventually reduce the abstinence symptoms and the addict is discharged as cured. Patients discharged from custody after several months of supervised abstinence are cured only in the sense that they can get on without the drug for a period. They have no longer the extreme anxiety which has regularly followed each dose after a term of hours. When, however, the original source of unrest recurs, relapse is possible. The drive of abstinence has been reconditioned, but not the original drive.

Characteristic mental states are associated with many other known organic causes besides alcohol, drugs and syphilitic infection in brain and spinal chord. Encephalitis lethargica, cerebral embolisms, brain tumors, the degenerative changes of senility as well as temporary states like fever or chronic diseases like tuberculosis all have characteristic effects on behavior. These are of more interest to medicine than to psychology and will not be dealt with here.

There remain two classes of psychoses of common occurrence in which the organic basis is today only suspected and not certain. These have been called since Kraepelin's time dementia praecox and manic-depressive insanity. They are based purely on symptom classification and not, like paresis, on a definitely associated organic cause.

Dementia praecox, which names a group of disorders which are not dementia and are not necessarily precocious, is also called *schizophrenia*. This latter term would indicate a split mind. This term is very little better as a description of the disorder than the original "dementia praecox." The cases to which these names are applied are marked neither by any "splitting of the mind" nor by any disturbance of the function of association. What does mark them all is what Janet calls a loss of the social sentiments or feelings. The patient may still perform the routine actions of everyday life, the primary adjustments to what goes on around him, but with a characteristic loss of normal sentiment. He is apathetic toward friends and relatives and toward their good or bad fortune. Pride in appearance and dress is lost and the patient becomes slovenly. The amenities of social intercourse are no longer observed and coarse language and bad manners appear. The patient withdraws from friendships and contacts with other persons. He spends much time in daydreaming. The impression he gives of dementia or actual mental impairment is misleading. There is no actual impairment of associations or of the learning process. But conversation is often unintelligible to others because it does not follow the usual course of talk and is often persistently directed at some topic which is obscure and private in nature. The schizophrenic is no longer concerned with argument and proof. These depend on social relations, and he is indifferent to the opinions of others.

It is customary to try to include all cases of schizophrenia under four varieties. *Simple schizophrenia,* in which little more than the apathy referred to is present, constitutes one type. Many cases which can be so classed are found among tramps and minor offenders. Associated with the loss of social feeling are often "ideas of reference." By this is meant a tendency to interpret the actions of other persons as referring to the patient himself. Bystanders are talking about him. He sees covert glances, nods, winks which are all concerned with him. Paragraphs in the news are obviously disguised references to the patient. A ship's radio operator tells me that he catches frequent snatches of messages that are spreading evil reports about himself.

The physical basis of this apathy toward human relationships remains obscure. Hoskins in his very comprehensive account of the endocrine glands called *The Tides of Life* considers the possibility that a deficiency of sex drive is involved. He mentions that McCartney's study of the group of eunuchs left behind when the imperial court in Pekin was abandoned describes these subjects as manifesting traits resembling the schizophrenic. In schizophrenia the sex life, he reminds us, is distinctly abnormal and usually has been for some time before the onset of the psychosis. Kempf's *Psychopathology* describes this abnormality of sex life as based on the functional establishment of perversions through learning and habit. There are a number of instances in which the onset of a schizophrenic condition coincides with a sudden interruption of perverse sex activity. That some kind of physical deficiency is prior to the functional disorder of sex interest and the social apathy which is its possible consequence would be indicated by the remarkable results of insulin treatment now being reported from many sources. As a consequence of induced insulin shock many schizophrenics have shown a prompt improvement or recovery.

Whatever the organic basis of the schizophrenic's condition, the fact remains that most of his behavior symptoms are his own adjustive response to his changed state. Simple schizophrenia has been described. It is sometimes complicated with a definite tendency toward silliness and an exaggerated inconsistency between action and social situation. The speech of the patient sounds to an observer quite incoherent and meaningless. But close attention will discover that this impression is caused by the patient's entire disregard of the observer and his social situation. The speech has to do with topics in which the observer is not interested, and the patient makes no effort to explain or prove or demonstrate. The speech of normal persons is a response to a situation in which the listener has a prominent part. The speech of the schizophrenic has inner sources and disregards the audience. No disorder of association lies behind its apparent incoherence. The essential activities that we call mind are not impaired, but only misdirected.

When the apathy of the schizophrenic is complicated by silly behavior in the presence of others he is described as *hebephrenic*.

If, instead of silly behavior, he manifests delusions which are usually delusions of persecution, he is referred to as *paranoid*.

The fourth group of dementia praecox or schizophrenic patients, the *catatonic*, is marked by a tendency to extreme withdrawal from social contact which may amount to a stuporous condition in which there is almost no evidence of response to the human environment. The patient is beyond communication in speech. This stuporous condition may last for months during which no word will be exchanged with those about him. After recovery from such a state the patient himself is sometimes able and willing to describe what has been going on about him during his withdrawn period and this can often be done with great detail. The condition that he has been in is obviously not genuinely a stupor. He must have been noticing and commenting to himself on external events the whole time.

Kempf describes many cases in which the habitual postures of the catatonic which are held for long periods can be understood as a pose which is related to his fantasies. He is an Egyptian deity and sits all day with arms extended on the arms of his chair looking directly ahead. Or he has become a stone and impersonates the behavior of a stone. In other words, the catatonic posture is consistent with the rôle that the patient has adopted.

This connection with rôle holds true of another characteristic response of many catatonics, a tendency to hold a posture into which they have been set by the physician. If the physician grasps the patient's hand and places it in an awkward position, this position will be maintained for several minutes and the arm will gradually return to its resting posture. Janet was quoted in an earlier chapter to the effect that this also is determined not by any involuntary reflex postural adjustment but by the patient's notion of his relations to the physician. The behavior will not be manifest when the wrong person attempts to elicit it. It is as if the patient had said, "Oh, well,—if the doctor wants it," and then paid no further attention to the posture. That this is the real nature of the so-called waxy *flexibility* of the catatonic is indicated by the fact that many of them instead of being so complaisant are negativistic and will immediately oppose without evident reflection most commands of the doctor or any attempt to mold the position of the arm. Both the negativism and the corresponding automatic obedience as well as catatonic attitudes may be interpreted as refusals to be bothered. The negativistic or the obedient attitude is assumed once for all and *avoids the necessity for a discriminating response.* We saw that much of the behavior of the hysteric is an attempt to conserve effort and simplify his life by disregarding stimuli. The schizophrenic tends to *conserve effort by limiting response.* Social reactions are the most difficult of all the reactions we are called on to make. They depend on intricate personal relationships and on the expressive behavior of others. By refusing to make such discriminations and by sticking to one line of conduct toward others, the schizophrenic avoids troublesome decisions.

The total picture of schizophrenia gives the appearance of a lack of physiological drive which would account directly for the apathy. The behavior of withdrawal, the catatonic postures, the negativism could all be readily explained as adjustments to this deficiency. By refusing to be involved with others the schizophrenic compensates for a social disability. His stupor is a protection against the bother and annoyance of friends and busybodies surrounding him. Consistent refusal to answer gives relief from troubling questions. It is therefore the last attitude associated with such questions. The attitude, once taken, becomes itself a habit and is self-maintaining, much as balkiness in a horse is self-maintaining and will resist the whip or other stimuli usually effective in getting action. The chair in a corner of the asylum ward may be a refuge if the world has become too difficult. I have been at times much struck with the resemblance of my own reaction to the inevitable and indefatigible activities of the organizers of deck sports on an ocean liner and the reaction of the schizophrenic to the social pressures about him.

It has become fashionable to speak of schizophrenia as a disorder of regression and to define regression as a sort of turning back of the calendar to the days of infancy. This doctrine has no psychological justification. An occasional patient may adopt "baby talk" and behave like an infant, but this is a device, a rôle, adopted because it has served as an escape from the present situation. There is no unwinding of the skein of habits of intervening years, and there is very little actual resemblance of the pretense to infantile behavior. When a 140-pound woman crawls about the hospital floor and acts the infant, the actual muscular habits required are very different from those used by a ten-months-old child, and it is fantastic to believe that we are confronted with an actual revival of infantile patterns. It is astonishing that so many physicians and psychologists have been "taken in" by the performer.

Besides the schizophrenics there is another large class of psychotic patients with radically different symptoms. These are referred to as manic-depressives. They are marked by states of excitement and depression which tend to be episodic and to be followed either by a return to a normal level or by excitement or depression. In these psychoses also there is no clear evidence of an organic cause. The psychoanalysts with their predilection for functional explanations hold that schizophrenia is a flight from reality, a withdrawal from struggle which follows on the discovery that basic desires are hopelessly barred from gratification. We have agreed that it is a flight and a withdrawal, but have suggested that a physiological deficiency may lie at the bottom of the trouble, rather than excess drive which meets resistance. These two explanations are not in absolute contradiction because there is always a possibility that the physical deficiency may have been in some obscure fashion the consequence of hopeless blocking. The psychoanalysts also hold that manic-depressive behavior is essentially the behavior of struggle and of exhaustion brought on by similar blocking of essential desires. Both are interpreted as cases in which sex perversions have developed and outlet for perverse interests is denied. In one case the reaction is retreat; and in the other, rage and struggle with possible delusions of triumph.

In this interpretation there is probably considerable truth. It neglects only the great probability of cooperating causes in the form of organic defects in drive and in the mechanisms for emotional reinforcement. As in schizophrenia, the onset of trouble is often some crisis in personal affairs. But it is probable that an equal crisis could have been weathered if the individual had been in good working order. The typical onset of a manic attack is merely an exaggeration of exciting emotion. The individual grows restless and animated. Action is speeded up. Usually there is a strong tendency to talk. Exciting emotion normally introduces variety into behavior by its reinforcement of action. In slight mania this may be noticed by others only as a sudden access of wit and brilliance, because the manic's speech is quickened. He answers before the questioner has finished his question. And the reply is often new and incongruous and evokes laughter in hearers on this account. As the attack progresses these symptoms are exaggerated. Eventually speech seems incoherent but this incoherence is largely a question of point of view. It derives from the fact that the manic rushes from one topic to another too rapidly for his hearers. The topic may change in the middle of a sentence and the result be a word salad. But there is no real dementia or breakdown of learning. And if the manic is held to one purpose for a time, as, for instance, by being shut in a room, he will be as effective as the next man in his efforts to escape. The manic excitement generally includes a strong feeling of well-being, a euphoria. The patient feels splendidly well and strong, equal to anything. The hospital is a fine place. Everything is prospering.

In nearly all such crises the state passes off to leave the patient somewhat exhausted and below his normal weight. In many cases there will be other attacks after intervals of months or years. In some persons the period of excitement is followed by depression, slight or acute. Action is impeded and everything is now as gloomy as it was previously bright. The patient is silent and morose instead of talkative. His voice may be almost inaudible. Convictions of guilt and disgrace are present.

In both manic states and depressed states we have only an exaggeration of changes of mood which are common to all persons. And there are all degrees of this exaggeration. Manic states may not reach the point of interfering with daily affairs and may be manifest only as a transient excess of energy and well-being during which much creative work may be accomplished. The depression may only amount to a period of reduced work and reduced interest, of discouragement.

In the interpretation of manic-depressive psychoses the distinction between organic and functional causes tends to become very tenuous, as it does in schizophrenia. We are obviously confronted with disturbances of the physiological mechanisms of emotional reinforcement of action. The psychosis is abnormal only in the sense that this reinforcement appears to be for a time independent of the situation. Many psychiatrists believe that this independence is only apparent and that the prolonged excitement is a response to a prolonged conflict of desire and interference, that the emotional mechanisms are operating normally and abnormality lies in the situation. It is more correct to view manic and depressive states as states in which the physiological mechanisms for reinforcement and depression are at least running wild and are not subject to normal control. Whether the attack is due primarily to antecedent physical disorder or not cannot now be answered. It is certain that behavior crises can release a manic period. There are also cases in which the patient has distinctly the appearance of "letting himself go" and these are close to the border of hysterical behavior. Sometimes an illusion of victory over an obstacle leaves the individual with energy to waste. His manic attack resembles the behavior of triumph. Only the undue prolonging of excitement and the evident actual exhaustion of energy reserves lead us to suspect that something more than the stimulus situation is responsible, that some portion of the physical equipment for action is running without its governor.

In the psychoses the brain mechanisms responsible for learning are physically impaired or there is impairment of some form of drive essential to normal behavior, or the central regulation of excitement and depression is not in proper working order. But the outstanding features of the insane patient's behavior are only the indirect results of these physiological defects. Behavior continues to be adaptive, but the outstanding adaptation is to the organic defect, and it is this adaptation that constitutes insane behavior.

XXVIII———

PSYCHOTHERAPY

WHEN a man is distressed by hunger, food would appear the obvious and the only cure. This is not the case. The distress may be alleviated, a certain amount of resignation may be encouraged, by what common sense would call "working on his mind." By this would be meant efforts to distract him from hunger, to lead him to form new attitudes toward hunger which would rob it of its capacity for keeping him wrought up. He may be induced to tighten his belt and stop complaining by preaching "guns instead of butter." Men may be led to starve to death with serene minds. When they die, they die in good mental health. The hunger strike and the religious fast both represent triumphs of mind over the material sources of drive, the stomach spasms whose "natural" result is to impel a man to such activity and new behavior that something or other will eventually be swallowed, even if it is his own boots.

We might describe the means by which we lead a man to adapt to hunger without having recourse to food as a "mental cure." It consists in leading him to form new habits and new attitudes which rob a natural source of distress of its capacity for troubling. The cure is "mental" because it uses the man's own capacity for forming new adaptations to disturbing stimuli. And if such striking results can be achieved with a source of distress so widely shared, so firmly established in the original structure of men, it would appear that similar "mental" treatment could be used for those instances of distress whose impelling causes are not natural drives but acquired habits and desires, for the hysterical paralysis that is motivated by the arduous conditions of the front line, for the social indigestion that is founded on an annoyance which is, like the beetles in the baseboard, a very special and private habit and not a primary and original drive. If hunger can be deprived of its terrors by the adaptive capacity of men, surely the conflict of two desires which are both adventitious habits of an individual can be prevented from leading to the agonizing tension and ultimate collapse that we call nervous breakdown.

If we tried to use the word "psychotherapy" for all the devices by which men have attempted to lead others to adjust to trouble through habit adaptation, the word would mean entirely too much. It would include all advice and reassurance, all the forms of encouragement, all the comforts of religion, all exchange of information, all the applications of science and many of the devices of medicine. That is obviously too much for any word to mean and still be useful. Psychotherapy must not be allowed to mean any treatment that uses the patient's mind. It must be restricted to those efforts at treatment which are consciously (in so many words) based on a knowledge of the ways of the mind, those treatments in which we are aware of the psychological explanation of the distress and of the principles of the adaptive habits that we are establishing as a cure.

If we thus restrict the meaning of "psychotherapy" we may omit all forms of religious cures, the healing shrines and healing saints, the healing cults, the exorcizings, incantations, witches' broths, shaman's rattles, magic formulas, Yogi breathing. We may omit also the modern flood of books with simple formulas for happiness or directions for controlling the "unconscious mind." We omit all of these from the meaning of the term "psychotherapy" not because these devices are without effect. They do achieve their effects. Otherwise they would not exist or endure. But they achieve their effects without being conscious of how they achieve them. They cure distress in many forms and they cure by devices that make use of the capacity for progressive adjustment that we have called mind. Faith in their efficacy has rid many a person of anxiety over his condition and bolstered up self-confidence, or has resolved a distressing conflict. The excitement of the shaman's rattle and weird ceremonies has probably stirred an occasional patient out of despair or the conviction that he had been bewitched, as well as performing an occasional service to the tribe by ridding it of an invalid through death.

Janet's *Psychological Healing* undertakes to examine some of the reasons why these unsophisticated methods are in so many cases successful. But a great deal more attention could be given to such "cures" with profit to psychology and to the psychotherapist. Behanan's recent account of Yogi leaves a reader with the impression that the self-discipline and the physiological effects of the practices of that cult would make almost impossible many of the varieties of neurotic breakdown now current in the United States. Yogi cannot, unfortunately, be prescribed for business men or society women because if they had adopted its mystic formulas and its exercises in time they would not have become business men or society women in the first place.

The most convenient classification of the forms of treatment of functional nervous disorders which make use of psychological devices is that suggested by Janet in his *Psychological Healing*. There he distinguishes methods of cure which depend on *rest and isolation*, those which depend on *economizing effort*, others which rely on *stimulation*, and, most important and difficult of all, those which depend on *reeducation* and the reorganization of interest and desire.

The rest cure was made popular in the United States and later in Europe by the work of a Philadelphia novelist-neurologist, Dr. S. Weir Mitchell, about the turn of the century. Mitchell put his neurasthenic patients to bed for six weeks in a darkened room and allowed them to see no one but the doctor and the nurse. Since the most common complaint of the victims of a nervous breakdown is of feelings of utter exhaustion, this appeared a natural method. It was followed by temporary recovery from the neurotic symptoms in enough cases to give the treatment a considerable vogue. By separating the patient from his family he was often relieved of the inciting cause of his distress. Family stresses and strains are responsible for a substantial proportion of neurotic incidents. The jealousies, resentments, rivalries, hostilities that develop in a family are sometimes the final aggravation when they are not the primary source of trouble. Removal from the family is a removal from the cues for trouble. But the method of rest and isolation has the disadvantage that the patient cannot be kept in bed forever. Mitchell added to his treatment a diet that put on weight. When the fattened patient returned home it would be found that there was comparatively little forgetting of the troubling responses to difficult members of the family and the history of the breakdown would be repeated because the same causes were operating that served to bring it on in the first place. The prescription of ocean travel and change of scene often has the same temporary effect, with the possibility that on the return new habits and attitudes may be established; but the treatment makes no provision for this.

By cures through economy of effort Janet refers to the fact that adjustment is far easier to a comparatively monotonous routine than it is to the unpredictable change involved in meeting new persons and new situations. The *déprimé* is inadequate to complicated living, to making choices and decisions. In a round of minor duties which are the same day after day, almost no such choices need be made. The same items of food, the same friends, the same arrangement of furniture, the same succession of movements may be confronted repeatedly with routine habit which demands no decisions. The depressed neurotic finds that he can preserve his mental health and avoid the expense of tension and anxiety by living the simple life. The job of an insurance salesman is indefinitely harder for such inadequate persons than is a job as a bookkeeper. Each prospective customer is a new problem. I am told that the reading rooms of city libraries have an undue proportion of salesmen during the day, many of them reading books on salesmanship; but this is only an excuse for getting away from the onerous task of selling. Sales managers are forbidden to use the lash, but they use what substitutes for it they can find. Prizes, competitions, ridicule, even a systematic encouragement to get into debt are used in many large firms. No such spurs are needed for men in routine jobs.

The depressed neurotic often learns without outside help to simplify his life. He dines always at the same place, plans to spend each week as he did the last, avoids the new. The number of persons who have fled from the life of cities and from friends and relatives to obscure corners of the world is astonishing. The recluse gets rid of his distressing neurotic symptoms because he is living a life to which he is equal. In Catholic communities the effectiveness of an economy and simplification of life is recognized in the use of the retreat or the convent. Every great city has its virtual hermits, because it is possible to be as alone among strangers toward whom one has no social responsibilities as it is among the trees of the forest.

Relinquishment of exacting ambitions has the same effect. Often an improvement in mental health marks the time when the sufferer has been led to recognize his own limitations. Ceasing to kick against the pricks, recognizing the inevitable as inevitable, require training. I once surveyed with a Norwegian carpenter friend some work that we had planned for the day. It was covered with a fresh fall of snow and a cold wind was blowing. "Well," he remarked, "we will have to do now what they do in Norway when it snows." "What is that?" I asked. "We yust let it snow," he answered. When we complain bitterly of the weather, nine-tenths of our upset state may be in response to our own grumbling which makes the weather an issue all day long and prevents us from turning to an occupation that would not be interfered with. The complaining attitude is self-maintaining, like all attitudes. In the person for whom the retraining of attitude would be difficult as it is in nearly all depressed persons, the only recourse may be retreat from the annoyance.

Much of hysterical behavior is the result of a blind and unreflecting discovery of some method of economizing effort by disregarding stimuli. An hysterical deafness is a simplification of life. The hysterically blind patient is not so different from the restaurant waitress whose attention seems impossible to attract when we are ready for our second cup of coffee. If she should see us her life would become suddenly more burdensome.

There are many persons capable of living comfortably at one level of complication who will promptly break down when faced with the necessity of living at a higher level. There is in this a striking analogy to Cannon's cats which could lead normal lives although their sympathetic nerves which are directly concerned in the emergency reinforcement of action were completely eliminated. But such cats do not survive when they are no longer carefully protected in the laboratory from radical changes of temperature and other disturbances. Many neurotics are in the same state. They can meet adequately a life free from the strain of choice and decision, but will break down under a slight increase in the complexity of their affairs. The reason that such cures by economy of effort are not formally recognized by most writers on psychotherapy is that they are so often self-achieved. The patient learns to make his own simplification. There is a real sense in which the schizophrenic who sits apathetically all day long in the ward of the hospital and responds almost not at all to what is going on around him can be said to have achieved his cure. From his own point of view his troubles are ended, cured by his economizing of social effort, by his withdrawal from a world that is too much for him. It is now his friends and family and the taxpayers who are in distress. They are the ones who suffer from schizophrenia, not he.

What Janet calls cures by stimulation are like the cures by economy of effort, in that they are frequently self-discovered. He had noticed something that will be recognized by everyone, once attention is called to it. This is that many neurotic patients rise to emergencies and behave normally when friends or family are in danger. The hysterically deaf person can respond nobly to the cry of "Fire" and the case of functional paralysis may reach the exit neck and neck with his deaf companion. The neurasthenic may in an emergency be stimulated to energy adequate for decision. Janet cites two cases of women who had severe neurotic symptoms and were regular visitors in the clinic at Salpétrière. Both of them had an intermission of symptoms and failed to appear for long intervals. When they did return with their old troubles it was discovered that a period of normal mental health had coincided with a career of stealing from the Paris department stores. The risk and excitement of daily thefts had restored them temporarily to health. Janet quotes Dubois, a Swiss psychotherapist, to the effect that it is a great pity that danger is so dangerous. Otherwise it could frequently be used as a prescription. But, unfortunately, a patient who died of his cure would be no great comfort to his doctor. The outstanding literary illustration of such cures by stimulation is Elizabeth Barrett. Years of invalidism which had fixed innumerable invalid's habits upon her (and corresponding habits upon her family) were ended by the excitement of her love affair with Robert Browning. A life well marked by frustration and discontent and indecision, victimized by the perverse interest of her father which required her continued invalidism to render her dependent on him had failed to stir her to that point of excitement necessary for the break-up of habit and the resolution of her decision. The needed extra stir was furnished by the poet. She became in a short time capable of taking things into her own hands.

Behind these cures by stimulation lies the fact that the sufferer is inadequate in the emotional reinforcement of action. In this condition, whether it is brought on by constitutional deficiency or by some failure of the glandular or other organs furnishing reinforcement, or is brought on originally by the exhausting effects of some major conflict, the addition of new sources of excitement may serve to change chronic restlessness and anxiety to a surge of energy equal to the difficulty.

If the neurotic state has its chief cause in a physical condition, the results of stimulation will be temporary. The transient character of many religious cures is an example. Under the stress of unusual excitement pains and aches and weakness may be forgotten. A soldier in action may be only vaguely aware of a serious wound which would have had all his attention if it had happened at his breakfast table at home or while listening to a lecture. Under stress of great excitement cases with paralysis caused by cerebral lesions may move or walk. When the excitement subsides, the paralysis returns. I have seen a healer holding forth in a tent-meeting in the presence of a thousand or more persons "heal" a man with a bad lameness. The tremendous excitement brought about in him as he stood up on the platform before the crowd and the confusion of the healer's harangue enabled him to walk from the platform with a firm step.

Not until the excitement was over and he had returned home did he need his crutches which had been discarded at the meeting. When the disability is a habit it is quite possible that temporary stimulation may effect its cure. Even when the disability has an organic basis, the stirring conditions of such faith cures may bring about an adjustment of attitude to the disability. It may be now accepted or ignored.

There are many persons who become dependent on certain sources of excitement for maintaining that normal level at which they can face their world and its decisions. Deprived of the noise and stir of the city where they have been living, or of the gay and reckless company they have been keeping, they go into a "slump" which may include many of the symptoms of inadequacy. Decisions become hard to make. Their attention turns to their own health. They become neurotic invalids. One such person, a woman, had with her husband built up a thriving retail business. She kept the books of the firm and supervised the stock. She quarreled with her husband and they separated. A divorce left her with full ownership of the business. She was then offered for it a very substantial sum, and she accepted. For years she had believed that she wanted leisure and freedom from the routine and confinement of the shop. With a generous income she now set out to enjoy her leisure. But she had few interests; and the hiring of a maid, a new apartment, many chocolates and much light literature represented the only real additions to her life. A very serious unrest developed. This had various sources, but the point is that occupation with the business had proved an effective outlet up to the time of her retirement. She developed distressing gastro-intestinal attacks and about twice a week required the services of a physician. Although as a routine measure he used the stomach pump to relieve the immediate distress, he could not prevent recurrences of the attack. Eventually the physician rebelled at the unpleasant routine and reasoned that the excellent health which had prevailed until retirement from active business indicated the real source of the difficulty. He persuaded her to buy back a half-interest in the shop and to resume her job as bookkeeper. This proved effective and the functional disorder promptly ended.

The cure could probably have been effected by establishing new interests of almost any sort—religion, travel, anything that would direct attention away from minor aches and pains and furnish a certain minimum of stimulation.

A typical complaint of neurotics is that life is not worth living, that nothing is worth doing. They are, of course, quite right in this complaint. Whether anything is worth doing depends on the interest of the doer. Worth and value depend on human desires. In a depressed state active desires are at a minimum because the strength of a desire depends on the amount of emotional reinforcement available to it. Nothing is in itself desirable. But when interests can be aroused by new stimuli, life becomes again worth living. Boredom, ennui, complaints about the worthlessness of life would all disappear temporarily if the patient could be placed in a large cage with a slightly decrepit lion, one that was hostile but could not run very fast. Exertion and exercise would cease for a time to be distasteful. A school of psychotherapy that depended on the use of lions or on the milder but more persistent exciting effect of fleas would find no patients in a democracy, but if patients could be drafted, such a school would be able to point to a certain proportion of therapeutic successes.

A generation ago a great deal was made of psychotherapy by suggestion. Before considering Janet's fourth type of psychological methods of healing, treatment through reeducation, we may undertake to examine the nature of this suggestion which was believed to be the chief hope of psychotherapy. In the writings of psychologists and sociologists of that day suggestion was accepted as a mysterious "force" or as an instinctive tendency of mankind. It was defined as the acceptance of ideas (and action) without adequate logical reason. People were regarded as just naturally suggestible and no attempts were made to explain the nature of the phenomenon. Suggestion was looked upon by many writers as Locke looked upon association, a low form of response which inferior persons, or superior persons in their weaker moments, were likely to exhibit. Suggestion was contrasted with the use of reason and logic. But a close examination of the notion of suggestion discloses the fact that it is not a special tendency of man or a particular weakness of certain persons. It is only a rather vague description of one of the aspects of associative learning.

The learning of a language consists in acquiring associative connections between words and acts. When the word has become a cue for the act, the word may serve as a symbol. The act may be partly inhibited and the word serve only to organize the beginnings of action whose overt expression will depend on the rest of the situation. All thoughts begin in action and were at first acts. Words with their associated beginnings of movement may be used in place of action. The hen that is in a quandary rushes about. The human thinker is also rushing about, but he is doing his rushing with the verbal substitutes for action and he does not commit himself to action until some experimental course turns up in words and is not inhibited by its associations or by the forbidding elements of the situation.

Now it is very true that human action can be guided by suggestion. But this only means that in some cases the words of other persons can evoke action. All of us are essentially suggestible in many situations. We can be made to turn from our food by words associated with disgust. We can, if it does not conflict with our own attitude at the time, be cajoled, persuaded, urged, commanded, or threatened, discouraged, forbidden. But there is no essential difference between persuasion with logic and persuasion without logic. Logic and grammar are only certain basic forms conventionally observed in the use of language. The popularity of the notion of suggestion derived from its connection with hypnosis. Suggestion under hypnosis is still effectively used in psychotherapy. The mystery and awe which attached to hypnotism were quite unnecessarily attached also to suggestion.

An excellent account of the history of hypnosis is included in Janet's *Psychological Healing*. A very adequate description of its details and the methods for inducing it is contained in a chapter on "Sleep" in Dorcas and Shaffer's *Textbook of Abnormal Psychology*. Hull's *Hypnosis* recounts many careful laboratory studies of the phenomenon. No feature of human behavior has been associated with so many glamorous and awe-inspiring misconceptions.

Although similar phenomena are described in Latin and Greek authors, the modern conception of hypnosis originated in the work of Mesmer, a healer who operated in Paris during the last years of the eighteenth century and who was investigated by a royal commission of which Benjamin Franklin, then ambassador to France, was a member. Mesmer had his patient recline on a divan in a darkened room. Dressed in an astrologer's robe and to the accompaniment of appropriate music, he stroked the patient lightly with a metal wand and produced a state which seems to have resembled mild erotic excitement, the Mesmeric trance. Some patients had a "crisis" in which convulsions appeared. The "crisis" was supposed to be followed by a cure of whatever disorder had brought the patient to the clinic.

In 1784 Maxime Puységur printed an account of a magnetic treatment of a young shepherd who, instead of going into convulsions, had fallen apparently asleep and could not be waked. He then rose and walked about like a sleepwalker. In this state he proved to be amenable to the directions of the experimenter, to obey automatically and without hesitation all manner of suggestions. When he waked he had forgotten all that had passed. Puységur called this somnambulism.

A tremendous popular interest was finally aroused in this phenomenon. During the early years of the nineteenth century many journals were devoted to it; and by 1840-1850 experiments had established that operations could be performed on subjects in the trance, now called hypnosis, without pain being felt by the subject. But in that decade anesthetics were discovered and their more certain results caused a loss of medical interest in hypnosis. In the meantime hypnosis had so captured public attention that alarming numbers of crack-pots and charlatans were concerned with it and many superstitions developed about it. The hypnotized subject was supposed to be clairvoyant and to be able to perform at command skilled acts which had never been practiced.

As a result of this wild growth of superstition, orthodox medicine left hypnosis strictly to the charlatans. But during the years from 1880 to 1890 it was again brought before the attention of medical men largely through the work of Charcot, head of the clinic for nervous and mental diseases at Salpétriêre near Paris. Charcot attempted to show that there were objective clinical tests for hypnosis, that the subject passed through three stages— a relaxed lethargy, a cataleptic state in which his members would hold any position in which they were placed, and a final stage of somnambulism in which he would automatically carry out the ideas of the hypnotist.

In 1884 Bernheim published a short account of hypnosis in which he showed that the state was the result of suggestion and that Charcot's three stages were present or not according as the subject had been led to believe that they would or would not appear. He reported that subjects would carry out suggestions after the period of hypnosis was over and that they could be given "negative hallucinations" or led to disregard objects present if this were suggested. One of his experiments reported in 1883 was very illuminating. The public had been convinced that subjects could be made to commit the most atrocious crimes under the influence of the hypnotist. Bernheim found that if he gave a subject an imitation dagger and explained that standing against the door was an enemy who had insulted him, the subject would attack the door with the dagger. Many imaginary persons were slaughtered thus, but it was soon discovered that the slaughter of real persons could not be induced. When given a loaded revolver whose cartridges had been made harmless by removal of the powder charge, the hypnotized subject cannot be induced to aim at a person and pull the trigger. A number of séances have been suddenly terminated by suggesting that the subject disrobe.

But there is no doubt that hypnosis represents a definite and unusual state. It has much in common with ordinary behavior. It may, in fact, be described as an exaggeration of certain very familiar ways of behaving. It is misnamed hypnosis because it has only a superficial resemblance to sleep. In sleep relaxation prevails and reflexes like the knee jerk are absent. In hypnosis such reflexes are undiminished.

The outstanding characteristic of hypnosis is a restriction of attention, usually a concentration of attention on the experimenter and his directions. The various methods for inducing hypnosis such as having the subject gaze at a bright light, stroking his head, talking of sleep, etc., have been most satisfactorily explained by Curt Rosenow (*Amer. Jour. of Psychol.*, 1928, 40, 205-235). He points out that all the methods used must include giving the subject conflicting directions. If a bright light is fixated it should be above the level of the eyes so that these will be in the position they have during sleep with the lids closed. There is consequently a strong tendency to close the eyes and this opposes the tendency to fixate the light. If the subject is told that he is falling asleep he must at the same time be well aware that he is not at liberty to fall asleep. He remains in a divided state between assuming the posture of sleep and keeping awake. In this state of mutual inhibition other irrelevant attitudes and postures are ruled out. It is all that the cooperating subject can do to manage his two mutually conflicting actions. This state is peculiarly favorable to a responsiveness when any new clear and unambiguous direction is given by the experimenter.

In the fact that the subject is not in an attitude of resistance or criticism lies the utility of hypnosis as a method of treatment. Tendencies to behave in ways appropriate to the experimenter's words have minimum opposition because the mutual inhibition and interference in the hypnotizing directions have eliminated "sales resistance" to the suggestions. The patient may visit the physician steeled to maintain his air of ill health or to act his part of an invalid. During hypnosis he is off his guard, absorbed in his efforts to do two quite incompatible things at once. In this state a new attitude can be suggested by merely naming it.

Much of the behavior that attends a toothache is not a direct response to the stimuli from the tooth but a response built up on this original pain. We make a wry face and this is now a stimulus added to the aching nerve. We acknowledge that we have a severe pain and this articulate notice carries with it the behavior appropriate to a pain. We act the part of a man with a toothache. We could have the ache without much of this acting. This secondary behavior can be broken up by hypnosis or by ordinary conversation or by new intense stimuli. If the house proves to be on fire the tooth does not stop activating its nerve, but we step out of the rôle of "man with toothache" and play for a while at being a man whose house is on fire.

The interruption of such secondary behavior, attitudes of dejection, obsessional behavior, hysterical behavior of all sorts, by hypnotic suggestion is usually temporary. But it still may be highly useful in dealing with an occasional patient. The behavior affected can include almost the whole field of associative action and attitude. And this includes almost the whole range of behavior. It cannot include anything not amenable to ordinary persuasion or conversation under favorable circumstances. Suggestion merely has certain temporary advantages in the hypnotic preoccupation. The actual use of hypnosis in psychotherapy has receded because of the discovery that its effects are actually more transient than the results of skillful conversation without recourse to hypnotism. Not enough associations are established during the hypnotic state to insure its lasting reorganization of interests. This would require patient and extended discussion.

In describing the psychotherapeutic methods of rest and isolation, economy of energy, stimulation, hypnosis and suggestion we have accounted for the less important devices for bringing about adjustment and serenity. All of these methods have a temporary character. They enable the sufferer to avoid his problem or lash him to a point of energy that may be short lived. If adjustment is to be lasting it must be the result of a reorganization of habits, and reeducation must be the method.

A certain amount of neurotic behavior consists in fairly simple bad habits. Although phobias and hysteric ailments usually give evidence of underlying faults of personality, this is not always the case. There are instances of isolated phobias or isolated items of hysteric reaction in persons who are otherwise in good mental health. The problem is in these simple cases only the problem of getting rid of a specific habit tendency. The methods for doing this have been stated at some length in the chapter on habits. To break a habit it is first necessary to know the stimuli responsible for its release. It is then necessary to use whatever arts one has to cause the person to do something else in this situation. This is the full recipe. The situation will now itself lead to the substituted act.

If this seems easy to say but hard to do, the reason is only that it takes observation and practice to be sure that one has found the responsible stimulus pattern. The habit may be "side-tracked" by interrupting it in its very beginning and causing this beginning to be followed by some other action. Or the patient may, by having the action deprived of success in the sense that it removes the motivating stimulus, bring about by trial and error behavior his own substitution for the unwanted act. In all these cases we are merely insuring that a cue which was once followed by the undesirable action is once followed by something else. If practice of the substitution is required, this is because the undesired act had more than one cue and it is necessary to recondition all its cues.

An illustration of stimulus-response analysis making possible such substitution of good for bad habit is furnished by a young man who once called at my office to ask advice about a severe digestive disturbance which he suspected might have a mental origin. He had seen active service during the war. His call was approximately five years after his discharge from the army. The symptoms of his "attack" included a rapid pulse, and a state of tense anxiety as well as the digestive upset. He had for several months made careful notes of what he had eaten just before such attacks. He assumed that some item of food was responsible for his acute distress. He would then decide what seemed the food item most likely to have been responsible and eliminate this from his diet. During the school year he had gradually reduced to an absurd few the number of items that he could allow himself. But the attacks continued.

We talked over his symptoms for some time and he was encouraged to give something of his history. At his third visit we uncovered a fact which he had failed to notice in his preoccupation with food. This was that each attack had followed a visit to a friend who had served with him at the front. The two had been during this time members of the same infantry squad. There seemed no doubt that it was the occasional evening spent with this friend talking over their war experience that served to revive a state for which front-line service was originally responsible. The service at the front had ended in a breakdown undoubtedly functional and he had been hospitalized.

In this student's case the stimulus situation which gave the associative cues for the distressing response was fairly definite and controllable. By keeping away from his friend the attacks could be avoided. By discussing the same events with a psychologist who took care to guard against the onset of emotion, negative adaptation was established and after a short period the ex-soldier was able to visit his friend without distress.

This is very like what is often accomplished by a psychoanalysis. The original circumstances of the association were not, of course, unconscious as the psychoanalytic account demands, but the ex-soldier was not aware of the connection and the original experience had not been discussed with anyone other than the companion and the psychologist. When the student became aware of the connection between visits and his attacks this was not enough to destroy that associative connection. The trouble did not disappear just by virtue of the awareness, but the awareness enabled both the student and the psychologist to set about the substitution of another habit attitude in place of the distressing one.

Freud has himself called attention to many such substitutions accomplished by the individual himself. Many odd habits whose meaning is now lost were originally substitutions for embarrassing or forbidden actions. The individual has succeeded in postponing or avoiding masturbation with some substitute activity, an odd movement of the foot or a gesture. This has now become a tic and its history sometimes, though by no means always, forgotten. Kempf in his *Psychopathology* describes many such substitutes for perverse sex habits, substitutes which at the same time block the desire and give evidence of its presence. In many cases the subject's unawareness is better described as reticence. He could, if the right occasion were provided, give the history of the association himself. Acknowledgment to another person waits on the establishment of confidence.

In the case of hysteric habits a cure is made harder by the fact that the unwanted habit represents a solution of a difficulty, a means of controlling and subjugating other members of the family, a means of saving face. If the hysteric is cured of the habit she is in a different situation, fully habituated to getting her own way or attracting attention. A cure of the habit would leave her unadjusted and without a means of escape or triumph. It is usually necessary to do much more than attack the individual habit. She must be given new interests and a new personality. Her attitudes toward friends or toward duties must be remodeled. This can sometimes be best accomplished through establishing a new rôle.

A girl of thirteen who was far above average intelligence proved almost the undoing of her teacher by violent rages and an extreme hostility shown at the most trivial or reasonable requests of the teacher. Her first encounter with the teacher had been unfortunate and left antagonism on both sides. Her superior intelligence was at the service of this hostile attitude and in the contest the teacher was handicapped by her responsibility for the rest of her room of pupils. The teacher finally, on advice, succeeded in persuading the girl to accept part of the responsibility for the class, to take some part in teaching. She was put in charge of several classroom activities. The new rôle

brought about a thorough reorganization of her attitudes and
ended her trouble. She was now the teacher's ally, no longer
interested in teasing and humiliating her. They exercised a joint
authority over the class. This management of rôle is, of course,
a device used in all control of persons. It has been a recourse
of government and industry always.

In the egocentric person we are dealing usually with a physical defect of energy and the first care should be that a thorough
physical examination discover any possible correction. Egocentrism is the natural result of deficient energy. It is an economy of interest and effort which is the only basis on which the
individual can continue without disaster. Reeducation here is
directed at certain old-fashioned virtues. Generosity is not a
native trait but must always be learned. It is essential to many
social adjustments. The ability to take another person's point
of view is a late acquisition in normal childhood and represents
a difficult problem in learning. Piaget found that five-year-olds
may be able to tell which is their own right hand but not which
is the right hand of another. A boy of less than six or seven
may acknowledge that he has a brother, but that he himself is
a brother he may quite fail to grasp. Many an adult, visiting a
foreign country, never achieves the realization that he himself
is an alien, a foreigner. He may visit Mexico and find himself
thinking of it as populated with foreigners. Because such taking
of the other's point of view is difficult, many persons never
emerge from a thorough egocentrism in their own thinking and
this is reflected in their behavior to others.

In the depressed individual the chief problem of reeducation
is his habits of failure based on experience of failure. The only
way out is to substitute the habits and attitudes of success. To
bring this about, it is usually necessary to so manage their activities as to lead them to undertake new tasks *in which success
is within their capacity.* These must be activities which have

tangible results. Success must be made evident to the worker and to others. For the more severe cases in the hospitals occupational therapy which begins with undertakings in basket weaving, furniture making, and the like helps to reestablish confidence and the habit of attacking work.

One of the uses of reeducation is in establishing in the neurotic insight into his own case, in making his blind resentments and blind desires articulate and manageable. This requires patient and sympathetic help and much discussion. It is this task to which most of the psychoanalyst's efforts are devoted. To enlist the patient's cooperation and overcome his resistance against intrusion of another into his history and affairs, the psychoanalyst undertakes to win the patient's love. There is no doubt of the efficacy of this method and all physicians are aware of the readiness of some patients to take this attitude toward a sympathetic and interested listener. The psychoanalytic literature is slightly reticent about the difficulties to which this may lead and the ease or difficulty with which the attitude is abolished when it has been made use of.

Of far greater effectiveness and importance is reeducation which leads to a corrected rôle, to the assumption of a part which is both within the capacities of the individual and fitted to the environment in which he must live. I have known many instances in which the more or less accidental discovery of a new interest brought about a remarkable change in personality and the replacement of neurotic traits with the signs of mental health. A shy and unattractive student, given to embittered criticism of associates, without interest in college work, unable to express himself in conversation, with frequent despondent moods, eventually hits upon a new interest. The new interest may be a laboratory science, or it may be a student organization, a job as student assistant which carries some responsibility, or a hobby like the camera. The new interest is sometimes the beginning of a thorough reorganization of personality. Associations which encourage loyalties and friendships go far to give point to living.

Many attempts at psychotherapy lead inevitably beyond the patient to the need for reconstructing his environment, particularly his human environment. It is often the family rather than the individual that is maladjusted. Or we may become convinced that it is the social order he lives in that is at fault. Bad company may have led to his bad habits. The motion picture and magazines may have aroused the wants which lead him into trouble or they may have stimulated erotic interests against which social tabus and economic limitations are an effective barrier. School may encourage ambitions that are inevitably vain for the great majority, or it may have prepared for a life in a well-ordered Utopia which makes the world of adult business and industry a great surprise when it is encountered.

So far as the psychologist knows, man can adapt himself to a great variety of political systems and social orders. He can do this unless his childhood training fails to prepare him for the real world. In the United States tradition dictates that many features of this real world be carefully suppressed. We conceal death in the mortician's parlor. Love is mentioned only in a romanticized and falsified version. The textbook of civics gives not a hint of the way in which an American city is really governed. The average child gains his competence in living and his adjustment to the adult world through an extra-curricular training that is not so circumscribed.

Habit can be depended on to adjust us to any cultural order provided that we are given our chance to confront its realities early and provided that it does not change more rapidly than our habits can be led to change. In both Fascist and communist dictatorships it is the middle-aged for whom the times are out of joint. We may deplore both kinds of régime, but the fact remains that the generation reared under that régime does not deplore it. From the psychologist's point of view the order must be judged first on the basis of its stability.

When we can face the realities of the world in which we live and put in order the example we set to the next generation, teaching them virtues which will fit their world and interests which will be attainable, many of the problems of mental health will have been solved.

SUGGESTED READINGS

CHAPTER I

Cannon's *Wisdom of the Body* and Haldane's *Organism and Environment* are accounts of the constant or homeostatic states essential to life, and of the means by which these states are defended from change. Hoskins' *The Tides of Life* describes the rôle of the endocrine glands in the body's economy. Rignano's *The Nature of Life* undertakes the definition of life and a general description of vital processes.

CHAPTER II

Lloyd Morgan's *Mind at the Crossways* is a brilliant treatise on the philosophy of mind in which associative learning or conditioning is represented as its most primitive manifestation. Morgan holds that reflective thinking and planning with reference to the future is an emergent capacity of a higher order. Rignano's *Biological Memory* treats of life and mind as defensive change.

CHAPTER III

Sherrington's *Integrative Action of the Nervous System* (1906) was the pioneer work in the description of the integrative functions of the brain and spinal cord and remains one of the best general accounts of the means by which neural integration is achieved. Herrick's *Brains of Rats and Men* and the same author's *The Thinking Machine* are more recent accounts of the rôle of the central nervous system in behavior. Pieron's *Thought and the Brain* should be also read.

CHAPTER IV

Association theory has had a long history which is recounted in Warren's *A History of the Association Psychology*. E. S. Robinson's *Association Theory Today* is a thoughtful essay on

394

associative learning. Pavlov's *Conditioned Reflexes* and his *Lectures on Conditioned Reflexes* summarize his own work and that of his Russian followers on conditioning. Guthrie's *Psychology of Learning* is a more extended statement of the theory offered in the present book. E. B. Holt's *Animal Drive and the Learning Process* carried explanation of learning in terms of association farther than it had been used previously. G. H. S. Razran has published a very comprehensive bibliography on conditioning in the 1937 volume of the *Psychological Bulletin*. In the same volume Hilgard has a very able and very thoughtful review of the present state of experiments on conditioning.

CHAPTER VI

Dunlap's *Habits, Their Making and Unmaking* has a clear and detailed statement of his own method of negative practice in breaking unwanted habits, as well as a discussion of habit formation.

CHAPTER VII

On the topic of emotional reinforcement of action Cannon's *Bodily Changes in Pain, Hunger, Fear and Rage,* and his *Wisdom of the Body,* and Cannon and Rosenblueth's highly technical *Autonomic Neuro-Effector Mechanisms* describe the mechanisms of reinforcement.

CHAPTER VIII

Edward J. Kempf's *The Autonomic Functions and the Personality* (1918) attempted to furnish a physiological basis for psychoanalytic doctrines of wish and desire. In a brilliant essay published in the *Medical Record* between February 6 and November 20, 1935, with the title, "Physiology of Attitude—Emergence of Ego-Organization," Kempf has extended and improved his earlier account.

CHAPTER IX

Dunlap's *Civilized Life* undertakes an account of the nature of desire and wish. For the psychoanalytic view of desires and for psychoanalytic theory in general Healy, Bronner and Bower's *The Structure and Meaning of Psychoanalysis* is the most enlightening source.

CHAPTER XII

Gordon W. Allport's *Personality: A Psychological Interpretation* is a well-written and extremely inclusive and thorough account of the attempts of psychologists to describe personality and to measure personality traits. Murphy and Jensen's *Approaches to Personality* and the extended report of experiments with tests and other measures of personality in Murphy, Murphy and Newcomb's *Experimental Social Psychology* should be consulted.

CHAPTER XIII

Janet's *L'évolution psychologique de la personnalité* is, in the writer's opinion, the best modern account of the nature of the self and of voluntary action.

CHAPTER XVII

For the description of the actual effects of inadequate emotional reinforcement (which he interprets as deficiency in mental *force*) Janet's *Psychological Healing* offers a multitude of cases and very enlightening comment.

CHAPTER XVIII

For a popular account of the nervous breakdown written in common-sense terms, the late W. Beran Wolfe's *Calm Your Nerves* serves very well. G. V. Hamilton's *An Introduction to Objective Psychopathology* has the best statement of the general nature of nervous breakdown.

CHAPTER XIX

Janet's *The Major Symptoms of Hysteria* remains the best description of symptoms.

CHAPTER XXI

Janet's *Psychological Healing* deals with many cases of inadequacy and with his theories of energy level. Hollingworth's

The *Psychology of Functional Neuroses* and his *Abnormal Psychology*, and McDougall's *Outline of Abnormal Psychology* have excellent descriptions of these neuroses.

CHAPTER XXII

Psychoanalytical theories of dreams are presented in Freud's *The Interpretation of Dreams* and his *Psychopathology of Everyday Life*.

CHAPTER XXIII

Morton Prince's *The Unconscious* describes a number of cases of amnesia. Amnesias are also dealt with in the textbooks of abnormal psychology mentioned above. Bartlett's *Remembering* contributes some new light on the nature of memory. Janet's *L'évolution de la mémoire et de la notion du temps* is abundantly illustrated from its author's experience with abnormalities of memory which has been undoubtedly more extended than that of any other man.

CHAPTER XXV

Hamilton and McGowan's *What Is Wrong With Marriage* undertakes to analyze the sources of marital difficulties on the basis of an extended questioning of 200 cases.

CHAPTER XXVII

Hart's *Psychology of Insanity* and the more recent *Psychology of Mental Disorders* by Abraham Myerson are clearly written accounts.

CHAPTER XXVIII

The outstanding work on psychotherapy is Janet's *Psychological Healing*. Shaffer's *Psychology of Adjustment* is an introduction to psychotherapy which improves on all earlier accounts through the use of a more clear and explicit theory of learning on which to base suggestions of therapeutic method.

REFERENCES

Adler, Alfred. *The Practice and Theory of Individual Psychology*. New York, Harcourt, Brace, 1925 (revised, 1929).

Allport, Gordon. *Personality: a Psychological Interpretation*. New York, Holt, 1937.

Allport, G. W., and Odbert, H. S. *Trait Names. Psychological Monographs*. 1936.

Cannon, W. B. *Bodily Changes in Pain, Hunger, Fear and Rage*. New York, Appleton-Century, 1915.

Cannon, W. B. *The Wisdom of the Body*. New York, Norton, 1932.

Cannon, W. B., and Rosenblueth, W. *Autonomic Neuro-Effector Mechanisms*. New York, Macmillan, 1937.

Dorcus, Roy M., and Shaffer, G. Wilson. *Textbook of Abnormal Psychology*. Baltimore, Williams and Wilkins, 1934.

Freud, S. *General Introduction to Psychoanalysis*. New York, Boni, 1920.

Freud, S. *The Interpretation of Dreams*. New York, Macmillan, 1913.

Freud, S. *New Introductory Lectures on Psychoanalysis*. New York, Norton, 1933.

Freud, S. *The Psychopathology of Everyday Life*. New York, Macmillan, 1914.

Guthrie, E. R. *The Psychology of Learning*. New York, Harper, 1935.

Haldane, J. S. *Organism and Environment*. London, Oxford University Press, 1917.

Hamilton, G. V. *An Introduction to Objective Psychopathology*. St. Louis, Mosby, 1925.

Hamilton, G. V. *Research in Marriage*. New York, Boni, 1929.

Hamilton, G. V., and McGowan, K. *What Is Wrong With Marriage*. New York, Boni, 1929.

Healy, William. *Mental Conflicts and Misconduct*. Boston, Little, Brown, 1917.

Healy, William; Bronner, Augusta F.; and Bowers, Anna M. *The Structure and Meaning of Psychoanalysis*. New York, Knopf, 1931.

Hollingworth, Harry L. *Abnormal Psychology*. New York, Ronald Press, 1930.

Hollingworth, Harry L. *The Psychology of Functional Neuroses*. New York, Appleton-Century, 1920.

Holt, Edwin B. *Animal Drive and the Learning Process*. New York, Holt, 1931.

Holt, Edwin B. *The Freudian Wish and Its Place in Ethics*. New York, Holt, 1921.

Hoskins, R. G. *The Tides of Life; the Endocrine Glands in Bodily Adjustment*. New York, Norton, 1933.

Hull, Clark L. *Hypnosis and Suggestibility*. New York, Appleton-Century, 1933.

Humphrey, George. *The Nature of Learning and the Living System*. New York, 1934.

Janet, Pierre. *The Major Symptoms of Hysteria*. New York, Macmillan, 1924.

Janet, Pierre. *Principles of Psychotherapy*. New York, Macmillan, 1924.

Janet, Pierre. *Psychological Healing*. New York, Macmillan, 1925.

Janet, Pierre. *L'évolution de la mémoire et de la notion du temps*. Paris, Cahin, 1928.

Janet, Pierre. *L'évolution psychologique de la personnalité*. Paris, Cahin, 1929.

Jung, Carl G. *Contributions to Analytical Psychology*. New York, Harcourt, Brace, 1928.

Kempf, E. J. *The Autonomic Functions and the Personality*. Baltimore, Nerv. and Mental Disease Pub. Co., 1918.

Kempf, E. J. *Physiology of Attitude*. Medical Record during 1935.

Luria, A. R. *The Nature of Human Conflicts*. New York, Liveright, 1932.

McDougall, William. *Outline of Abnormal Psychology*. New York, Scribners, 1926.

Malinowski, B. *The Sexual Life of Savages*. New York, Halcyon House, 1929.

Max, L. W. An experimental study of the motor theory of consciousness. *Journal of General Psychology*, 1935, 13, 159-175.

Menzies, R. *Journal of Psychology*, 1937, 4, 75-120.

Morgan, C. Lloyd. *Mind at the Crossways*. New York, Holt, 1930.

Morgan, J. J. B. *The Psychology of Abnormal People*. New York, Longmans, Green, 1928.

Murphy, Gardner, and Jensen, Friedrich. *Approaches to Personality*. New York, Coward-McCann, 1932.

Murphy, Gardner; Murphy, Lois; and Newcomb, T. M. *Experimental Social Psychology*. New York, Harper, 1937.

Myerson, Abraham. *The Psychology of Mental Disorders*. New York, Macmillan, 1927.

Pavlov, I. *Conditioned Reflexes*. London, Oxford University Press, 1927.

Pavlov, I. *Lectures on Conditioned Reflexes*. New York, International Publishers, 1928.

Prince, Morton. *The Unconscious*. New York, Macmillan, 1915.

Prosser, C. L., and Hunter, W. B. The extinction of startle responses and spinal reflexes in the white rat. *American Journal of Physiology*, 1936, 117, 609-618.

Razran, Gregory H. S. Bibliography on Conditioning. *Psychological Bulletin*, 1937, 34, 191-256.

Robinson, E. S. *Association Theory Today*. New York, Appleton-Century, 1932.

Rosenow, Curt. *American Journal of Psychology*, 1928, 40, 205-235.

Schjeldrup-Ebbe, T. Beitrage zur Socialpsychologie des Haushuns. *Zsch. f. Psychol.*, 1922, 88, 225-264.

Seward, G. H., and Seward, J. P. *Psychological Review*, 1937, 44, 351.

Sherman, M., and Sherman, I. C. *The Process of Human Behavior*. New York, Norton, 1929.

Sherrington, C. S. *The Integrative Action of the Nervous System*. New Haven, Yale, 1906.

Smith, G. Mennon. *Character and Personality*, 1937, 5, 331-337.

Thurstone, L. L. *The Nature of Intelligence*. New York, Harcourt, Brace, 1924.

Tolman, E. C. *Purposive Behavior In Animals and in Man*. New York, Appleton-Century, 1933.

Warren, H. C. *History of Association Theory*, New York, 1921.

Watson, J. B. *Psychology from the Standpoint of a Behaviorist*. Philadelphia, Lippincott (2d edition), 1924.

Woodworth, R. S. *Dynamic Psychology*. New York, Columbia, 1918.

Wendt, G. R. An interpretation of inhibition of conditioned reflexes as competition between reaction systems. *Psychol. Rev.*, 1936, 43, 258-281.

INDEX

Index